BEYOND BOUNDARIES

BEYOND BOUNDARIES

Cyberspace in Africa

Edited by

**Melinda B. Robins
and Robert L. Hilliard**

HEINEMANN
Portsmouth, NH

Heinemann
A division of Reed Elsevier Inc.
361 Hanover Street
Portsmouth, NH 03801–3912
www.heinemann.com

Offices and agents throughout the world

ISBN 0–325–00184–7 (Heinemann cloth)

British Library Cataloguing-in-Publication Data is available.

Library of Congress Cataloging-in-Publication Data

Beyond boundaries : cyberspace in Africa / edited by Melinda B. Robins and Robert
    L. Hilliard.
        p. cm.
    Includes bibliographical references and index.
    ISBN 0–325–00184–7 (cloth : alk. paper)
    1. Information technology—Social aspects—Africa.   2. Internet—Social aspects—
Africa.   3. Cyberspace—Africa.   I. Robins, Melinda Beth, 1953–   II. Hilliard,
Robert L., 1925–
HN780.Z9 I563   2002
303.48'33'096—dc21   00–053918

Printed in the United States of America on acid-free paper.

05 04 03 02 01 SB 1 2 3 4 5 6 7 8 9

Contents

Preface

While much of Africa has long been considered extremely weak in its efforts to move into the modern communications age, many nations are beginning to leap-frog the more established media into cyberspace. Some observers have noted that media structures—essentially print, radio, and television—could not be expected to grow optimally in Africa because their roots are not indigenous, but were imposed by colonial exploiters or imported from the industrial West. This perspective tends to ignore the fact that African nations today are not isolated cultures. They reflect, as does the rest of the world, economic and social contrasts, infused by communications and transportation, with First World and Third World potentials and problems. The media reflect the disjunctions, both as promise and as problem.

This book will examine how a new and growing use of the Internet as a means of communications is developing across Africa. Who is using the Internet? For what reasons? What are the demonstrated and anticipated effects? Who is benefiting and who is not? What are the current issues and problems, as well as the potentials? How is the Internet affecting the efforts to promote democracy and an open market in Africa? What are the underlying political, social, economic, and cultural conditions and philosophies that affect the development and use of cyberspace and that will be affected by its growth?

An underlying theme of this book is to show how the use and potential use of cyberspace have begun to dissolve and will continue to break down the sometimes externally—and sometimes internally—imposed boundaries of language, religion, geography, and political alliances; and how cyberspace, as an expansion of cross-border uses of radio and television, is helping to disprove many political, social, economic, and cultural stereotypes.

The value of using cyberspace is undeniable. It offers citizen groups and individuals, as well as organizations, government offices, and business and industry, the opportunity to access information and education from all over the world and to disseminate information, beliefs, and concerns. It offers a means for sharing alternative philosophies. It provides an opportunity for establishing broader political bases outside of the purview of controlling authorities.

Some of the critical issues are: access to information, especially for women (Chapter 3 is dedicated to this subject); building networks for research; information dissemination; technology transfer; and health, education, and small business development. For example, nongovernmental organizations (NGOs) have information technology needs that will permit them to promote cooperative initiatives that can lead to economic, legal, and social reforms; these initiatives can be local, regional, and global.

Most African nations are still struggling to develop the basic mass media resources of radio and television. Yet, even as these countries democratize and permit more and more independence for their media, many of them have begun to jump across existing communications systems into the media mode of the twenty-first century: cyberspace. Publications are in many instances moving from manual typewriters and antiquated presses directly to computers. Since the beginning of 1997, for example, an estimated more than 50 newspapers in Africa have gone on-line.

It is not easy. Basic communication systems lag badly behind the rest of the world. With about 13 percent of the earth's population, Africa has only 2 percent of its phone lines; sub-Saharan Africa, the focus of this book, has about 10 percent of the world's population and only about one-half of 1 percent of its phone lines. At the beginning of 2000, Africa had approximately 200 radios and 50 TV sets per thousand people; by contrast, North America had some 2,000 radios and 1,000 TV sets per thousand; Europe 750 radios and 475 TVs; South America 375 and 200; and Asia 225 and 85. Even with positive economic growth, it would appear most difficult for Africa to catch up with the rest of the world in accessing even traditional media, even though the 1990s showed substantial growth in the establishment of new mass media systems and in training programs for their effective use. Depending on the availability of economic resources, cyberspace provides a means for many African countries to catch up through instant use of the new medium.

However, the term "economic" is the key. Africa is a continent of "haves" and "have-nots." The costs of operating a computer are high, higher if connected to the Internet. In terms of basic incomes, electricity costs in Africa are daunting. The paucity and unreliability of the phone lines needed to connect a computer to the Internet pose additional problems. Connection to the Internet requires a service provider as well. Most such providers in Africa are owned by the countries' elite; these companies have fought aggressively for customers who are able to pay their high fees, and they have developed few plans through which the less affluent might achieve access.

Cyberspace as a priority in African countries continues to be debated, especially in poorer nations that find it hard to provide their citizens with basic needs such as education, health care, and clean water. Most critical, as the new century begins, is AIDS. The African continent accounts for 75 percent of the world's HIV/AIDS infections.

While some African countries may soon become full participants in cyberspace's global matrix of minds, others will have to struggle to become connected. Connection will be crucial to fostering expanded communications with other countries on the continent and around the globe. As cyberspace increasingly becomes a principal means of international communication, a lack of connectivity will place these basic-commodity-producing countries into a further disadvantageous position in the world's marketplace.

This book concentrates on key countries that typify the use (and nonuse) of cyberspace in their regions. The bulk of the book, chapters describing the status of cyberspace in specified countries, is written by experts from those countries. As coeditors, we have written opening and closing chapters designed to provide an overview, set the stage, and arrive at conclusions. Coeditor Robins wrote the chapter on women's e-initiatives. She was a 1989 Fulbright Professional Scholar in Uganda, and has worked with women and the media in Tanzania. She has presented papers on Africa at educational and professional conferences. Coeditor Hilliard has given lectures and conducted workshops in Africa (including some for US AID and USIA); has consulted for African governments, NGOs, education, and industry on communications development and laws; and served as liaison with visiting African media officials when he was a federal government official in Washington, D.C. The individual country analyses provide background on those nations, including communications and cyberspace infrastructure, and the relationship of the Internet to selected social, political, economic, cultural, and philosophical issues, problems, and potentials.

We hope this book not only provides information on cyberspace in Africa to students and scholars in the field of African studies, and to the general reader interested in the potentials of that continent, but that it makes some contribution toward spurring the growth of the Internet throughout the region and, especially, in the economically deprived sub-Saharan area, including its use to fight AIDS. Further, if this book contributes to cyberspace development as a tool to breaking down artificial boundaries and moving the countries of Africa toward peaceful cooperation or, at least, accommodation, our personal purposes in writing the book will be fulfilled.

We wish to express our thanks to Emerson College, our professorial affiliation, for awarding us a faculty research grant that helped us complete the manuscript for the book. We appreciate, too, the encouragement and assistance of our editor at Heinemann Publishers, Jim Lance, and of our production editor, Lynn Zelem. And, not least, our appreciation to our old and new friends and colleagues who wrote the chapters on the individual countries of Africa.

Melinda B. Robins and Robert L. Hilliard

1

Getting Ready for Cyberspace

Robert L. Hilliard

If Africa is the world's sleeping giant, cyberspace has begun to make it stir and stretch out its arms, embracing itself and the rest of the world. More than any other technological development in history, the Internet has provided every country in Africa with the means to communicate its cultural, educational, political, social, and commercial messages and needs to every other country on the continent, bypassing previously imposed barriers that separated many countries from their neighbors and from other nations on Earth.

The Internet offers the opportunity for a giant leap forward for the nations of Africa. Over 30 years ago, before the reality of cyberspace communications, U.S. President Lyndon B. Johnson's Task Force on Communications Policy noted the importance of communications in the world:

> A truly global communications system could help knit the family of nations into a living community, based on mutual understanding and the universal diffusion of knowledge and skills. . . . Improved communications are essential to a growing world economy. They are vital to the progress of advanced and developing nations alike. New services promise to revolutionize customary patterns of business and finance, learning, entertainment and leisure, and the processing, storage and retrieval of information. Above all, they offer the citizen everywhere the opportunity to acquire the knowledge and the insight essential to mature exercise of [their] responsibilities. Within each nation, and among nations, the wise use of telecommunications is a key to success in building and reinforcing a sense of community which is the foundation of social peace: a sense of community based on freedom, and on tolerance of diversity; a community which encourages and appreciates the unpredictable richness of human imagination; but a community, nevertheless, faithful to its own rules of civility

and order. . . . . improved telecommunications generally promise important contributions to the less developed world.[1]

The development of Internet use in the intervening years showed that this form of telecommunications could do even considerably more than what was envisioned by the President's Task Force. In 1999 the *Boston Globe* editorialized that the Internet might well help end the extreme poverty that affects many nations of the world, a disproportionate number of them in Africa. The *Globe* stated, "One ambitious theory is that the Internet could revolutionize awareness of global poverty and turn awareness into action. Forget the fleeting images on nightly news broadcasts. A Web site could provide vivid details—facts, video clips and firsthand accounts, along with background reports and progress updates."[2]

The *Globe* goes on to suggest that once people throughout the world learn about these problems and are given specific routes of action, they will feel more empowered than they do now to do something to help. The *Globe* sees an even larger Internet role, enabling countries that missed the first industrial revolution—again, many of these in Africa—to become part of the information revolution: "If they had an education, people in extreme poverty could even be employed through the Internet."[3]

All of this sounds tailor-made for much of Africa, especially the sub-Saharan nations that suffered the greatest exploitation by colonial powers and inherited conditions that have kept them in dire economic straits, resulting in poverty for much of their populations. Cyberspace, by helping break down the artificial boundaries between and among countries, may well provide a new opportunity for them to become partners in the growing world economy.

Yet, becoming part of the cyberspace revolution, even getting ready for it, is not an easy task for most African countries. The historical exploitation of African nations by other countries, principally European powers, left the relatively recent—in terms of historical time—independent African countries with little infrastructure, inadequate economic resources, lack of planning and development programs, inapplicable regulatory models, and few pertinent training programs. It is not surprising, therefore, that of the estimated 200 million Internet users throughout the globe in 2000, Africa has, according to several estimates, only about 1 percent. However, when one considers that the United States and Canada have more than half of the total, Europe more than 20 percent, and the developed nations of Asia and the Pacific region almost 20 percent, the figures for the developing countries are as good as might be expected at this time. It should be noted, too, that the most sought-after market for on-line commercial enterprises in the first decade of the twenty-first century is China. One may well assume that Africa will be next, thus providing an incentive for foreign capital investment into Africa's Internet structures.

The countries that moved most quickly into cyberspace are those with the strongest economies and—importantly—the telecommunications base that made the addition of and transition into cyberspace relatively easy. As the new century began, the per capita yearly incomes of most African countries were among the lowest in the world.

A direct correlation exists between established telecommunications systems and growth of the Internet. Here, too, African countries started with a disadvantage, compared to much of the rest of the world. The year 2000 saw a world ratio of about 400 radio sets and about 200 television sets per 1,000 people. In Africa the ratio was about 200 radios and about 50 TV sets. This compares with over 2,000 radios and almost 1,000 TVs in North America, about 750 radios and 475 TVs in Europe, 375 radios and 200 TVs in South America, 225 radios and 85 TVs in Asia, and over 1,000 radios and 500 TV sets in Oceania.[4]

Telephone system infrastructure also is essential for Internet growth, and here, too, Africa is lagging, especially in its sub-Saharan region, the focus of this book. Sub-Saharan Africa has 10 percent of the world's population, but only one-half of 1 percent of the world's telephone lines. Excluding South Africa, there are only three million lines in the rest of the region, one telephone for every 17,000 persons. Further, telephone rental for a year averages about 20 percent of the average per capita income of the region. Compare that to the world average cost of 9 percent of average per capita yearly income and one telephone for every 600 people.[5]

Does this mean, then, that there is little hope for Africa's full participation in boundary-breaking cyberspace? No. Although the figures above paint a relatively bleak picture, they becoming misleading taken out of the context of recent developments in Africa that may very well put most of the continent in a position to move forward. As one expert notes:

> Africa is emerging. In the last 10 years we've seen what you might call Renaissance, the second independence of Africa. It's a time of economic growth. Most countries on the continent now have returned to the column of net growth beyond their population growth rate . . . some years ago . . . the infrastructure was so rudimentary for communications. It was so costly . . . only the elite had telephones. Now it is different . . . phones connect a whole village.[6]

Given the opportunity, much of Africa has begun to take up the Internet, bypassing the development of more traditional communications modes such as television and radio, whose cost denied them past opportunity for satisfactory growth. The Internet offers distance learning more effectively than television has, providing education to those unable—because of geography, physical condition, lack of funds, or distance from an educational institution—to obtain an education. Africa is principally a rural land, with most of its citizens isolated from educational centers. Many on-line educational services are already in operation, such as Kenya's Distance Learning Center. On-line universities open up new vistas. The Internet also permits reliable and relatively inexpensive communication among individuals. "E-mail is so important to the developing world, not least for the planet's poorest continent. It is the only mode of international telecommunication that Africa can afford on any reasonable scale."[7] Continuing costs of other forms of direct communication are more expensive.

A look at the telecommunications infrastructure of some of the regions of Africa provides a base for estimating the problems and potentials of Internet development. First, it should be emphasized that Africa is a continent of "haves" and "have-nots." In some parts of the continent, such as north Africa and African countries that are part of the mideast, not only are economies good, but telecommunications have been developed to a point where it is an easy move into cyberspace. In other parts of the continent, most especially sub-Saharan Africa, poverty is rampant, with national communications systems ranging generally from fair to very poor, with a few exceptions, notably South Africa, which in recent years has expanded its television and, especially, community radio coverage.

Sub-Saharan Africa, excluding South Africa, is one of the poorest regions in the world. While some countries were left a remnant of a telecommunications infrastructure upon which to build, by the colonial powers that occupied them for many years—in the east it was the United Kingdom, in the west it was France—most were left with nothing but a poorly run, underfunded, technically deteriorating radio system. After they gained their independence, the former British and French colonies used whatever systems they had in the same way the colonial powers had used them: to maintain control over the people through nationalistic education and propaganda. In some countries television was introduced on the basis of an event that the public wanted to see—or the government wanted them to see—such as the Olympics, the visit of a world dignitary, the ceremonies of a presidential inaugural.

Strong national and even regional differences mark the countries of Africa. Most of the continent falls into the Third World category, nations struggling to emerge from decades and even centuries of economic subjugation and exploitation. In sub-Saharan Africa many of the countries are too poor to develop effective television systems, and radio remains the principal means of mass communication. Even in the north, where the economy and educational opportunities are better, radio is still the key medium. Large parts of Africa are rural, with individual tribes and much of the population relatively isolated from the facilities of cities and towns. Further, electricity is scarce, if not nonexistent. Where it does exist, it is extremely expensive. Batteries are likewise costly, making it very difficult for any one family to own and operate a radio, no less a television set. In many places radio and television are heard and seen by extended family groups— for example, a set in a public square in a village, sometimes operated by a foot-powered generator.

Individual countries, no matter how poor, make special efforts to provide radio and television programming to their citizens. The high rate of illiteracy leaves radio and television as the principal means with which a government can reach its people with information and ideas designed to affect their minds and emotions in ways considered desirable by the party in power. A problem encountered in most countries is the multiplicity of languages spoken by different tribes. Although English in the south and French in the west are the official languages, and in some areas Kiswahili crosses internal and external borders as a second language, many isolated groups know only a tribal language. In such cases it is necessary to program several radio services in several key languages, or to provide programming in different languages on the one existing service. In some cases television, being visual, compensates for a lack of verbal understanding, but the higher cost of TV broadcasting and receiving makes it a far less desirable medium from an economic standpoint and, consequently, there are many fewer TV sets and stations in any given country than there are radio sets and stations. Language, however, is an important long-range factor in cross-border Internet use; in the short-term, users have been and will be the business, govermnent, and educational elite who know the regional languages of English and/or French, but as computer availability and access begins to spread, this will not necessarily be the case with the average user.

The content of radio and television, with few exceptions, is carefully controlled by the respective governments, even where private stations have been authorized. Most systems are still owned and operated by the government, although in a number of countries statutory public systems have been established. The systems usually operate from a central transmitter with relay stations in strategic parts of a country carrying the signals to rural areas. For example, Madagascar uses its one national station to feed 36 low-power relay transmitters.

South Africa is an exception to the Third World limitations imposed on most other nations in Africa; despite its economic difficulties, unemployment, and tribal strife, it is in a considerably better communications situation than most nations on the continent. Prior to the end of apartheid, its broadcasting system was simply a propaganda arm of the National Party. Since then it has been changed to accommodate the needs of a larger public. Radio, especially, has been growing, with the establishment of a large number of community stations, operated by community groups. William Siemering, who took a leading role in the development of community radio in South Africa, states that the country "has the potential to develop the most diverse and effective radio system in the world." He cites as reasons the high rate of illiteracy giving radio dominance, the oral tradition of the majority of the people, the lower cost of the medium, and its easier accessibility to the public.[8]

Countries with well-developed radio and television services would appear to have the infrastructure necessary to move easily into Internet services. Some have done just that, but, ironically, by putting their priority communication resources into cyberspace, they have slowed or delayed the expansion of their other telecommunications systems. Countries without well-developed traditional communication systems would appear to be at a disadvantage in relation to cyberspace. However, many have chosen to bypass the further development of radio and television systems and to move directly into Internet services, by necessity putting their limited economic resources into cyberspace rather than into the more costly traditional communications services. There is no question that cyberspace is the coming medium of choice for Africa and, with appropriate foreign investment, it will grow exponentially in the next decade, bringing all of Africa into the global communications market.

A look at the telecommunications facilities of African countries at the beginning of the twenty-first century may provide an understanding of both their economic resources for communications and the likelihood of their short-term expansion into cyberspace services.[9]

Algeria, with a population of 30.5 million, has 3.5 million radio sets, with broadcast signals from some 25 locations, and 2 million television sets, with the government-operated system using some 19 sites. Algeria also operates a short-wave radio system.

Angola's 11 million people have a half-million radios, with broadcasting emanating from about 14 government locations, plus some 20 provincial stations. The government television system has about 7 repeater sites for the country's fewer than 100,000 TV sets. It also has a shortwave operation. The per capita yearly income of $700 makes it one of the continent's poor countries, limiting the ability of its citizens to obtain needed communications-receiving equipment.

Benin has just over 5 million people and government-run communications systems: a radio network and about 10 regional stations reaching fewer than a half-million radios and a TV system reaching fewer than 100,000 TV sets. Its yearly per capita income of $1,400 is higher than that of most African countries and indicates some potential for media growth. Chapter 4 details Benin's cyberspace progress.

Botswana has a small population of about 1.5 million. Its 600,000 radios receive three government stations from some 12 sites and its fewer than 50,000 TVs receive signals from a private station.

Burundi's 6 million people, deep in genocidal wars, have a barely operational radio and TV system and few sets. Its per capita yearly income of $600 and continuing internal strife do not indicate a likely change soon.

Burkina Faso has 11.5 million population, with a per capita income of $700 per year. It has a number of radio facilities: a government network, 2 religious stations, 3 commercial stations, and 5 private stations reaching somewhat over a half-million radios. It also has a government television system, but fewer than 100,000 television sets.

Cameroon's 15 million people have 6 million radios, receiving signals from a government system emanating from some 16 sites, and over a half-million TV sets served by a government facility. Its per capita income of $1,200 makes it marginally economically viable for communications growth.

Canary Islands' small population of 1.7 million does well in communications, with over a half-million radios receiving signals from about 75 sites and over a quarter-million TV sets served by a public system and 6 private stations.

Cape Verde has a population of only a half-million and its 60,000 radios are served by a government system and a religious station. Its 10,000 TV sets are served by a national government system. Its per capita income is above the mean, at $1,100.

Central African Republic has 3.3 million people, whose per capita income is only $800 per year, with a poor infrastructure of broadcasting. There are fewer than 200,000 radios and not much more than 10,000 TVs, both media served by government stations.

Chad has 7 million people with a per capita yearly income of $600, and its 1.3 million radios and less than 50,000 TV sets are served by government stations.

Comoros, a Federal Islamic Republic, has about 650,000 inhabitants and about 65,000 radios that receive the government station.

Congo (Democratic Republic of, formerly Zaire) has about 49 million people, whose per capita income of $400 per year makes it one of the poorest countries in the world. It has 3.5 million radios served by a government system, and 2.2 million TVs, which are served by a government network from about 18 sites, and by 2 commercial stations.

Congo (Peoples Republic of) has 2.6 million inhabitants whose $3,100 per capita income would appear to make it one of the more economically viable nations in that part of Africa. Yet, it has fewer sets than one might expect, with about a quarter-million radios and 20,000 TVs, both served by government stations.

Côte d'Ivoire has 14.8 million population, with 1.6 million radios receiving programs from a government network and a private station, and over 800,000 TV sets served by a government system operating from about 14 sites. Its per capita income is moderate for Africa, about $1,500 per year.

Djibouti is small, with about 575,000 people, who have only about 35,000 radios and about half that number of TVs, with a national radio network and one government and one pay-television station. Its per capita income is $1,200 per year.

Egypt, an Arab nation, is one of the largest in Africa, with a population of 64 million. It has one of the most extensive telecommunications systems on the continent, with a government network of about 75 AM sites and about 15 FM sites reaching over 16 million radios and a government television system operating out of 48 stations serving over 5 million sets. It also has a large shortwave operation. Its per capita income is $2,760 and it is expected to be one of Africa's leaders in cyberspace development and use.

Equatorial Guinea has fewer than a half-million people and a per capita income of $800. But it makes extensive use of radio, with over 200,000 sets and 1 national public and 1 commercial radio service. It has barely begun television development, with only a few thousand sets in operation, served by a government station. It also has a shortwave station.

Eritrea, covered extensively in Chapter 5 of this book, has about 4.6 million people and 2 government radio networks.

Ethiopia, one of the poorest countries with $400 per capita income, has over 61 million population, with 9 million radios served by a government network and about 200,000 TV sets served by a government system with about 28 stations. It also has a shortwave operation. Chapter 6 details Ethiopia's Internet status.

Gabon has 1.3 million people whose $5,200 yearly per capita income makes it one of the more well-off countries in Africa. It has about 160,000 radios with 1 government network and 1 commercial station, and about 50,000 TV sets with a government system of 3 stations. It also has a commercial shortwave operation.

Gambia has 1.1 million people and about a half-million radio sets, a high ratio on the continent. It has 1 government and 1 commercial radio station, and 1 TV station for its fewer than 10,000 TV sets.

Ghana has extensive telecommunications services for its 19.5 million people, with 12.5 million radios programmed to by an autonomous government-authorized network and by 6 private stations, and over 800,000 television sets that receive signals from a national system with some 11 stations. Its per capita income is $1,400 per year, the combination of income and its broadcasting infrastructure suggesting that it could become a strong Internet user.

Guinea (Republic of) has 7.4 million population with government networks serving a quarter-million radio sets and 65,000 TV sets, the latter from 6 sites. Its per capita income is just over $1,000.

Guinea-Bissau has 1.1 million people, with only 40,000 radios, its programming coming from a government system.

Kenya, with 29.7 million people, has a per capita yearly income of $1,300. Its 5 million radios are served by a national broadcasting company with 12 AM, 7 short-wave, and 7 FM stations, and by 1 commercial FM station. It has almost 1 million TV sets served by a government commercial system with 6 stations and by 1 commercial TV network. It has also begun cable service. Chapter 7 covers the Kenyan situation.

Lesotho has 2.2 million people with a per capita income of $1,450. It has a good ratio, for Africa, of 1 radio for every 2 inhabitants and a quarter-million TV sets, all served by government systems.

Liberia has 3 million people, and is just recovering from internal wars. Its per capita income is only $770. It has 2 national networks, and 2 commercial, 1 religious, and 1 private station for its 600,000 radios, and 1 government commercial station for about 50,000 TVs.

Libya has one of the continent's highest per capita yearly incomes, $6,510, for its 5.4 million people. One government radio network, with about 17 sites, reaches 1 million radios, and a government TV network with about 12 stations reaches about 550,000 TV sets. It also has several shortwave sites. With a broadcasting infrastructure in place and a comparably good income for its citizens, it should be able to fairly easily develop cyberspace capacity.

Madagascar has 14.4 million inhabitants and a per capita income of $820. It has 2.3 million radios with 1 government system and 2 private stations, and a quarter-million TV sets with a commercial national system.

Madeira, a Portuguese possession, has 300,000 people and 200,000 radios, with a national system emanating from about 10 sites, plus 2 commercial and 6 private stations.

Malawi has 10.6 million people and 1.1 million radios with 1 national statutory system operating from about 15 sites.

Mali has only a $600 per capita income for its 10.2 million people. It has 1.6 million radios, which receive programs from a national statutory network operating from about 8 sites and from 12 community radio stations. It has just over 10,000 television sets served by 1 national station.

Mauritania has 2.3 million people with a per capita income of $1,200. A government radio system serves its 1 million radio sets from 4 sites and a government TV station broadcasts to about 50,000 TV sets.

Mauritius has the highest per capita yearly income in Africa, $9,600, for its 1.2 million inhabitants, suggesting a promising economic base for developing Internet use. A partially commercial national system serves 400,000 radios and a commercial system with 5 stations serves some 230,000 television sets.

Mayotte, a French territory, has 112,000 population, with national systems broadcasting to 50,000 radios and several thousand television sets.

Morocco has 30 million inhabitants, with a per capita income of $3,000. It has 5.1 million radio sets, with signals from 1 government system, 1 government commercial system, and 5 commercial stations. A government television system uses about 26 stations to serve 1.7 million television sets, some of which also receive programs from a commercial station. The government operates 2 shortwave systems, 1 of them commercial.

Mozambique has 19.8 million people, whose per capita yearly income is $700. It has 1 government radio system programming to 5 million sets from about 25 stations, and it also has 9 provincial stations. One government station programs to about 50,000 TV sets. The government also runs a commercial shortwave station.

Namibia's 1.9 million people have a per capita yearly income of $3,600. Its 230,000 radio sets receive programs from a national system with 6 sites, 2 commercial stations, and 1 community station. Its 40,000 TV sets receive programs from 1 national public system with 5 stations. Chapter 8 details the situation in Namibia.

Niger is one of the region's poorest countries, its 9.1 million people having a per capita income of $600 per year. Its broadcasting systems are small, with only about 440,000 radio sets served by a government system with 5 stations and 35,000 TV sets receiving signals from a government system with 11 stations.

Nigeria is one of the world's largest nations, with 123 million people. Its per capita income is $1,300. Nigeria has attempted to develop an extensive broadcasting system, despite its largely rural nature, and has 17.2 million radios served by a national system operating with about 45 sites, and by a statutory public system. It has 9.3 million TV sets served by a government system. It also has a statutory corporation operating a shortwave system. Chapter 9 details its cyberspace situation.

Reunion has 680,000 inhabitants earning an annual per capita income of $4,300. Its 170,000 radios receive programs from a national system that has about 45 sites, and from more than 40 private stations. Its 91,000 TV sets receive signals from 1 public system and 4 private commercial stations.

Rwanda, torn by genocidal strife, has 5.5 million people and 1 national radio system.

São Tomé and Principe is a small country with 152,000 people and 1 national radio system broadcasting to 31,000 sets and 1 TV station broadcasting to about 21,000 sets.

Senegal has 9.1 million people with a per capita income of $1,600. It has 850,000 radios, which receive programs from 1 national system with about 10 sites, 2 shortwave stations, and 1 commercial FM station using 5 sites. It has a quarter-million TV sets and 1 government TV station and 1 pay-TV service. Chapter 10 details the Senegalese situation.

Seychelles Islands, a small nation, is one of the more economically advantaged in Africa, with a per capita income of $6,000 for its 78,000 inhabitants and an excellent ratio of 50,000 radio sets and 14,000 TV sets, both served by national radio and television systems. It also accommodates one of the largest shortwave operations in the world, a religious missionary station.

Sierra Leone has an underdeveloped telecommunications system for its 5.2 million people, whose yearly per capita income is $960. It has 1 million radio sets served by 1 government system and 7 private commercial stations, and about 210,000 television sets served by a government commercial station.

Somalia, a poor country torn apart by internal factions that have destroyed virtually all national infrastructures, has 11.4 million people earning a per capita yearly income of $500. Its 5 radio stations are controlled by different political factions and reach about 300,000 radio sets. It also has 1 television station.

South Africa, as noted earlier in this chapter, has been developing an extensive radio system as well as a television service. Because of the isolation of many of its tribes, it has only 7.5 million radios for its 44 million people. One national radio system uses some 160 sites, in addition to which there are numerous community stations, metropolitan stations, regional stations, and a number of commercial stations. The South Africa Broadcasting Corporation programs to 5.3 million television sets through 3 major channels utilizing some 170 stations, in addition to which there is a private commercial pay-TV service. South Africa has extensive shortwave operations and has moved ahead strongly in cable, with some 20 percent of television homes cabled at the beginning of 2000. Its yearly per capita income is $4,800. South Africa already has more than half the Internet users in all of Africa and its cyberspace connections will continue to grow.

St. Helena is a British possession with just 6,000 people whose 2,500 radios are served by a government channel.

Sudan has 32.3 million people whose per capita income is $800. One national radio system broadcasts from about 15 sites to 5.8 million radios and 1 government commercial system serves about 1.5 million TV sets. The government also operates a shortwave system.

Swaziland is one of the better radio-served countries with a half-million sets for its 1.1 million people, with programming provided by 3 commercial systems, 1 government, 1 private, 1 community, and 1 religious station. Its 15,000 TV sets receive signals from 1 government station and 1 independent station. It also accommodates a large religious shortwave operation. Its per capita yearly income is $3,700. Its economy and communications infrastructure suggest that it is ready for serious Internet development.

Tanzania has 31 million people whose per capita income is $800. Its government has attempted to develop both radio and television systems in recent years, permitting private station licensing because of a lack of public funds. The capital city of Dar es Salaam, the capital, has 5 television stations—1 government and 4 private—more than in London. The country has about 80,000 TV sets. Tanzania's 4.5 million radios are served by a government system sending signals from 10 sites, and by 3 private regional stations. Zanzibar, the island part of the nation, has its own government station.

Togo has 4.6 million population, and a per capita annual income of $900. A government radio system and a regional station program to its 720,000 radio sets, and a government television system serves its 150,000 TV sets. Chapter 11 covers Togo.

Tunisia has a population of 9 million and a per capita income of $4,250. It has 1.7 million radios that receive broadcasts from 1 national radio system that operates 7 AM and 8 FM sites. It also has 650,000 TV sets that receive signals from a government system with some 19 stations.

Uganda has 30 million people and 10 million radio sets that receive signals from a government system with 4 AM and 4 FM sites. Its 200,000 TV sets receive programs from a government network with 8 stations. It has also begun to wire TV homes with cable. Its per capita income is $900 per year.

Zambia's 10.3 million people have a per capita yearly income of $900. A national statutory corporation operates 18 AM, 4 FM, and 3 shortwave radio sites. Additionally, a Christian radio system and a private station program to the country's 1.3 million radio sets. A government system with some 9 stations programs to the approximately half-million TV sets. Chapter 12 details Zambia's situation.

Zimbabwe has a population of 11.8 million. Its per capita income is $1,620. The 1.3 million radios receive programs from an independent statutory corporation with 5 sites. Its 450,000 television sets are served by a commercial system with about 16 stations.

Ownership and control of telecommunications by governments is the norm in Africa. Although in recent years a number of countries have authorized the licensing of privately owned facilities, many of them either exercise direct control over these systems or maintain close supervision. They try to preclude any content or activity they do not deem favorable to the government's aims and reputation. For many governments, the authorization of private facilities is an economic necessity; without the infusion of private capital, in most cases from foreign sources, it would not be possible to build the country's communication infrastructure. The same general problem and approach have marked the development of the Internet, although the Internet is not as controllable as are other media. It is extremely difficult to monitor communication from any given computer linked to the Internet.

Economics is not necessarily the principal motivating factor, although it appears to be the most obvious. The history of colonialism is marked by government control over all media. Only as a given country becomes democratically stable—and there is a dependency upon economic stability as a prerequisite—has it been able to lessen its grip on telecommunications. The poverty of most of Africa made it difficult, if not impossible, to find affluent enough private enterprise within a given country able to develop telecommunications systems, thus ceding that responsibility to the government. The high rates of illiteracy, poverty, illness and disease, mortality, hunger, and births—much higher than that of the Western nations—require ubiquitous means of reaching out to widely scattered and geographically isolated groups with information and education, as well as propaganda, in order to maintain a base of economic and cultural development. Not least is the governments' need to control the media as a means of staying in power.

In the year 2000, as a new millennium promised breakthroughs in many areas of life for Africans, an unexpected scourge threatened to destroy much of the progress made in education, economics, health, and the environment during the previous half-century. Sub-Saharan Africa is the world's principal victim of AIDS. At the beginning of 2000, it accounted for almost 25 million HIV/AIDS infections, compared to fewer than 6 million in South and Southeast Asia, fewer than 1.5 million in Latin America, less than 1 million in North America, just over a half-million in Europe, and less than 400,000 in the Caribbean. In many African countries, about 80 percent of the deaths of people between the ages of 25 and 45 is tied to AIDS. The adult infection rate continues to grow. In Botswana and South Africa, it is over 35 percent, in Swaziland and Zimbabwe over 25 percent, in Lesotho over 23 percent, in Zambia and Namibia 20 percent, in Malawi 16 percent, and in Kenya and the Central African Republic 14 percent. Throughout the world, 13.2 million children have been orphaned by AIDS, 12.1 million of them in Africa.[10] When you read this, the figures are likely to have become considerably higher.

Despite this holocaust that is devouring Africa—and perhaps to some degree because of it—increasing numbers of the population, having had greater exposure to information and ideas of the outside world through radio and television, seek even greater contact with countries, people, and cooperative assistance outside their own borders. This has been spurred through the reception of signals in some parts of Africa from stations broadcasting from the European continent, from signals picked up from other African countries, and for those who can afford it, from satellite reception, opening up for them access to the entire rest of the world.

The budgeting for telecommunications in Africa is essentially the same as for other regions of the world. However, user fees—one approach used extensively in other parts of the world, particularly Europe—does not work because of the low incomes of much of Africa. This has left two major funding sources, government and advertising. The lack of government funds in many countries has resulted in commercialization of many telecommunications systems, either the government retaining control and selling advertising or, as is increasingly happening, the establishment of private commercial stations and, in some areas, cable. In some countries, such as Kenya, the government provides a yearly budget to add to the advertising income of stations in order to keep them operational, necessitated by the low incomes of the population precluding substantial and profitable selling of advertising time by the stations. This, of course, maintains a dependency of the station on the government and facilitates continuing government control, even of private stations.

Other countries that do not provide subsidies make certain that all content, even commercials, do not in any way reflect negatively on the government's policies. This is true even for those countries that have moved away from dictatorships or monarchies into democratic systems. For example, in Uganda, President Yoweri Museveni moved the country toward democracy, following the tyrannous reigns of Idi Amin and Milton Obote. Yet, in 1996, as part of a new constitution, he tightened control over the media by establishing requirements for all journalists that enabled the government to allow employment only for those who supported the government's policies. In Tanzania, a significant example of new democracy in Africa, the government developed new telecommunication laws, its rules and regulations emulating those of the freest, uncensored systems in the world, principally those of the United States and the United Kingdom, and even going beyond them in some instances with proconsumer provisions. Yet, one clause in the new law states that final determination of the application of the new rules and regulations would be by the Minister of Information, thereby keeping ultimate control of communications in the hands of the government. A typical example of government fears and control was the action of the Liberian government in closing down one privately owned radio station, Star, and suspending another, Radio Veritas, citing "security reasons" as the grounds for its actions. Accusing "agents provocateurs" of using the media to disestablish the government, it stated: "The government of the Republic of Liberia views with grave concern the rising incidence of inflammatory statements, comments and radio programs filling the airwaves in recent times which appear to be creating tension in society."[11] In comparable form, almost every country in Africa has taken similar action against one or more arms of the media, despite almost invariable strong protests from members of the media, especially journalists' associations.

Aside from maintaining political power, the control over media by governments is also a colonial-era reaction to what some critics have labeled an economic recolonization: the control of a country's resources by foreign investors. On one hand, a lifeline for many African countries, foreign investments also provide a foothold that threatens Africa's economic renaissance at the beginning of the twenty-first century. Particularly vulnerable have been television systems, as noted earlier requiring large amounts of money to become viable. The same is true for cable, actually so-called "wireless cable" that operates on an ultra-ultra-high frequency and is less expensive for equipment and operation than broadcast television. Satellite use would appear to be a good internal solution, but a number of African countries have in the past expressed opposition to uncontrolled cross-border communication in order to protect their own political or cultural monogamy. Nevertheless, internal cross-border communication moved forward significantly in 1995 with the launching of PanAmSat PAS-4 satellite, the footprint of which included southern Africa, leading to the subsequent additional satellite services, at the end of the decade numbering at least seven and reaching the entire continent. Not only is there a fear of external intrusion of ideas by some countries, but international satellite reception has tended to lessen the audiences for domestic television programming and, consequently, advertising revenue for domestic stations. Nevertheless, media advances have made it increasingly difficult for any African country to maintain a communications isolation, and most have not only accepted a potential role in international communication exchange, but have embraced it through the new media, most specifically the Internet.

One of the motivations for African countries to develop telecommunications systems that reach not only across their borders but also beyond the continent is the misperception of much of the rest of the world about Africa. The stereotype of Africa as a conglomeration of backward Third World countries comes mainly from Western media, including both news and entertainment programs. To counter this, Africa needs to reach out with its own information. Indeed, even some of the poorer countries have external media services, broadcasting on shortwave not only to other African nations but to other continents. These include Algeria, Angola, Egypt, Ethiopia, Ghana, Libya, Mozambique, Nigeria, Sudan, and Tanzania. Morocco reaches Europe with Radio Mediteranée Internationale. South Africa reaches other countries on the continent with its Channel Africa, and beams broadcasts to other parts of the globe.

Cyberspace opens the door considerably further and more easily and cheaply than using traditional telecommunications. Providing material through the Internet to the non-African world may be easier sometimes than reaching one's own citizens. As noted earlier, language differences may inhibit common bases of understanding; in sub-Saharan Africa some 1,200 languages, excluding dialects, are spoken, and there are some 850,000 villages to be reached, many with their own cultural traditions and dialects. South Africa is a good example of solution-seeking for this problem. Under apartheid all media outlets were controlled by the white minority, offering virtually no access to majority groups. By the beginning of 2000, South Africa had some 20 separate radio services that included an English-language service, an Afrikaans-language service, a bilingual national commercial service, services aimed at different sections of the country such as the Transvaal, the Western Cape, the Natal region, and the Orange Free State, and services with languages of the indigenous peoples of the country such as Radio Zulu, Radio Swai, and Radio Ndebele, and to nonindigenous groups, such as the Indian population.

In addition, African nations have become increasingly involved in international and regional communication organizations. These include the International Telecommunications Union (ITU), the world's oldest such organization, founded in 1865, of which African countries are equal members. The ITU coordinates telecommunications policy and technical considerations for 184 nations. Thirty-nine African countries are members of the International Telecommunications Satellite Organization. Many African countries are represented in the Association for International Broadcasting, an industry group, and participate in the International Institute of Communications, a professional group. There is a Union of National Radio and Television Organizations of Africa (URTNA), with 48 active members who promote cooperation, coordinate studies, and collaborate on news coverage. A number of countries participate in the World Association of Community Radio Broadcasters (AMARC), which has an African branch office. There are regional groups, as well, such as the Arab States Broadcasting Union and Southern Africa Broadcasting Association (SABA). In 2000, representatives to the annual meeting of the Organization of African Unity signed an agreement to establish an African Union, a possible first step toward the creation of a United States of Africa. The motivation and groundwork are clearly there for the transition—for some the leap—into cyberspace.

However, one problem still remains. As communication systems have grown, particularly private telecommunications services, governments have become increasingly concerned about their lack of control over content. They all are aware of the axiom that whoever controls the media of a country controls its politics. Therefore, with very few exceptions, all governments in Africa retain tight control of content, mostly through direct censorship, as discussed earlier in this chapter. This has created, for some, concern about the growth of the Internet. Where a traditional mass medium can be monitored from a central source to be certain that everything emanating from it conforms to the government's vision of truth or, at least, acceptability, it is extremely difficult for a government to monitor the communication from or to any given computer linked to the Internet. Although control of ISPs (Internet service providers) does allow a government to establish rules concerning web sites, it is virtually impossible to enforce them without hordes of people monitoring Internet communications, checking not only web sites and chat rooms, but even the e-mail that each person sends or receives.

Writing in Munich's *Suddeutsche Zeitung*, Michael Bitala states that the "Internet is regarded as one of the greatest achievements on the African continent. It offers a connection to the outside world, to information that Africans haven't known existed."[12] Bitala notes that the media in Africa are mostly government controlled, with independent reporters threatened, detailed, and even killed. "The Internet breaks this state control on information," he writes. "Now, Africans can even read accounts posted by exiled journalists and ousted rulers."[13] As Bitala points out, with the notable exceptions of Eritrea, Libya, Tunisia, Sierra Leone, and Sudan, people in most countries have limited access to the Internet because their governments control and censor it. *World Press Review* editor Alice Chasan confirms the impact of the Internet in erasing artificial barriers and the fears this engenders in some governments. "The Internet's interconnectivity," Chasan editorializes, "has begun to blend formerly distinct media—witness the proliferation of radio and TV web sites—and is fast making any form of cultural hegemony obsolete." She adds that "nationalism, as much as any high-brow perspective, motivates some regimes to control what people see and hear . . . e-mail can carry dangerous ideas like democracy and skepticism of authority."[14]

This problem—loss of control over communications content—has prompted some countries to have second thoughts about rushing headlong into the exciting new world of cyberspace.

Nevertheless, the Internet's potentials for increased trade, exchange of information, greater educational opportunities, international exposure, and participation in more global organizations and activities have motivated both citizens and government officials alike to move ahead—cautiously for some, aggressively for others—into the new world of cyberspace.

NOTES

1. From the Final Report of the President's Task Force on Communications Policy, Dec. 7, 1968.

2. *Boston Globe*, Aug. 17, 1999, A16.

3. Ibid.

4. *World Radio-TV Handbook* (Milton Keynes, UK: WRTH Publications, 1999). Some figures extrapolated.

5. MikeJ@sn.apc.org. Michael Jensen is a key provider of information on telecommunications in Africa.

6. "Conversation with Professor Willard Johnson," *Boston Research Center for the 21st Century Newsletter*, Nov. 13, 1999, 10.

7. Michiel Hegener, "Telecommunications in Africa," http://som.csudh.edu/cis/press/devnat/general/africa.html, April 10, 1999.

8. Personal statement to a coauthor.

9. *World Radio-TV Handbook*, op. cit.

10. Edward Hopper, "How AIDS Was Unleashed upon Africa." *Observer*, July 9, 2000, 20–21.

11. *Boston Globe*, March 16, 2000, A30.

12. From the *Suddeutsche Zeitung* of Jan. 5, 2000, as cited in *World Press Review*, March 2000, 15.

13. Ibid.

14. Alice Chasan, "Hegemonic or Homogenized, We're Connected," *World Press Review*, March 2000, 3.

2

The Structure of Cyberspace

Robert L. Hilliard

The figures don't tell the real story. Africa, at the beginning of the new century, had only about 1 percent of the more than 200 million Internet users in the world. In the United States about one in every two persons was using the Internet, in Europe about one in four, and the world average is about one in 38. In Africa the figure is about one in 1,500.[1] Nevertheless, the continent was on the cutting edge of cyberspace development.

Cyberspace in Africa started late and developed late, largely owing to the residue of colonialism that left the newly independent countries shorn of much of their economic and natural resources and with tattered infrastructures. The necessity to keep people alive with food and shelter became the priority. To the problem of economic poverty were added the state control of telecommunications without an adequate infrastructure; the lack of telephone lines and services and, where there were connections, exorbitant costs; the lack of electricity and the high charges for that service where it was available; and the generally low literacy levels.

It is estimated that there are only about 20 million telephone lines in all of Africa, most of them in South Africa and Egypt. Only people with high incomes can afford a computer and Internet charges. Consequently, the vast majority of Internet connections are in universities, government agencies, NGOs (nongovernmental organizations), and private business and industry offices.[2]

Even so, it's growing. MIT Professor Nicholas Negroponte states: "The next wave of E-commerce is likely to hit the third world and Africa and Latin America in particular . . . the driving force . . . will be the need for radical solutions to inefficient distribution, educational and telecommunications infrastructures which currently impede commerce in these regions. E-mail in particular has been the means of linking individuals and groups, taking information and ideas beyond the borders of African countries for the first time on a scale that bypasses traditional political, cultural, and economic boundaries."[3]

Professor Negroponte cites examples of Internet use to simplify trade procedures and customs clearances in southeast Africa, and Internet use by COMESA (Common Market for Southern and Eastern Africa) to facilitate a free trade agreement. He notes that use of the Internet makes it possible for "eventual monetary harmonization, food security, better natural resource utilization, more reliable transportation, and communications on the larger scale."[4]

Jean Sutherland, the editor of the newspaper *The Namibian*, states: "Access to the Internet allows us to determine what news coverage is beamed into cyberspace from our countries. We can decide what images we project. This is particularly important at a time in Africa when the widespread view is predominantly one of disease, suffering, war, famine, and poverty. We now have the opportunity to provide a more complete picture of the people and events in our countries."[5]

The Internet is seen by many political activists as a tool for social change. For many people the Internet may be their sole or primary source of information. For governments the Internet provides an immediate and informal means for intergovernmental communication, whereas traditional communications require formal and time-consuming bureaucratic processes. The Internet also makes possible much better coordination of international relief efforts.[6] It further materially upgrades the distribution of health and medical information, educational opportunities for isolated people, a means for human rights organizations to obtain and disseminate data and even to organize concerned citizens, and a way for journalists to bypass censorship restrictions in obtaining and reporting the news. One problem, however, is that some governments, in attempting to control the Internet for political purposes, even restricting the development of the Internet in the given country, can do so easily by exerting a monopoly over the Internet service providers (ISPs).[7]

International aid, foreign investors, and nonprofit donors are necessary for the growth of cyberspace in Africa. Lisha Adam, coordinator of the Capacity Building Project for Electronic Communications in Africa, notes that "national economic crises of African countries which forced them to set priorities in the needy areas such as agriculture, relief, and rehabilitation, also created a wall for the development of other sectors such as electronic communications."[8] Where internal funding is available for communications, some countries are still trying to expand their voice communication systems, with little or no funds left for data (i.e., Internet) communication. An increasing number of countries, however, have been able to find investments for a growing number of ground stations for connection to the Internet.

The United Nations, INTELSAT (International Telecommunications Satellite organization), and the ITU (International Telecommunications Union), among others, are playing significant roles in providing international support for cyberspace in Africa. UNICEF, for example, has set up satellite stations with direct feeds between Africa and the United States and Western Europe, among other areas. There is a United Nations Special Initiative for Africa (UN-SIA) group devoted to developing information technology for the continent.[9]

Another, the United Nations Development Programme: Sustainable Development Networking Programme, launched a networking program in 12 pilot countries in 1992 and currently is helping 40 developing nations and 36 small island developing states connect national networks to the Internet, including a number in Africa such as Angola, Cameroon, Malawi, Mozambique, and Togo. A USAID (United States Agency for International Development) initiative, the Africa II Gateway Project, is connecting 20 African countries to the Internet and helping develop the continent's ISP industry. Another USAID project, AfricaLink, is establishing electronic communication between U.S. and African collaborators, with the goal of connecting more than 100 African institutions to the Internet.[10] An offshoot of this project is the AfricaLink Directory (http://hawkeye.info.usaid.gov/africalink), a directory of African Internet Service Providers, with a comparison of ISP prices. Another excellent site for locating African ISPs, with maps and links to web sites, is http://www3.sn.apc.org/africa/.

One of the most ambitious and key projects related to the development of telecommunications and the Internet in Africa is Africa One, an undersea fiber-optic system circling the continent designed to provide all countries with far-reaching telecommunications capabilities. Also called the Africa Optical Network, it was viewed with great expectations in the mid-1990s, but its progress has been less than anticipated, with fewer countries than expected evidencing cooperative enthusiasm. As the decade ended it was still far from complete. Its web site is http://www.africaonesystem.com/.

INTELSAT, which for over 20 years has been the leading provider of international satellite services to Africa, has in the past few years focused on the Internet, with more than 45 African nations using INTELSAT for Internet connection at the start of the 2000 decade. The World Bank is building "world-class degree programs for the education of scientists, technicians, engineers, business managers, health care providers, and other professionals" to be transmitted by Internet to African universities, with lectures by professors in the United States and Europe.[11]

A number of cooperative and self-aid projects for the development of the Internet have been developed within Africa itself. The African Information Society Initiative (AISI) was established by the Economic Commission for Africa (ECA) in 1996 to build Africa's information and communications framework. Working with a number of international and regional organizations, including UNESCO and the ITU, AISI has set a 2010 goal of helping all African countries build information and communications infrastructures, eliminate legal and regulatory barriers to the use of information technologies, establish an environment for the free flow of information, apply information and communications technologies where they may have the highest impact on socioeconomic needs, develop locally based low-cost and widely used Internet services, develop human resources for the new technologies, increase access to information and communication facilities with priorities in rural areas, and service to disenfranchised groups, including women.[12] Information on its activities may be found at its web site, http://www.bellanet.org/partners/aisi/.

Other African projects, some with international cooperation, others through regional or local African initiatives, include the following:

HealthNet Africa is part of a computer-based telecommunications system, SatelLife, that links health care workers worldwide. It provides current medical information, e-mail connections, electronic conferencing, and other services, using a system of satellites, ground stations, and radio- and telephone-based computer networks. Its web site is http://www.healthnet.org/hnet/africa.html. HealthLink is a similar operation, but oriented primarily to South Africa and established by South Africa's Health Systems Trust. It uses dial-up rather than satellite connections. Its web site is http://www.healthlink.org.za.

The International Development Research Center's Connectivity Southern Africa project helps formulate strategies for promoting Internet connections in countries in southern Africa. Its web site is http://www.idrc.org.za/connectsa/index.html.

NSRC is the Network Startup Resource Center, an organization that provides technical and engineering assistance to groups seeking the development of public access to Internet networking. It is based at the University of Oregon in the United States and concentrates on assisting academic and research organizations and NGOs in developing countries, including Africa. Information on its work can be obtained at http://www.nsrc.org/.

Two projects assisting scientists through the Internet, including those in Africa, are ORSTOM, a French public service agency that helps establish and run scientific networks in a bulletin-board-type system on the Internet (www.orstom.fr/), and RIO, ORSTOM's intercontinental computer network, which maintain e-mail contact among scientists in tropical countries (www.rio.net/).

SANGONeT is an African regional electronic information and communications network for those working with development and human rights projects. Its purpose is to network the key people in NGOs, community-based groups, government, and the private sector for the dissemination and exchange of information. It calls itself an "Internet service provider with a difference—we promote development and social justice through affordable and accessible communications and information. We also promote open and accountable government through networking and the distribution of government information." Its web site is http://wn.apc.org/.

The International Internet Society, established in 1991 for "global coordination and cooperation on the Internet," has a number of chapters in African countries, including Benin, Gabon, Ghana, Guinea, Nigeria, Senegal, South Africa, Mali, and Uganda.[13] An East African Internet Association promotes cooperative electronic communications and networking in the region. The Africa Internet Developers Association provides information on Internet development. The Africa Internet Group is developing an African Regional Network Information Center.

Africa One is an undersea fiber-optic system developing a ring around Africa designed to provide all countries with far-reaching telecommunications capabilities. The Advisory Network for African Information Strategies (ANAIS) facilitates the distribution of information about the Internet. NGO-NET, Internet for NGOs in East Africa, is an organization to enable NGOs to use the Internet and distribute information at the lowest cost through cooperation on a local and regional basis. UNESCO provides information on the "top 50" African web sites (http://www.woyaa.com/topweb/). There are many other internal initiatives, some in cooperation with outside organizations, some self-contained. In addition, there are frequent workshops and conferences on cyberspace in almost every country. One example is the Internet Technology Workshop and Expo, which took place in Nigeria in April 2000. Some endeavors are limited to a given country or even a city. An example of the former is the Namidef Foundation in Namibia, an organization of Internet users seeking through cooperative action to lower costs in such areas as the government's high tax on computers, which are considered luxury items, and connection service fees.

As in the case of many Third World countries where the technical, economic, and political resources limit the access to telecommunications, including radio and television, Internet development has prompted group use, that is, public interest centers for Internet use. Just as some villages have one radio or one television set and make it available so that everyone in the village has access, in some urban areas Internet cafés (coffee bars or shops with computers providing Internet access) have sprung up. Some of the better known ones are in Ghana, Kenya, Senegal, South Africa, and Zimbabwe.[14] Other forms of public Internet access include adding personal computers to community phone centers, schools, police stations, and medical clinics, resulting in a sharing of costs and the accommodation of a larger number of individual users. Phone shops—a necessity in much of Africa—in rural as well as urban areas are adding Internet access to their traditional services. Hotels and business services centers increasingly are providing PCs with Internet access.[15]

Another cost–saving approach taken by some countries' national posts-and-telecommunications offices is the establishment of a special area code on local levels that is used for Internet access and that charges local call tariffs. This permits national Internet interchange, including connection with remote areas, at greatly reduced costs.[16] Another cost-saving approach is the availability from a number of ISPs in Africa of lower-cost e-mail-only services. Many users avoid even that charge by signing up with one of the free e-mail service such as Hotmail, Yahoo, and Excite, most of which are in the United States. Sometimes the free service is offset by the additional on-line time required to maintain a connection to the remote site.[17]

E-mail is the key to Internet growth in Africa. The average estimated traffic is one outgoing and one incoming e-mail message per day per connection, aver-

Table 2.1
Internet Use in Africa

Country	# of Users	Percent of Population	Growth Jan.–May 1999
Algeria	2250	.01	3X
Angola	12000	.11	7X
Benin	6000	.01	3X
Botswana	3000	.02	3X
Burkina Faso	2700	.02	4X
Burundi	450	.01	3X
Cameroon	6000	.04	3X
Cape Verde	150	.04	3X
Central African Republic	600	.02	3X
Chad	900	.01	4 1/2X
Comoros	600	.11	3X
Congo (Kinshasa)	1500	.01	8X
Djibouti	900	.02	3X
Egypt(July 1999)	400,000	.06	10X
Equatorial Guinea	600	.13	3X
Eritrea	900	.02	3X
Ethiopia	7200	.01	3X
Gabon	3000	.24	3X
Gambia	450	.03	3X
Ghana	15000	.08	3 1/2X
Guinea	900	.01	3X
Guinea Bissau	450	.04	3X
Ivory Coast	6000	.04	6X
Kenya	45000	.16	3X
Lesotho	600	.03	3X
Liberia	225	.01	3X
Madagascar	4500	.03	7X
Malawi	6000	.06	3X
Mali	1500	.01	3X
Mauritania	300	.01	3X
Mauritius	39000	3.3	39X
Morocco	120000	.4	6X
Mozambique	12000	.06	3 1/2X
Namibia	9000	.55	4 1/2X
Niger	900	.01	4 1/2X
Nigeria	9000	.01	9X
Reunion	1500	.21	3X
Rwanda	300	.01	3X
Senegal	7500	.07	3X
Seychelles	3000	3.79	3X
Sierra Leone	450	.01	3X
South Africa (August, 1999)	1,622,000	3.74	since Dec. '98: 1/3+

Table 2.1 (continued)

Sudan	900	.01	3X
Swaziland	2700	.27	3X
Tanzania	7500	.02	3X
Togo	5100	.1	since Jan. '98:17X
Tunisia	48000	.5	7X
Uganda	9000	.4	3X
Zambia	9000	.09	3X
Zimbabwe	30000	.27	3X

aging three to four pages in length. E-mail is becoming the preferred alternative for other traditional forms of personal communication exchange, with about 25 percent of e-mail replacing faxes, about 10 percent replacing telephone calls, and the remaining 65 percent representing an increase in communications per se, communications that would not have been made if there were not an e-mail system.[18]

The largest multinational ISP in Africa is Africa Online, mainly serving the capital cities. Many African Internet sites have U.S. or European servers; the major international Internet service providers in Africa are AT&T, Global One/Sprint, UUNET/AlterNet, MCI, NSN, BBN, Teleglobe, Verlo, and France Telecom/FCR. Charges are high in terms of the African economy. While ISP charges vary greatly, ranging from $10 to $100 a month, they average about $60 per month in Africa for five hours of local dial-up access. Compare that with 20 hours of access for $29 in the United States, $74 in Germany, $52 in France, $65 in the United Kingdom, and $53 in Italy—keeping in mind that in the latter countries that buys four times as much access and the average income is more than 10 times that of the average income in Africa.[19]

In the listing on pages 24 and 25 of Internet use in each country,[20] the numbers of users are miniscule in most countries and hardly impressive in others. The real story is in the rate of growth. Except where otherwise noted, the figures given are for May 1999; the multiple (i.e., 3X) represents the rate of growth since January 1999, a period of only five months. (Angola, for example, is listed as having 12,000 Internet users, barely over 1 percent of its popu lation; however, the figure 7X indicates that the number of people in Angola connected to cyberspace increased 700 percent, from about 1,700 users, in the previous five months.) With the multiples increasing at a rapid rate in almost all African nations, it is expected that substantial use, comparable to much of the rest of the world, will be in operation by the end of the first decade of the century.

All of the 54 countries and territories in Africa have Internet access in their capital cities. All but 12 had more than one public-access ISP at the end of the 1990s. Eighteen countries (Angola, Benin, Botswana, Cameroon, Egypt, Ghana, Guinea, Kenya, Madagascar, Morocco, Mozambique, Namibia, Nigeria, South

Africa, Tanzania, Tunisia, Zimbabwe, and Zambia) had local ISPs or other dial-up access to the Internet in secondary towns. Fifteen countries had nationwide local dial-up access to the Internet (Benin, Burkina Faso, Cape Verde, Chad, Ethiopia, Gabon, Malawi, Mali, Mauritius, Mauritania, Morocco, Senegal, Togo, Tunisia, and Zimbabwe). Half of the countries had public-access centers to the Internet, such as cyberspace cafés and telecenters, with the numbers growing every day. An increasing number of airports and hotels were providing Internet-access facilities. One indication of the Internet's growth, importance, and out-reach is the number of traditional entertainment and information facilities, such as radio stations, turning to the Internet. At the beginning of 2000 radio stations in 14 African countries (Algeria, Angola, Benin, Egypt, Gambia, Ghana, Kenya, Madagascar, Morocco, Senegal, Tanzania, South Africa, Tunisia, and Uganda) were broadcasting on the Internet.[21]

The following chapters are analyses of specific countries in sub-Sahara Africa, examples of cyberspace growth and potential that appear to mark Africa as a whole, with emphasis on the role of the Internet in taking the peoples of each and every country beyond the traditional boundaries that separate them from their neighbors. Opening up the lines of communications and the exchange of information and ideas necessitates not only access for dissemination, but access for reception. The "have" nations begin with a distinct advantage, whether in the realm of international politics or e-commerce. The "have-not" or developing nations must be given both the opportunity and the resources to become part of the new communications infrastructure of the world. The United Nations issued a statement stressing the need for inclusion of all countries in the emerging global information society, a statement that has special significance for the nations of Africa. The statement is presented in its entirety in the Appendix to this chapter.

Notes

1. http://www3.sn.apc.org/africa/afstat.htm, cited from on the UNDP *World Development Report*.

2. Ibid. for site, cited from ECA information.

3. "E-Commerce to Hit Developing Countries," *ZDNet*, March 25, 1999.

4. Ibid.

5. www.Namibian.com, *The Namibian Online*.

6. Lisha Adam, "Prospect for Upgrading the Ethiopian Network to the Internet," http://www.electriciti.com/~adisaba/lishan2.html, April 8, 1999.

7. Mike Jensen, "African Internet Connectivity," http://www3.sn.apc.org/africa/afstat.html#tables, April 7, 1999.

8. Lisha Adam, "Regional Electric Communication Projects," op. cit.

9. http://www.undp.org/rba/intrinit/inter/page2.htm.

10. http://www.info.usaid.gov/aink/welcome.htm.

11. http://www.avu.org.

12. http://www.bellanet.org/partners/aisi/.

13. http://www-sul.stanford.edu/depts/ssrg/africa/elecnet.htm. This site provides web addresses for many African information sites, including those of the Internet Society chapters.

14. Information on Internet cafés may be found on http://netcafeguide.com/africa.htm and on http://www.netcafes.com.continent.asp?continent=africa.

15. Mike Jensen, "African Interrnet status, ICT Developments, Policies and Strategies," http://www3.sn.apc.org/africa/afstat.htm.

16. Ibid.

17. Ibid.

18. Ibid.

19. Ibid., statistics cited from the Organization for Economic Cooperation and Development.

20. www.nua.ie/surveys/how_many_online/africa.html; figures compiled by SANGONeT.

21. All of the figures in this paragraph, under the title of "Continental Connectivity Indicators, July 1999," may be found at http://www3.sn.apc.org/africa/partial.html.

Appendix: ACC Statement on Universal Access to Basic Communication and Information Services International Telecommunication Union[1]

1. The world is in the midst of a communication and information revolution, complemented by an explosive growth in knowledge. Information and knowledge have become a factor *sui generis* in societal and economic development. As generic technologies, information and communication technologies (ICT) permeate and cut across all areas of economic, social, cultural and political activity. In the process they affect all social institutions, perceptions and thought processes. Globally the information and communication sector is already expanding at twice the rate of the world economy. Decreasing costs of increasingly powerful, reliable hardware and software, as well as the fact that much hardware has become a desktop item, will continue to drive the use of information and communication technologies, facilitating access by ever wider segments of society. But this tendency can have profound benefits only if gains in physical access are accompanied by capacities to exploit these technologies for individual and societal development through production and dissemination of appropriate content and applications.

2. The communication and information revolution opens up entirely new vistas for the organizations of the United Nations system; it will bring about a dramatic shift not only in the way our organizations will operate in the future, deliver services and products, but also collaborate and interact with each other and other actors. Indeed, the multilateral system as a whole—and specifically development cooperation—has reached a threshold where our future orientations, strategies and activities have to be revisited and adjusted to the new circum-

stances and opportunities. We are resolved to respond readily and effectively to these new challenges.

3. We recognize that knowledge and information:

- represent the life blood of the emerging global information society and its attendant infrastructure;
- are the principal resources of the burgeoning information economy;
- are at the heart of the intensifying globalisation trends—and drive the emergence of a tele-economy with new global and societal organizational models (telework, telecommuting, teleservices, telemedicine, distance education, teletraining, teleshopping, telebanking, business facilitation, trade efficiency, trade information, etc.); in many instances, physical location is becoming irrelevant for the ability to receive or deliver products and services;
- will increasingly affect the international division of labour, determine the competitiveness of corporations and national economies and generate new growth patterns and paradigms; and
- will have strategic consequences for the global power constellation. Knowledge, more than ever, is power. Information about what is occurring becomes a central commodity of international relations—and determines the efficiency and effectiveness of any intervention which is a particular challenge for multilateral actors.

4. Information is not a free good. Comparative advantages are henceforth expressed in the ability of countries to acquire, organize, retrieve, and disseminate information through communication, information processing technologies and complex information networks to support policy making and the development process. Abilities in these areas may allow the prevention and resolution of regional and other conflicts or deal with new challenges like international crime, terrorism, proliferation of weapons of mass destruction and environmental damage by charting better informed decisions—all of which are of utmost concern to the organizations of the United Nations system.

5. We are profoundly concerned at the deepening mal-distribution of access, resources and opportunities in the information and communication field. The information and technology gap and related inequities between industrialized and developing nations are widening: a new type of poverty—information poverty—looms; Most developing countries, especially the Least Developed Countries (LDCs), are not sharing in the communication revolution, lacking as they do:

- affordable access to core information resources, cutting-edge technology and to sophisticated telecommunication systems and infrastructure;
- the capacity to build, operate, manage, and service the technologies involved;
- policies that promote equitable public participation in the information society as both producers and consumers of information and knowledge; and

- a work force trained to develop, maintain and provide the value added products and services required by the information economy.

We therefore commit the organizations of the United Nations system to assist developing countries in redressing the present alarming trends.

6. Over the past decades, the organizations of the United Nations system have carried out many projects at various levels incorporating communication and information technologies. However, today we must acknowledge that often this was done in a rather uncoordinated manner. We therefore perceive an urgent need for a more strategic and systematic approach to ICT and information management, based on a strengthened collaboration among the organizations of the UN system.

7. We have concluded that the introduction and use of ICT and information management must become an integral element of the priority efforts by the United Nations system to promote and secure sustainable human development for all; hence our decision to embrace the objective of establishing universal access to basic communication and information services for all. ICT and effective information management offer hitherto unknown possibilities and modalities for the solution of global problems to help fulfill social development goals and to build capacities to effectively use the new technologies. At the same time, infrastructure and services of physical communication, in particular postal services, are a means of communication widely and universally used throughout the world, particularly in developing countries. Postal services are vital and will remain, for the foreseeable future, essential to promoting trade, industry and services of all kinds. Indeed the value of postal services will be further enhanced as new services gain ground.

8. Individually and jointly, our organizations are already carrying out or are planning at the national level to embark on various projects and activities to highlight the catalytic role multilateral organizations can and must play in this increasingly vital area. We pledge to do more by joining forces in a variety of fields, e.g. in agriculture, education, health, natural resources and environment management, transport, international trade and commerce, employment and labour issues, housing, infrastructure and community services, small and medium enterprise development and strengthening of participatory arrangements. . . . It is our intention and determination to demonstrate the viability and suitability of the new technologies and effective information management—especially by reaching out to and targeting the rural areas and most impoverished segments of society so often bypassed by the benefits of technological progress. Unless we are able to show that ICTs make a difference and reach out to more poor people or deliver better services to larger segments of society, the potential of ICTs and information management would remain just that.

9. Harnessing and spreading the potential of the new communication technologies to countries, especially in the developing world, in a timely, cost-effec-

tive and equitable manner will be a daunting challenge. The telecommunication infrastructure is weak in virtually all developing countries. The 59 lowest income countries (which account for about 56 percent of the world's population) share only 7 percent of the world's telephone mainlines. Excluding China and India, the 57 lowest income countries (which together account for one-fifth of the world's population) have 100th of the global telephone main lines. Wherever there is connectivity, it is limited to major cities, the waiting lists are long and there is no indication that the situation will improve dramatically soon. Within the limits of its resources and priorities, the UN system stands ready to assist governments in designing national policies, plans and strategies to facilitate and guide the development and management of an appropriate national information infrastructure in accordance with their needs and traditions.

10. ICT hold the prospect of an accelerated introduction of certain state-of-the-art technologies superseding the step-by-step process of transferring know-how and technologies which has dominated industrialisation processes. Successful leapfrogging will allow developing countries to advance, bypassing stages of technology development. While being aware of the considerable practical hurdles, we are nevertheless determined to assist our developing country partners in this quest.

11. We are equally conscious of the imperative to build human and technical capacities to enable societies to facilitate access and make best use of the new multimedia communication resources. The rapid expansion of the Internet and its interactive character have introduced a dramatic paradigm shift in retrieval, handling and dissemination of information. The technologies make it possible for those who need information and knowledge to look for it on an electronic network and download what they need, when they need it. The explosion of the Internet and the World Wide Web (WWW) have created an easy to use communication interface for linking together computers in every part of the world for communications, information and data exchange for those who can afford it.

12. The emphasis on networks such as the Internet should however not distract from the potential role and contribution other ICT can make in advancing sustainable human development. Advances in CD-ROM technology, for example, have made multi-media and large-scale data transfers accessible to developing countries, even to areas where there is no telecommunication connectivity. Many of the multimedia options—and especially the Internet—depend on the availability of reliable, powerful telecommunication connections with a sufficient bandwidth—as well as access to electricity grids or renewable energy (e.g. solar power), which are other limiting factors in the poorest areas. Widespread illiteracy, diverse cultures and linguistic differences pose yet different obstacles for the introduction of new technologies on a universal basis.

13. Massive investment in telecommunication networks worldwide has helped to link most developing countries to international telecommunication networks,

albeit in most cases only their capital cities. Thus far this connectivity invariably bypasses rural areas and hinterlands of developing countries, where the incidence of poverty is highest. We believe therefore that the expansion of domestic telecommunication infrastructure to rural areas and its connection to reliable international networks must become a top priority for governments, the private sector and multilateral and bilateral development organizations. Unless telecommunication systems can be expanded, access will be confined to an urban, literate elite in developing countries, bypassing rural areas and the poor. Here, rapidly emerging digital satellite systems offer new solutions.

14. An indication of the magnitude of investment required is seen by the estimate that in Sub-Saharan Africa raising teledensity to 1 telephone mainline per 100 inhabitants (from the current 0.46 mainlines per 100 inhabitants) would require an investment of US\$ 8 billion. The estimate assumes, however, that the cost of a mainline closely mirrors the prevailing international prices, whereas experience shows that typically the cost tends to be about three times higher in Sub-Saharan Africa. The enormity and scale of the challenge to provide universal access in basic communication and information services to the developing world would thus make it advisable to focus on the community level and on reinforcing major development missions such as education, rather than the household or individual level. Even so, harnessing and spreading the potential of the new information and communication technologies to developing countries will be a daunting challenge.

15. The organizations of the United Nations system alone cannot undertake this massive and exceedingly costly investment. Such investment will help alleviate poverty and create new livelihoods and open up new markets. We call upon the private sector, governments, civil society and other development organizations to engage with us in a purposeful and systematic endeavour to shape and manage this process by:

- establishing and promoting a common global vision and broad-based awareness of the changes upon us and articulating a compelling vision and strategy of how new technologies can be made to benefit all countries, particularly the poorest;

- building of national human, technical and economic capacities to facilitate access to and utilization of ICT in developing countries;

- promoting multimedia ICT in the delivery of programmes advancing sustainable human development, especially to rural areas; and

- promoting with the participation of the private sector, the creation, management and dissemination of strategic information and data pertaining to the various dimensions of development—globally, regionally and nationally and at the community level.

16. We are conscious of the fact that modern communication links—and especially Web-based approaches—will materially impact on programmes,

programme content, modalities and quality of delivery—and hence on the future of multilateral cooperation and technical assistance per se. For our part, we will accelerate our ongoing internal reform and change processes to create modern, cost-effective and globally networked organizations involving a strengthening of our in-house technical capacities and changing staff attitudes and perceptions, especially among senior managers. Another objective will be to strengthen ties and intensify communication among our far-flung offices opening up opportunities for decentralisation and for an instantaneous presence of technical backup and support.

17. Beyond, we intend to harmonize and coordinate our strategies for modernising and enhancing capacities and effectiveness. The objective will be to create a United Nations system-wide Intranet (Internet for internal usage) to facilitate cooperation among the organizations to ensure integrated exploitation of competencies of organizations and coordination at national level. We shall seek to promote cooperation among our respective organizations through the use of compatible systems which we already pursue through the separate mechanism of the Information Systems Coordination Committee. We aim to ensure the compatibility, accessibility and convergence of communications and computer-based systems.

NOTE

1. http://www.itu.int/acc/rtc/acc-rep.htm.

3

Linking Africa's Women

Melinda B. Robins

Africa's women journalists are expected to do more than just report the news. Having overcome the barriers to entering that traditionally male-dominated profession, they are considered duty-bound to address and help alleviate the problems of women in every level of society. "Women media workers," as they are often known across the continent, have been an important part of the development process; they have played a crucial role in championing legal rights, and advocating for women's increased access to education and other resources. Now, they are doing the same to reap and share the informational and networking benefits of the Internet. For all women, the Internet is another promise that they can transcend traditional barriers of culture, education, and poverty to take their rightful place in society. Whether the promise will be delivered is another question.

In recent years, as more African women gain access to higher education, they have entered formerly all-male professional bastions. The many new commercial newspapers and broadcasting stations started during Africa's wave of democratization in the 1990s have opened the door of the newsroom to women journalists. The crusading agenda of women journalists is apparent in the extensive reporting they do on women's issues, bringing news about women's problems to the public at large, and disseminating important information. However, their work goes beyond their journalism jobs to their actual personal involvement in planning and carrying out projects that help women, for example working with a rural legal clinic (as in Uganda), providing housing for battered women (as in Tanzania), or helping rural women go on-line and start their own businesses (as in Mauritania).[1] Now, the tremendous growth of on-line resources is offering a powerful new conduit for the dissemination of information, the sharing of resources, and networking among women across the continent and the world.

This chapter will discuss the current status of African women journalists; the use of the new information and communication technologies (ICTs) by women journalists and development organizations; cooperative e-initiatives that seek to advance the legal rights, participation in the public sphere, and quality of life for African women; and questions of access and equity.

MEDIA WOMEN AND WOMEN IN THE MEDIA

In recent years, an explosion in private mass media in countries that have turned to a market economy has opened up new possibilities for the educated African woman. In the journalism profession, not that long ago considered a man's domain in which women reporters were vilified, this increase in commercial media outlets has forced editors desperate for trained talent to hire women en masse. As a result, women are changing the face of the newsrooms.

However, the rising number of women in journalism does not address the distribution of jobs and assignments in the newsroom. A survey of the employment status of women in the southern African media, conducted by the Federation of African Media Women,[2] confirms that women are greatly outnumbered by men in senior-level posts. Problems faced by female journalists included confinement in low-paying jobs, negative gender-related attitudes, sexual harassment both in the office and on assignment, and relegation to covering trivial stories.

In a 1995 survey conducted by the International Women's Media Foundation[3] women journalists identified "balancing work and family" as the number-one obstacle to their advancement. Women said they had to be twice as good as male journalists to be recognized. A lack of role models and mentors in top positions was the second major concern.

In 1995, a global media monitoring project to determine women's participation in the news found that even though women comprised 43 percent of journalists worldwide, they accounted for only 17 percent of interviewees, of whom 29 percent were victims of accidents, crime, and war. In stories about politics and government, only 7 percent of interviewees were women.[4] A second monitoring project was to be conducted in 2000.

Therefore, despite recent advancements by women journalists in general, their continuing marginalization has serious implications for both the quality and quantity of information disseminated about women—and, by extension, for the use and content of the new media. In a 1999 on-line discussion sponsored by the United Nations Development Program, one journalist[5] detailed persisting negative representations of women in the media. She noted that while more stories about women could be found in Malawian newspapers by 1997, these often focused only on their work as housewives and mothers. Stories about women seldom were found on the front page; when they were, they focused on women as victims of rape or battering, or as recipients of government awards. Stories about prostitution or rape treated these serious problems lightly; for example, a cartoon of a man chasing visibly terrified women accompanied a story about a serial rapist.

Discussion participants agreed that very little has changed in the portrayal of women in media since the Fourth World Conference on Women, held in 1995 in Beijing, whether in advertising or news media. At the turn of the millennium, negative, stereotyped, inaccurate, and violent images of women are pervasive. Some groups of women are simply invisible, such as those from minority populations. Women are described in terms of appearance rather than abilities. A summary report noted: "Moreover, the increased commercialisation of every medium has intensified the visibility of negative images, from billboards to television to newspaper. New media are perpetuating and accentuating much that is negative about the portrayal of women, notably computer games and music videos."[6]

Activists believe that one way to alleviate chronic negative representation of women is to advance the status of women journalists. The African Women's Media Center in Senegal (awmc.com) notes that while male journalists often enhance their visibility and career opportunities when they socialize with colleagues after work, this kind of networking is still considered inappropriate for women in Africa. African women who go to bars usually are seen as sexual fair game. To counter this situation, the AWMC found that new media associations for women journalists are creating opportunities in which they can meet to discuss common work concerns and to develop strategies for overcoming personal and professional obstacles.

Over the past decade, a number of such women's media organizations has been formed to offer members training, more access to resources, and a unified voice to counter mainstream journalists' unions, which are dominated by men. For example, the Zambia Media Women Association (ZAMWA) monitors media coverage of women, and conducts training on gender issues. The African Women's Media Center lists a number of other women's media networks that have been formed in Africa over the past decade, including the Tanzanian Women's Media Association, the Association of Media Women in Kenya, and the West African Media Network.

The AWMC itself was formed in 1997 to conducting workshops and conferences, and as a clearinghouse for information. It has sponsored cyber-conferences to address the lack of women in media leadership roles, and held workshops to help women journalists improve their computer skills, explore how to use electronic resources in their jobs, set up e-mail accounts, and design web pages.

The organization's use of the Internet is just one example of the many new groups with an on-line presence that offer information and networking to those with access to the Internet. Its resources directory, for example,[7] is a comprehensive guide of links to help women journalists strengthen their skills and enhance their professional standing within the media. It notes: "Because women are often excluded from informal networks within newsrooms, and from access to information about training and resources, it is important that they have a set of tools developed specifically to meet their needs. [This resource directory] has been designed as a vehicle to link women to the institutions and opportunities that can offer them support, training, knowledge, and connections."

Another organization, the Women's Institute for Freedom of the Press,[8] details the philosophy behind its media initiatives as they relate to development work. "[Our attempt] to advance the role of women in the media is based on the belief that no press is truly free unless women have an equal voice. In all of our work, we actively seek comments and opinions of women journalists around the world on the status of the media, media companies, and . . . on obstacles and challenges that women in the media face."

DEVELOPMENT NEEDS AND GOING ON-LINE

Some 40 years after independence from colonial rule for many African countries, international organizations such as the United Nations, the Economic Commission for Africa (ECA), and the Southern Africa Development Community (SADC) note that the continent's chronic problems of poverty and lack of literacy, education, health care, and employment are still prominent. Meanwhile, newer ills like AIDS have broken down traditional family and community networks of support and caused much suffering. These organizations have been paying particular attention to women owing to their crucial role in subsistence agriculture and family life, and therefore to overall development planning.

A report issued by the Africa Policy Information Center[9] notes that any discussion of women's access to and use of the new technologies in Africa must take into account the gendered nature of the social, economic, policy, and technology systems that frame opportunities for women:

> Women's place in African society is markedly distinct from that of men in almost all parts of life. Views of women's capability, purpose, and needs are strongly held, defining the boundaries of what women expect of themselves and what they are expected by the rest of society to achieve. . . . girls and women take on second-class status in the home, developing fewer skills used outside the home, setting more limited goals for themselves, and gaining less access to education and health care. For this reason, a strongly articulated issue for African women is the need to change traditional attitudes, and for women to recognize within themselves the capability of transcending the limits socially ascribed to them.

If meeting basic needs and addressing the lower status of women are still top priorities in Africa, why focus on expensive new technologies? Those who advocate Africa's embracing of the new media say access to and control over information are central to positive change, especially for women. Despite access and connectivity problems, and the expense of the new technologies, the on-line sharing of information and the creation of new cyber-communities are seen as crucial to women's education, organization, and action. The senior communication adviser at the ECA has called the emergence of an international information society an opportunity for Africa's women to overcome some of the systemic and traditional disadvantages they have faced.[10]

In 1995, Section J of the Beijing Platform for Women, which focuses on women and media, identified the need to help women gain access to and use the new technologies of communication. However, Sophie Huyer of Women in Global Science and Technology (WIGSAT) notes that most of the positive effects of the information revolution so far have bypassed women. "The 'information highway' is still predominantly male-oriented, and often a forum for gender discrimination, intimidation, and even harassment. The profound, gendered implications of [information and communication technologies] for both men and women in employment, education, training, and other productive and personal development areas of life mean that women need encouragement and support to take their place in the information revolution."[11]

Huyer finds that men are crowding out women's access to training in the new technologies. Women's work with computers is concentrated in clerical work, endangering the chance for participation in employment or political networking. The report stresses that the Internet and World Wide Web are important not only for the distribution of equitable portrayals of women, but for the sharing of information, and for allowing women to find allies around the world. Huyer gives one of many examples of this kind of use: a woman in South Africa working on a campaign for women's reproductive and health rights posted a message to a women's mailing list. Women responded with information about legislation and resources that could help the advocacy campaign in South Africa.

Another area of concern is the increasing consolidation of multinational media corporations, the fusion of telecommunications and media backed by powerful economic interests, and the resulting gobbling up of local media and attendant self-censorship. The decentralized and instantaneous nature of the Internet is seen as a way to circumvent this situation, and an inducement for women to publicly articulate their views. As an example, Huyer details how the Internet was used as a tool for networking—and for the subversion of Chinese government restrictions—at the UN Fourth World Conference on Women held in Beijing in 1995. Web sites set up to disseminate information on the conference received some 160,000 requests before the conference even began. Mailing lists and electronic conferences connected hundreds of thousands of women around the world. Meanwhile, Chinese organizers attempting to restrict and control access were met with an immediate negative global response that ended in a reversal of the restrictions. The report noted:

> [The new technologies] allow the exchange of views, opinions, and news that might not be possible in other media under government censorship and control. They have also been used to protect unpopular leaders in authoritarian countries: through

publication of their ideas, up-to-the-minute status reports, they provide a vehicle for international expressions of concern and demonstrate to authoritarian governments that their actions are visible to the world. For example, during apartheid, the reporters of Africa Information Afrique (AIA) in South Africa (many of whom were women) used modems and computers to transmit news reports out of the country.[12]

BARRIERS TO WOMEN'S CONNECTIVITY

The barriers to access and use of the new communication technologies for both men and women in Africa are many and well documented. The Huyer report[13] cites the cost of equipment and on-line access, and the lack of training, technical information, and computer parts and repair. These barriers are worse for women because of their lower economic and social status, lack of training and literacy, concentration in lower-level and entry-level employment, and lack of autonomy and time.

The relevance of new technologies for women in the South also has been hotly debated. However, there does seem to be some consensus that it is not an either-or situation. Different media forms are seen to be complementary; therefore, the Internet should not be a technology just for the well-to-do and the North. Observers call for new strategies to provide access to women:

> Strategies for women should focus on e-mail and listserv/conference systems. Studies worldwide show that women tend to use e-mail more than other Internet services, for reasons of time, cost and level of technical ability. The African situation lends itself more to e-mail services generally . . . but again, women's situation and income tend to cluster them in the simpler technology systems. . . . The majority of women who have access today do so from research institutions, governments and some businesses. Access among poorer and rural classes is currently non-existent, but critical for Africa's development.[14]

A South African journalist notes that the profile of an Internet user in Africa—educated, wealthy, and male—has not changed since the continent went on-line a decade ago. African women have been marginalized, she writes, because technology has not been packaged for or presented to them. Women have not participated, "because women have not been to school, they are the majority of the poor, and they have no money to buy computers. It is a problem of the status of women in society."[15]

The late 1990s saw a slew of new initiatives being developed and instituted to address these problems. For example, the African Gender Institute's WomensNet initiative[16] set up an e-mail information exchange among librarians and documentarians working in gender equity and justice information. The Healthnet network in Uganda was beginning to examine women's use of and access to health information. Other projects were aimed at providing women with access to information on natural resource management and food production. According to WIGSAT,

> Currently, it is only middle- class and professional women who use [e-mail and the Internet]. In order to facilitate access for women from other classes and sectors, [these technologies] will need to be located in local institutions to which women have open and equal access, such as health centres, women's [nongovernmental organizations], women's employment centres, libraries, women's studies departments and institutes, and perhaps even churches. The location in these types of contexts also pertains to the practical, specific kind of information that women require as a result of their time constraints. For example, placing Internet access in a local health centre will facilitate women's access to the health information they need for themselves and their children, by providing access to information for which there is a specific need at the same time as making a health-related visit. When women can understand and experience the benefits of ICTs, they are quick to use them.[17]

Other individual programs are addressing the paucity of women computer users on the African continent. For example, new centers across the continent are beginning to teach women how to start their own businesses, and how to read, type, and use computers. The African Women Global Network[18] links institutions that work to improve the living standards for African women and their families.

In South Africa, a community radio pilot project conducted by WomensNet[19] worked with community radio stations and women's organizations to teach participants how to use the Internet as a research tool to generate gender-sensitive programming, to prepare radio- and Internet-ready content, and to develop partnerships with other community radio stations and women's organizations.

On a macrolevel, international organizations in collaboration with individual governments have been experimenting with telecenters, multipurpose communication sites being built in areas with limited telecommunications. For example, in Mali, a pilot center[20] has 11 computers and serves a regional population of 200,000 people. It offers copying, telephone, fax, and Internet services. It also helps local artisans set up web pages to sell their art and crafts in global markets. The telecenter serves a wide range of other community groups, such as teachers, rural radio workers, students, and librarians. Support for health care is another focus, with health workers trained to use the Internet to do research, and to communicate with doctors in outlying areas. The three-year project, which began in 1998, is run by technical staff and a steering committee that includes the mayor, business people, artisans, librarians, health workers, women's associations, and other members of the community. Ultimately, it is hoped that the center will expand to other rural areas, and be operated entirely by community members.

While such efforts are an attempt to provide access to the Internet for women, researchers warn[21] that while there is the potential to offer women's organizations important opportunities, the telecenters are male dominated, with the criteria for establishing them largely determined by men, often in isolation from women in communities the telecenters are meant to serve.

WOMEN JOURNALISTS AND DEVELOPMENT

In late 1999, an on-line working group to discuss women, the media, and new technologies was sponsored by Women Watch, a United Nations initiative created after the 1995 Fourth World Conference on Women, and Women Action, a network of organizations focusing on Section J of the Beijing Platform for Action. Section J urges that women be trained in and encouraged to use new technologies to disseminate information, produce content for the mass media, and strengthen women's participation in policy making.

Participants agreed that women's organizations must work with and through the media to get out their messages, for example, information about reproductive and sexual health (including family planning and HIV/AIDS prevention and care), inheritance rights, participation in government, and violence against women. They noted that such organizations often lack the savvy to gain access to the media in the first place, and then to provide usable information and story ideas to the press. Women journalists were seen as crucial partners to help these groups strengthen their communication and advocacy skills and define their messages, audiences, and media; and to show them how to use e-mail and the Internet to strengthen partnerships, find sources of funding, stay linked internationally, and learn from sister organizations.

One participant offered her experience with networks of women journalists working to promote debate about such problems as HIV/AIDS and legal rights, and to disseminate other important information. She found that these initiatives helped foster a sense of community and collective responsibility for the women journalists, nurtured a serious interest in and understanding of gender-media issues, and helped them work to counter sexist representations of women and poor coverage of women's issues.[22] The director of the Washington-based Women's Institute for Freedom of the Press wrote that the Internet has allowed her organization to quickly communicate internationally with its associates, bypassing slow, expensive, and often unreliable "snail mail" and telephones. Also,

> The Internet has allowed the greatest expansion of our voices. This media discussion we are engaged in is truly a dream come true: a way we can communicate globally about what needs to be done, about media and democracy, about how we can communicate with each other about the issues vital to our survival. These discussions and initiatives will help bring about changes that will affect women globally.[23]

A journalist from Zambia shared her experience in development work, and the need for on-line networking:

Information is power—power to influence, educate and form public opinion . . . the Zambia Media Women Association (ZAMWA) is working to advance the status of women at all levels by increasing their access to media and developmental information. ZAMWA promotes the use of media to sensitise society on gender issues and works with other women's rights organisations to advocate and lobby for legal changes that favour the rights of women and children. [However], women still have inadequate or no access to the media and are not reached by development information. Due to the high poverty levels and low literacy levels in women, there is a general lack of appreciation of information technologies.[24]

She went on to describe a consortium of women's nongovernmental organizations that has been created to use the new information technologies, and to get information out to women living in poverty or in rural areas.

The use of the new technologies to strengthen women's participation in the democratic process also was addressed on the discussion list. It was noted that women and women's groups in many countries use mailing lists to organize around particular issues and, sometimes, to promote or prevent a change in the law. Women's organizations have used mailing lists to organize demonstrations, sign petitions, stimulate public discussions, and do strategic planning across huge geographical areas. One such initiative is Women'sNet,[25] a program to help women use the Internet to find the people, resources, and tools to promote women's social activism.

However, a representative of Women Connect!,[26] which works to strengthen the communication and advocacy skills of women's rights organizations around the world, writes, "Clearly, wiring groups to the Internet is not sufficient to enhance communication capability or an organization's broader mission. Rather, we take the view that it is only by strengthening an organization's entire range of communication capacities that it will be able to clearly define its own mission and become truly sustainable."[27]

In Mali, the Panos Institute and Media for a Democratic West Africa have attempted to upgrade women's status in the media and reinforce their position as journalists and producers of information. The project[28] collects data on women's status in the media, identifies obstacles to their equitable representation and promotion, and conducts training. It also has set up a data bank and directory of women journalists in the region.

The Acacia Initiative[29] is an "international effort to empower sub-Saharan African communities with the ability to apply information and communication technologies to their own social and economic development." Among the resources available at the Acacia site is a report on supporting women's use of information technologies for sustainable development, which includes case studies on African women's use of ICTs.

CONCLUSION

Much positive work has been done to democratize the new technologies for African women at all strata. However, basic microlevel problems of access and training persist alongside the chronic macrolevel economic, political, and cultural problems of poverty, lack of power, and illiteracy that a gender analysis uncovers. In the report, "Information and Communication Technologies: A Women's Agenda," the Association for Progressive Communications (APC) notes:

> We are convinced that globalisation and the emerging information society will either advance the status of women in society or reinforce their marginalisation. If we do not engage and harness the tools which ICTs offer us, we will further marginalise women's concerns. . . . We believe that it is essential to engage more women in accessing and using information and communication technologies (ICTs) for equality and development in Africa. We believe that women should be able to use ICTs strategically in support of women's empowerment and agendas in order to facilitate networking and information exchange; support solidarity campaigns and collaborative actions; mainstream issues of concern to women; and ensure that women are able to participate equally in civil and public life.[30]

The organization—a global network of individual women and women's organizations that develops and disseminates information, provides regional support, and lobbies for policies that consider gender—notes that the development of the new technologies takes place in a global context of gender inequality:

> Gender intersects with many other differences and disparities, which also shape women's ICT needs and experiences, such as race, ethnicity, class, culture, age, history, sexual orientation, geographic location, and disability. Poverty, war, and endemic violence against women are ever-present realities in the lives of many women living in Africa. The new technologies have the power to bring profound change, influencing how people know, and understand the world. They change work methods and the ways in which we communicate. They affect how we access and share information. They are also an important source of power. By acquiring the equipment and skills to use them, we gain access to that power.

Groups such as APC that bring a gender analysis to the situation warn that if African women are not actively present at all levels of policy and implementation, new forms of marginalization could undermine other advances made by women over the years. While the information and communication technologies have great potential for women around the world, there is a danger of deeper exclusion for those who do not have access. The changes are taking place so fast that there may not be enough time to grasp their implications and respond with adequate policy measures. Women must take on these issues themselves, appropriating and using the technologies to access information, share knowledge, and form new communities in cyberspace.

NOTES

1. The list of organizations and projects cited in this chapter is by no means exhaustive. Readers can begin their own investigations by following the links supplied.
2. Federation 1999.

3. iwmf.org.
4. World Association for Christian Communication 1999.
5. Mutembo 1999.
6. womenaction.org/global/wmrep.html.
7. awmc.com/resources/resource.htm.
8. igc.org/wifp.
9. 1998.
10. da Costa 1998.
11. Huyer 1999.
12. Ibid.
13. idrc.ca/index.html.
14. Huyer 1999.
15. Mutume 1998.
16. womensnet.org.za/ict.
17. idrc.ca/index.html.
18. osu.edu/org/awognet/.
19. radio.womensnet.org.za.
20. tombouctou.org.ml.
21. idrc.ca/acacia/outputs/womenicts.html.
22. Mutume 1998.
23. Allen 1999.
24. Mutembo 1999.
25. womensnet.org.za.
26. piwh.org.
27. Meyer 1999.
28. Panos 1999,
29. idrc.ca/acacia/.
30. flamme.org/documents/apcstate.htm.

REFERENCES

Acacia Initiative. idrc.ca/acacia/.

Africa Policy Information Center (1998). "Report: Strategic Action Issue Area: African Women's Media Center." awmc.com.

African Women Global Network. osu.edu/org/awognet/.

African Women's Rights. africapolicy.org/action/women.htm.

Allen, Martha Leslie (1999). Posting to Women Watch on-line discussion. sdnhq.undp.org/ww/women-media. Dec. 12.

Association for Progressive Communications/Women-Africa. "Information and Communication Technologies: A Women's Agenda." flamme.org/documents/apcstate.htm.

da Costa, Peter (1998). Posting to afr-fem@tristam.edc.org. March 27.

Federation of African Media Women (1999). "Survey of employment status of women in southern African media." ijnet.org/Archive/1999/11/4-6234.

Huyer, Sophie (1999). "Supporting Women's Use of Information Technologies for Sustainable Development." idrc.ca/index.html.

International Women's Media Foundation. iwmf.org.

Meyer, Doe. Dec. 14, 1999. Posting to sdnp.undp.org/ww/lists/wandh/women-media/msg00285.html.

Mutembo, Ing'utu (1999). Postings to sdnp.undp.org/ww/lists/wandh/women-media/
    msg00252.html. Dec. 7 and Dec. 9.

Mutume, Gumisai (1998). "Changing the Profile of the Internet User." Inter Press Ser-
    vice, Harare, Zimbabwe. June 10.

Panos Institute/Media for a Democratic West Africa. (1999). "Project: Women and the
    Media." panos.sn/e/programmes/wmedia.html.

Women in Global Science and Technology. idrc.ca/index.html.

Women's Institute for Freedom of the Press. igc.org/wifp.

Women'sNet. womensnet.org.za/ict.

Women Watch (1999). Summary report of on-line working group on women, the media,
    and new technologies. UN Internet Gateway on the Advancement and Empower-
    ment of Women. womenaction.org/global/wmrep.html. Archives at
    sdnhq.undp.org/ww/women-media.

World Association for Christian Communication (1999). "Global Media Monitoring
    Project." wacc.org.uk/gmmp2.htm.

4

Benin and the Internet

W. Joseph Campbell

The United Nations' *Human Development Report* published at century's end—the tenth in a series begun in 1990—was replete with sobering data underscoring the imbalances between North and South in such comparative measures as educational attainment and per capita income. Especially striking was the report's analysis of new media technology as a force that threatens the further marginalization of the world's most impoverished states. "Those with income, education and—literally—connections have cheap and instantaneous access to information," the report noted. "The rest are left with uncertain, slow and costly access. When people in these two worlds live and compete side by side, the advantage of being connected will overpower the marginal and the impoverished, cutting off their voices and concerns from the global conversation."[1]

The report's gloomy tone has resonance for Benin, a small country with a population of about six million (1997 estimate) and for much of West Africa, where access to the Internet has been decidedly uneven, limited, and slow to develop. Benin in 1999 had perhaps 6,000 to 7,000 *Internautes*. Most are able to access the Internet in Cotonou, Benin's commercial center and largest city, and are associated with higher-education institutions or with nongovernmental organizations (Lohento 1998). As in much of the rest of West Africa, the access to and the extension of the Internet in Benin is constricted by multiple factors which, as this chapter will discuss, include:

- illiteracy and limited knowledge of English,
- limited and unreliable electric service and telephone connections,
- high costs of computer hardware,
- indifferent government policy.

What was not necessarily applicable to Benin was the bleak tone of the 1999 *Human Development Report*. To be sure, impediments to new media are many and imposing. But the media and media practitioners in Benin are remarkably resilient and have the capacity to defy long odds—attributes that render gloomy predictions precarious and may permit a measure of encouragement about the eventual role of new media in the country. This legacy of resilience has, notably, allowed for the emergence of an impressive variety of print and broadcast media independent of direct government control and influence. By late 1999, 12 daily newspapers and easily twice as many weekly, biweekly, and monthly newspapers were being published. Privately owned and operated radio and television stations were taking to the airwaves, rivaling the state-controlled outlets for audiences. The transformation of Benin's media landscape has been nothing short of stunning. As recently as 1987, there were no independent newspapers and no independent broadcast outlets in the country.

Benin's news media are both heirs to, and the manifestations of, well-established traditions that valorize the open expression of dissent—traditions that were shaped during the long period of French imperial rule and that have become central to a stunning transition from Afro-Marxism to multiparty democratic rule during the 1990s. Twice during the decade, Beninese voters turned incumbent presidents out of office—outcomes without precedent on the African mainland.

This chapter will review the legacies that appear likely to infuse and inform the emergence of new media in Benin. It also will discuss how new media may serve as tools to expand and nourish Benin's culture of dissent, and to bolster the country's experiment in democratic rule. The chapter also will outline the multiple impediments that face the growth of the Internet in Benin and consider prospective measures that may address such obstacles. First, the chapter will examine the legacies of expressing dissent through the news media, which were established during the decades when the French ruled Benin, at that time called Dahomey.

DISSENT THROUGH NEWSPAPERS

During the first decades of the twentieth century, newspapers became the principal way for a reasonably well-educated elite in Dahomey to call attention to the hardships and abuses of French imperial rule. In their "denunciation and agitation," the Dahomean newspapers "had no equal elsewhere" in French-ruled Africa.[2] They were the shapers of a flourishing, if fractious, culture of dissent that lives on in contemporary Benin.

Although no count of the colonial-era press is regarded as definitive, perhaps as many as 80 titles appeared in Dahomey from 1905 until political independence was attained in 1960. Most of the newspapers were short-lived. Many of them appeared during the late 1920s and 1930s, in the midst of a global economic depression; many others appeared after World War II and during the late colonial period, when political activity slowly was legalized throughout French West Africa.[3]

The colonial-era press in Dahomey was written by and for *les évolués*, a colonized elite who typically had received at least several years of schooling and who accepted, if not incorporated, aspects of French culture and values. Prominent among the Dahomean colonial elite were the "Brazilians," descendants of former slaves in Brazil and the Caribbean who had returned to Africa during the nineteenth century and settled along the Atlantic littoral.[4] The Dahomean elite also included indigenous Africans educated by Roman Catholic missionaries, as well as descendants of Portuguese arms and slave traders.[5]

The first Dahomean newspaper, *L'Echo du Dahomey*, was published in 1905 by French merchants in the colony's capital, Porto Novo. Their principal objective in starting the newspaper was to bring about the removal of the autocratic colonial governor, Victor Liotard. While short-lived, *L'Echo du Dahomey* demonstrated the potential power of an assertive, politicized medium: Liotard was recalled in 1906. The polemical style of *L'Echo*, moreover, represented a style later adopted by the press of the colonized elites in Dahomey.[6]

The first printed newspaper was *Le Guide du Dahomey*, a four-page weekly published under the logo "truth without fear" and "Dahomey for Dahomeans." It first appeared in December 1920. *Le Guide's* founder was a Dahomey-born naturalized French citizen, Dorothée Joaquim Lima, who served in the French infantry during World War I and afterward returned to Dahomey, seeking a position in the colonial administration. His overtures were rebuffed. For the better part of two years thereafter, Lima in *Le Guide* criticized the regime of the colonial governor, Gaston Fourn, assailing its administrative ineptness and its failure to keep its promises. Lima could be subtly clever while undeniably provocative. In *Le Guide's* inaugural edition, he wrote, "Our principal objective will be to push for indispensable reforms that effectively contribute to our ECONOMIC AND INTELLECTUAL EVOLUTION."[7] Lima from the outset also assailed the harshness and unfulfilled expectations of French rule, writing: "The native [Dahomean] is awaiting the great improvements promised when the French took possession of this country and while waiting, a hail of taxes has beaten down upon him, not to mention the fines often unjustly imposed, the bullying and humiliations of all sorts. He no longer understands. He still has recollections of his old king . . . and in those days no one demanded so many sacrifices."[8]

Le Guide ceased publication in late 1922 after 88 issues, a victim of the hard economic times then sweeping French West Africa. *Le Guide's* contributions to the emerging Dahomean press traditions, however, were important and lasting. The newspaper routinely called attention to the abuses and shortcomings of colonial rule, confirming the assertive, combative tone that characterized the short-lived *L'Echo du Dahomey*. In its weekly periodicity, moreover, *Le Guide* helped to establish the beginnings of a journalistic routine, setting a stage for the emergence of scores of other Dahomean newspapers.[9]

Le Guide's longest-running successor was *La Voix du Dahomey*, which appeared fortnightly beginning in 1927 and continued into the 1950s. Dorothée Lima was one of *La Voix's* founding directors and was its publisher from 1934 to 1938, a time when French efforts to suppress the newspaper were most pronounced.[10] From its earliest issues, *La Voix du Dahomey* cloaked its criticism of French rule in subtle cleverness. The newspaper regularly addressed the abuses and the incompetence of colonial administrators while insisting on its unquestioned loyalty to France. *La Voix's* critiques often were enveloped in lavish expressions of fealty to France. Such a tone was established in *La Voix's* inaugural issue in August 1927: "In founding this newspaper, our objective is to make heard the wishes and the modest and legitimate demands of a population which, attached to France by indissoluble links, has given France in all circumstances, particularly during the Great War, unequivocal proof of its staunch loyalty. . . . We do not want revolution but rather evolution in all senses: political, economic, social, material, and moral."[11]

Perhaps inevitably, *La Voix* ran afoul of the French rulers. In 1934, the newspaper, its editorial board, and several collaborators were named as defendants in what became the most celebrated press trial in French West Africa. The case was based in part on articles published in *La Voix* suggesting bribe taking in the colonial administration. The prosecution also maintained that the defendants included members of a secret society that was "clearly anti-French" and inspired by nationalist sentiment.[12] The defense replied by submitting scores of *La Voix* articles that praised the French, most of them written by defendants, such as Lima, who had fought for the French during World War I.[13]

The verdicts were announced in June 1936. Three defendants were acquitted and the others were found guilty. They were, however, ordered to pay little more than symbolic fines[14] and the verdicts were widely regarded as a repudiation of the colonial administration's inopportune attempt to crack down on what arguably was the colony's most upstart newspaper.[15]

Why French authorities did not routinely suppress the combative colonial press in Dahomey—particularly during the 1930s, when newspapers proliferated at what has been called "the high point" of French colonial power in Africa—has baffled scholars.[16] The absence of frequent proscription is especially puzzling because French authorities clearly regarded the Dahomean newspapers with keen suspicion, seeing in them the sources of incipient nationalism and extremism. One governor wrote in a report to authorities in Dakar: "Most of the papers published in Dahomey are improperly written, badly edited, poorly presented, tendentious, clearly hostile to the French administration. Without a definite political doctrine, they nonetheless display sympathy for certain extremist versions of communism. Their aim, not avowed but obvious, is to prepare Dahomey's emancipation."[17]

There appear to be several factors that, together, account for the disinclination of the French to crack down systematically or routinely on Dahomey's press. These factors include: the deftness of the press in obscuring criticism within praise for France and the decidedly ambiguous nature of its nationalist objectives; the frequent turnover of French colonial governors assigned to Dahomey; the increasing importance of educated Dahomeans serving as vital, midlevel administrators in French colonies throughout West Africa; and the constraints effectively, if indirectly, imposed on French colonial rulers by international human rights and political movements. Together those factors suggest broad-based difficulties that even authoritarian regimes encounter in suppressing a heterogeneous and politically vibrant press.

To a striking degree, the colonial-era press in Dahomey confronted chronic difficulties not unlike those encountered by the many nonofficial newspapers that appeared in Benin during the 1990s. These impediments include constricted circulation, limited sources of advertising revenues, widespread illiteracy, uneven training for journalists, and mechanical and production breakdowns.[18]

Despite the uncertain, improvised, and rather quixotic character of the colonial-era press, the newspapers were the centerpieces of a culture of dissent that came to define political life in Dahomey and, later, Benin. The Dahomean press after World War II was highly politicized and trained hostility on domestic political rivals as often as on French administrators.[19] Newspapers were the vehicles for pursuing political agendas that became increasingly fractious as the colonial period wore on and regional and ethnic cleavages emerged as crucial political variables.

In the years after independence, scores of political parties vied for power, and instability became chronic. From 1960 to 1972, Dahomey was the theater for six successful *coups d'état*, innumerable foiled plots, frequent student protest, and seemingly endless intrigue. The tiny country fully merited its title as Africa's *enfant malade* during those years.

The chronic instability ultimately gave rise to a harsh experiment in Afro-Communism that was set in motion by a military coup in October 1972 led by Major (later General) Mathieu Kérékou. Under pressure from student extremists, Kérékou proclaimed a Marxist-Leninist state in 1974 and subsequently declared that Dahomey would henceforth be known as Benin.[20] Kérékou crushed political opposition and tolerated no rivals to his regime's daily newspaper, *Ehuzu*, a self-styled "voice of revolutionary militancy."

Still, dissent percolated, if surreptitiously, during Kérékou's rule. Eventually, the press emerged as among the first, aboveground indicators of Kérékou's crumbling regime and of the resurgent culture of dissent.

THE "DEMOCRATIC RENEWAL"

Indeed, just as newspapers were the locus of political dissent and protest during Dahomey's colonial period, the nongovernmental press was a focal point of Benin's return to democratic rule during the late 1980s and early 1990s. The trigger for the transition from Afro-communism to multiparty democracy was the Kérékou regime's inability to stem economic decline. Unrest flared in early 1989, when students struck the National University of Benin to protest the nonpayment of scholarships and grants. The protesters were soon joined by civil servants, who had not been paid in months. Demonstrations in the largest cities, Cotonou and Porto Novo, became frequent and, increasingly, violent. By mid-1989, Benin appeared "virtually ungovernable."[21]

Amid that uncertain climate, newspapers independent of regime control had begun to appear, as Kérékou searched for ways to release pent-up grievances while retaining political control. The first nonofficial newspaper was *La Gazette du Golfe*, the inaugural issue of which appeared in March 1988 and sold out within seven hours. Other titles soon appeared. One of them, *La Récade*, declared itself an heir to the country's press traditions laid down during the colonial period.[22]

With power flowing inexorably away from his regime, Kérékou renounced Marxism-Leninism in late 1989 and announced that a national conference would be convened in Cotonou early in 1990 to which all sectors of Beninese society would be invited to consider the country's political future.

The National Conference, which met in February 1990, was the cornerstone for what came to be called Benin's *renouveau démocratique*, or "democratic renewal." The conference brought together more than 500 representatives from all parts of Beninese society, including military officers, religious leaders, intellectuals, trade unionists, students, exiles, and delegates from Beninese associational life. In perhaps their most significant decision, the participants declared their decisions would be binding, not advisory. They proceeded to strip Kérékou of most of his power, selected Nicéphore D. Soglo interim prime minister, and set in motion the overhaul of Benin's constitution. The rewritten constitution was approved by national referendum in December 1990, permitting presidential elections in March 1991, in which Soglo overwhelmingly defeated Kérékou. The former Marxist relinquished power without protest. He nonetheless maintained a watchful silence, and bided his time, away from public view.

The National Conference was a heady moment in the reemergence of independent journalism in Benin. On the final day of deliberations, the delegates adopted a message of congratulations to the press for its coverage and support of Benin's stunning and peaceful political transition. It was a time for unabashed self-congratulation. As one journalist wrote, "Beninese journalists . . . furnished during the National Conference proof that they are capable of conceiving and realizing, by themselves, . . . media campaigns worthy of their elders, precursors of the Dahomean free press such as . . . Dorothée Lima."[23]

The independent press during the first years of Benin's *renouveau démocratique* positioned itself as guardians of democratic values and of the culture of dissent. Close and critical reporting about Soglo produced sustained attention to his decidedly antidemocratic ways and to his penchant for appointing family members to important positions. Such reporting contributed to Soglo's repudiation in the presidential election of 1996.[24]

Although Soglo was ahead after the first round of voting, a coalition of political parties supported the resurgent candidacy of Kérékou in a runoff election. The former Marxist and born-again Christian won handily. Although Soglo protested that the election had been stolen from him, he ultimately acquiesced in the outcome and Kérékou returned to power.

During the election, Kérékou supporters established a site on the World Wide Web, to call international attention to his candidacy. Although the site was seldom updated, it nonetheless suggested a 1990s freshness to a familiar and once-despised personage who likens himself to a chameleon.[25] But it was hardly a case of the Internet's figuring in Kérékou's return to power. Since being elected president, Kérékou has done little to promote the extension of new media in Benin.

OBSTACLES TO INTERNET CONNECTIVITY

So imposing are the impediments that the Internet seems far-fetched to many Beninese—or, as a writer for the government daily, *La Nation*, described it, "a luxury and a myth." He added: "To buy a computer, a modem and to get connected just for 'surfing' seems like a dream for the average Beninese."[26]

Indeed, the Internet may seem mythical—unthinkably remote and of little immediate value—in a country where the economy is based on subsistence agriculture, cotton production, and cross-border trade (both legal and illegal) with Nigeria, its huge and powerful eastern neighbor. However, new media technology in Benin has its articulate and persistent advocates, such as Ken Lohento, the president of Oridev, a nongovernmental organization that seeks to promote the promise and benefits of new media in Benin. "If we don't take steps [to embrace new media technology] now," he has warned, "we will fall even farther behind and become even more marginalized."[27]

Lohento wrote his graduate thesis at the National University of Benin about the Internet, concluding that new media offer Benin the chance "to catch up" technologically, so long as "the stakes are readily understood and the conditions of development are established. The most important stakes that it offers for Benin are: economic survival, promotion of research, training of young professionals, the communication improvements among regions, and promotion of Benin and its democracy."[28]

While the Internet's potential may be impressive, the obstacles it faces in Benin are, as noted, multiple and diverse; Lohento's thesis catalogs many of them. Perhaps most significant is the pervasiveness of illiteracy in Benin. About 60 percent of Beninese 15 and older cannot read and write in French, the country's official language. Among women, illiteracy approaches 75 percent. But even literacy in French may be of marginal value in an on-line world, where as much as 90 percent of all content is in English—principally because the Internet was developed in the United States and because English gained wide use as the language of commerce and diplomacy well before the advent of new media.

Another obstacle in Benin is the limited access to reliable supplies of electric power and telephone service. Sixty-five percent of the country's 77 cities and towns have electric service, and the telephone network was extended to just 33,000 subscribers in 1997.[29] Moreover, the cost of computer hardware needed to go on-line—about 1 million to 1.5 million francs CFA, or $1,800 to $2,000—represents the equivalent of about six years of earnings for the average Beninese. In addition, an on-line account costs about 12,000 francs CFA (about $20), with the per-minute costs once on-line 51 francs, or 8 cents. Given such expenses, it is "practically impossible for the average Beninese to enjoy the Internet with a personal subscription."[30]

Lohento also reported that Internet development is further constrained by government indifference. "No government program exists for promoting the Internet in Benin," he wrote. "The only move in this direction was the installation of a server at the Planning Ministry. But this server vegetates in inactivity." Moreover, he wrote, most Beninese who are heard discussing the Internet "are confused about its capabilities."[31]

That shortcoming may be attributable in part to the limited attention new media have received in Benin's press. Lohento reported that in reading four daily newspapers during the first 10 months of 1997, he found just seven articles written by Beninese authors about the Internet. None of the articles appeared on the front page. And 1997 was a time of explosive growth of the World Wide Web in many Western countries.

Benin's print media, moreover, project only a rudimentary presence on the Web. The government daily, *La Nation*, posts a selection of its daily reports on-line. However, accessing *La Nation* through the Eloida server in Benin requires registration and a password, and the server is prone to delays and service interruptions. *Le Matinal*, a nonofficial daily newspaper, also makes a portion of its report available on-line. But, the *Le Matinal* site can be difficult to access and the updating of on-line content is sporadic.

The sites' cumbersome elements, limited content, and not-infrequent service disruptions do little to encourage frequent return visits, which, in turn, underscores another reservation about the Internet in Africa: African culture, values, and politics have limited presence on-line. "There are very few African political websites and it is important that African countries use this medium to ensure that the web is a democratic medium with different political views. It also needs more cultural and linguistic diversity to promote different values and viewpoints from other societies."[32] Such concerns certainly resonate in Benin, where it has been noted that "the number of sites devoted to disseminating African information and culture is quite insufficient."[33] Even so, *Internautes* in Benin appear to regard the technology as a valuable tool and are optimistic about its future in the country. They do not, however, perceive the Internet as necessarily crucial for Benin's economic emergence, at least not according to an informal survey conducted among 100 Internet users for Lohento's thesis. Although results of such a survey have limited external validity, they are nonetheless suggestive of measured, tempered confidence in the Internet, and of a reluctance to overstate the potential of new media in Beninese life.

The benefits of the Internet could be important and varied, however. Notably, an enhanced two-way flow of news and information facilitated by the Internet may give wider international prominence to Benin's experiment in multiparty democracy. Despite its exceptional nature, the fair and free elections in which incumbent presidents were turned from power are prone to being overlooked by Western news media. The *New York Times*, for example, published a despairing editorial in mid-1999 about the uneven course of democratic experiments in Africa: "Sub-Saharan Africa—aside from South Africa—illustrates the limits of the world's new emphasis on elections. From 1991 to 1993, Africa did have a handful of truly democratic elections. But democracy activists cannot think of a single case in the last six years in which an incumbent ran and lost."[34] Benin, of course, is just such a case—one clearly deserving more attention, if only for the lessons the *renouveau démocratique* may hold for states in Africa and elsewhere. The Internet is a well-suited instrument for enhancing such awareness.

Moreover, greater Internet connectivity could help obviate other misunderstandings about Benin. A simple example is revealing: The New York-based Committee to Protect Journalists erroneously included in its 1998 annual report, *Attacks on the Press*, the names of two Beninese journalists—Maurice Chabi and Pascal Zantou—as among the 118 reporters and editors who were imprisoned in the world at the start of 1999.[35] Chabi and Zantou indeed had been convicted in 1998 of defaming a former government minister, in a case that posed troubling potentialities for the Beninese press. But the verdicts against the two journalists were not imposed: As of late 1999, they had not been imprisoned. An embarrassing error such as that perhaps could have been averted through wider use of, and access to, the Internet.

The Internet certainly carries the potential to enrich Benin's thriving culture of dissent in that it could serve to expand domestic political discourse beyond the country's borders. Sustained contributions could be made from abroad, through the Internet. While such contributions would typically lack the relevant immediacy (and even the intensity) of domestic political discourse, they nonetheless could be expected to provide important examples of accomplishments and failings in democratic experiments elsewhere. After all, as Nancy Bermeo has observed, "Political elites have much to learn from the successes and failures of counterparts abroad."[36] Benin's democratic experiment, to be sure, is not without its stresses. The *renouveau démocratique* has given rise to more than 100 political parties, an unwieldy and perhaps even problematic number. While such a variety has the effect of encouraging coalition building, it also can lead to disruptive political participation, dividing as it can along ethnic and regional lines. Such cleavages were key variables explaining Benin's chronic political instability during the 1960s and early 1970s. Lessons communicated from abroad could prove useful in managing and accommodating Benin's fractious culture of dissent.

There are, to be sure, risks of overstating the potential of the Internet. It may fall well short of the visions of the optimists. Indeed, without "careful regulation, digital technology may devastate low-income communities and eliminate personal privacy. And repressive regimes may harness the Internet to increase their power over the people."[37] In any event, the conundrum of providing ready access to the Internet in Benin must be resolved if the new media technology is to have much reach and impact at all. While projecting developments in new media is a risky endeavor, there are some prospective developments that promise to bring the latest technologies closer to Benin and West Africa.

DEVELOPMENTS IN CONNECTIVITY

Mike Jensen, one of the leading international authorities on the Internet in Africa, has noted that the "biggest headache" for Internet service providers in Africa tends to be the telephone network. Telephones in Africa, he noted, "are a particularly scarce resource for both ISPs and their potential customers. Waiting lists for lines in some countries are many years long. Where lines do exist, most of them are concentrated in the . . . cities, so the 70 percent or more of Africa's population who live in rural areas are an even more inaccessible market to reach." Jensen added that Internet service providers in Africa "are increasingly turning to terrestrial wireless radio-communications technologies as a way of avoiding these problems. The technology has reached an acceptable level of maturity—a wide range of competing products are now on the market and the earlier lack of non-interoperability is now being addressed."[38]

Wireless systems in Africa are becoming more common, and Benin at the end of the twentieth century appeared poised to participate in the technology. Titan Corporation in the United States and Alcatel in France announced in June 1999 a multidimensional venture intended to provide mobile cellular service, digital switching equipment, and a satellite-based telecommunications subsystem, in a $60 million agreement with Benin's Office des Postes et Telecommunications. The press in Benin reported the deal as making the prospect of reliable telephony available "for the average Beninese."[39]

In addition, Benin has been designated one of two dozen landing points for a $1.6 billion undersea fiber-optic cable project that, proponents says, promises to bring a high-speed telecommunications "backbone" to Africa. The project envisions the laying of cable around Africa, with landing points in Benin as well as Senegal, Côte d'Ivoire, Ghana, Nigeria, Cameroon, Gabon, Angola, and South Africa. "The system will fully integrate the African continent into the global broadband telecommunications network," said the chairman of the consortium called Africa One that is developing the project.[40]

Such ventures offer promise, and may place Benin in a position to benefit from new media technologies in more than a tentative, superficial manner. However, Lohento maintains the Internet can take off in Benin only if citizens, the private sector, and government authorities devote themselves to its development. "The Internet," he writes, "will only realize growth in Benin once each citizen sees in this tool an instrument for national development."[41]

NOTES

1. *Human Development Report* 1999, 6.
2. Suret-Canale 1964, 553.
3. Campbell 1998.
4. Ronen 1974, 55–56.
5. Ballard 1965, 62.
6. Codo 1978, 80.
7. *Le Guide du Dahomey*, Dec. 11, 1920, 1. Emphasis in the original.
8. Ibid. 2.
9. Campbell 1998.
10. Codo 1978.
11. *La Voix du Dahomey*, Aug. 15, 1927, 1.
12. Glélé 1969, 62–63.
13. Adissoda 1973, 41.
14. Adissoda 1973.
15. Moseley 1975, 502.
16. Manning 1988, 83.
17. Moseley 1975, 466.
18. Campbell 1998.
19. Codo 1978.
20. Cornevin 1981, 519.
21. Heilbrunn 1993, 285.
22. Campbell 1998.
23. Agbota 1991, 5.
24. Campbell 1998.
25. Campbell 1998.
26. Sonon 1997.
27. Gozo 1999, 9.
28. Lohento 1998.
29. Ibid.
30. Ibid.
31. Ibid.
32. Naidoo 1998, 43.
33. "Internet: Une troisième révolution sans l'Afrique?" 1997, Sept. 23.
34. *New York Times*, 27 June 1999.
35. *Attacks on the Press 1998* 1999, 23.
36. Bermeo 1992, 283.
37. Shapiro 1999, 14.
38. Jensen 1998.
39. Mariano 1999, 9.
40. Whitehouse 1999.
41. Lohento 1998.

REFERENCES

Adissoda, Marie-Antoinette (1973). *La presse au Dahomey (1890–1939). Mémoire de maîtrise,* Université de Dakar (Sénégal).

Agbota, Sébastien (1991, October 14). "La presse d'état au Bénin: Les professionnels entre le marteau et l'enclume." *La Nation,* 5.

Ballard, John (July 1965). "The Porto Novo Incidents of 1923: Politics in the Colonial Era." *Odu 2* (1), 52–75.

Bermeo, Nancy (April 1992). "Democracy and the Lessons of Dictatorship." *Comparative Politics 24,* 273–291.

Campbell, W. Joseph (1998). *The Emergent Independent Press in Benin and Côte d'Ivoire: From Voice of the State to Advocate of Democracy.* Westport, Conn.: Praeger Publishers.

Bellarmin Coffi Codo (1978). "La presse dahoméenne face aux aspirations des 'évolués': 'La Voix du Dahomey' (1927–1957)." Thèse de doctorat, Université de Paris VII, 80.

Committee to Protect Journalists (1999). *Attacks on the Press 1998.* New York: Committee to Protect Journalists.

Cornevin, Robert (1981). *La république populaire du Bénin: Des origines dahoméennes à nos jours.* Paris: Maisonneuve & Larose.

Glélé, Maurice Ahanhanzo (1969). *Naissance d'un état noir: L'évolution politique et constitutionnelle du Dahomey, de la colonisation á nos jours.* Paris: Librairie Générale de Droit et de Jurisprudence.

Gozo, Armand Joël (1999, March 18). "L'Internet est un enjeu de développement. . . ." *Les Echos du Jour,* 9.

Heilbrunn, John R. (June 1993). "Social Origins of National Conferences in Benin and Togo." *Journal of Modern African Studies 31* (2), 277–299.

"Internet: Une troisième révolution sans l'Afrique?" (1997, September 23). *La Nation.* http://eloida.intnet.bj/chbin/main/text/lanation?name=1822-.

Jensen, Mike (April 1998). "Wireless in Africa." *Telecommunications 32,* S6–S8.

Lohento, Ken (1998). *Radioscopie de la connection du Bénin à l'Internet. Mémoire de fin d'études en sciences de l'information, l'Université du Bénin.* http://www.bj.refer.org.benin_ct/med/lohento/presenta.htm.

Manning, Patrick (1988). *Francophone Sub-Saharan Africa 1880–1985.* Cambridge: Cambridge University Press.

Mariano, Jules-Alex (1999, June 2). "Le téléphone pour le Béninois moyen." *Les Echos du Jour,* 9.

Moseley, Katharine Payne (1975). "Indigenous and External Factors in Colonial Politics: Southern Dahomey to 1939." Unpublished Ph.D. dissertation, Columbia University.

Naidoo, Kameshnee (1998). *Africa Media Online: An Internet Handbook for African Journalists.* Paris and Dakar, Sénégal: Institut Panos.

Ronen, Dov (1974). "The Colonial Elite in Dahomey." *African Studies Review 17* (1), 55–76.

Shapiro, Andrew L. (summer 1999). "Think Again: The Internet." *Foreign Policy,* 14–18.

Sonon, Stéphane (1997, September 23). "Internet: Le Bénin sur la Bonne Voie?" *La Nation.* http://elodia.intnet.bj/chbin/main/text/lanation?name=1822A.

Suret-Canale, Jean (1964). *Afrique moire occidentale et centrale: L'ère coloniale (1900–1945).* Paris: Editions Sociales.

"Undemocratic Elections" (1999, June 27). *New York Times* Sect. 4, 16. United Nations Development Program (1999). *Human Development Report: Globalization with a Human Face.* New York: UNDP.

Whitehouse, David (1999, June 23). "Circle of Light Is Africa's Net Gain." British Broadcasting Corporation. http://news2.thls.bbc.co.uk/hi/english/sci/tech.

5

Eritrea: Wiring Africa's Newest Nation

Asgede Hagos

The history of Eritrea's modern communication systems, its national identity, and its long struggle for freedom are closely intertwined. Its national identity has been indelibly shaped by the series of conflicts that characterize its history; this, in turn, has had significant implications for its communication processes and systems. After decades of war and international indifference, the Eritrean policy and practice of self-reliance has led its citizens to develop their strengths. This has had a great deal of impact on Eritreans at home and abroad. It has caused a tremendous growth of Virtual Eritrea, the Eritrean community in the Diaspora linked in cyberspace, as well as the spread of the Internet at home.

Eritrea's modern channels of communication came with colonialism. The first organized modern communication technology was introduced to Eritrea in the second half of the nineteenth century, first as an instrument of proselytization, but later as an important dimension to the Italian colonial state machinery. The modern press came to Eritrea in the early 1860s and was used first to produce religious publications. A quarter century later, Italian colonizers who took full control of Eritrea in 1890 saw and utilized it as an important part of the state machinery and means of control. It was also the same process that brought Eritrea's nine cultural groups under one national umbrella, planting the seeds of Eritrean nationalism.

The introduction of the modern press to Eritrea also contributed to the birth of Eritrean nationalism. What served as an instrument to consolidate colonial power and disseminate Eurocentric values—while destroying indigenous institutions that were perceived as obstacles to the process of modernization—had within itself the seeds that would eventually destroy the colonial structures it was used to build. "As in the case of many other colonized peoples, the new communication channels also served as vehicles of protest against colonial oppression. There is a strong link between the history of the Eritrean press and Eritrean nationalism. Many of the Eritrean publications of the 1940s fought against the growing Ethiopian interference in internal Eritrean politics."[1]

This became even more evident during the second half of the 1940s, which saw a burst of press freedom when the British colonial administration dropped censorship requirements. This triggered a great deal of press activity, including the publication of some general readership as well as political-party-affiliated newspapers, almost all of which contributed to the defeat of what can be considered the first major threat to Eritrean nation building: a partition plan, presented by the British in a United Nations resolution seeking to divide the former Italian colony between Ethiopia and Sudan.

During the 30-year war for independence (1961–1991), the group that successfully led the struggle, the Eritrean Peoples Liberation Front (EPLF), used the modern channels of communication to popularize important national symbols—including historic and national figures, the liberation army, and the martyrs of the war—and to increase broad mass participation not only in the war, but also in the development of the economy in the liberated areas. There is no question that EPLF's communication strategy—planned or implied in the objectives of the struggle—increased the national awareness of the people. The integrative capabilities of these channels seem to have had some impact on the psychocultural makeup of the nation. In addition to invoking common history, legacy, and destiny, as well as nationalism, the revival of the different Eritrean cultures after decades of Ethiopian government-sanctioned suppression is believed to have touched a collective nerve because it reinforced the people's sense of cultural and national identity.

Robert Kaplan, in an article published one month after Eritrea's war of independence ended in May 1991—after a 30-year brutal struggle with virtually no outside help against Ethiopia, then fully supported by the Soviet Union—noted that the Eritreans had "transformed the ideals of self-help and group cohesiveness into a new kind of ideology that resists classification . . . [but], they are, in every respect, a nation."[2] Many others have written about this strong sense of cohesive national identity among the Eritreans. A former Peace Corps volunteer who served in Eritrea in the 1960s when Eritrea was formally annexed by Ethiopia says that "Eritrea is a country with a vision and strong sense of identity, forged in merciless battles with Soviet-backed Ethiopian troops. . . . Although the modern infrastructure of the former Italian colony was destroyed, the protracted guerrilla war brought out the best in the Eritrean people. They learned to be completely self-reliant, to work together harmoniously with no thought except the ultimate goal of victory."[3] Journalist Dan Connell, who covered the struggle for several U.S. publications for more than 15 years, in a 1993 book on the revolution writes: "After a command attack in the besieged Eritrean capital triggers brutal reprisals, we travel behind the lines to meet the liberation fighters—engineers, doctors, teachers, flight attendants, auto mechanics, farmers and shepherds who make common cause not only to free their country but to recreate it."[4] More recently, the *Washington Post* called this former Italian and British colony "the most unified nation in Africa."[5]

This high sense of national identity and ideals of self-reliance are rooted mainly in Eritrea's history of struggle to determine its own destiny. Eritrea, one of the three former Italian colonies in Africa—Libya and Somalia being the others—was one of the early victims of the Cold War, the intense rivalry between the two superpowers that divided the world into spheres of influence. In what is considered unique even for this period of continuously shifting alliances, Eritrea had to face both superpowers at different times when they came to support Ethiopia's expansionist designs for access to the sea. During the early years of the Cold War following the end of World War II, there was a scramble for military bases, and Eritrea was caught in that superpower security frenzy. Thanks to Great Britain, which took control of Eritrea following Mussolini's defeat in 1942 and ruled it for 10 years, the United States set up a military and listening base in Asmara, the Eritrean capital, early in the postwar period. To ensure a permanent military presence in the strategic Horn of Africa, American foreign policy makers decided to permanently link this Red Sea territory to their ally Ethiopia, which was then ruled by Emperor Haile Selassie, who desperately wanted access to the sea. He was determined to acquire Eritrea's two Red Sea ports, Massawa and Assab.

The end of the war and the onset of the Cold War marked the beginning of the decolonization period in Africa. As a result, the United Nations, then dominated by the United States, began to discuss the disposal of the former Italian colonies. However, Washington's security needs and Ethiopia's willingness to go to great lengths to secure access to the Red Sea were to greatly complicate Eritrea's destiny. John Foster Dulles, then U.S. Secretary of State, expressed the policy: "From the point of view of justice, the opinions of the Eritrean people must receive consideration. Nevertheless, the strategic interests of the U.S. in the Red Sea Basin, and considerations of security and world peace make it necessary that this country [Eritrea] has to be linked to our ally, Ethiopia."[6]

Connell writes, "In the late 1940s, Washington became the main champion of Ethiopia's claim to Eritrea."[7] That decision by the United States had implications for the Eritrean people for almost the entire second half of the twentieth century. "The United States was not sure how the Eritrean nationalists would react to American military presence in Eritrea in the event that country became independent. . . . From the standpoint of military strategy, then, it was unwise to risk a future reality which might turn out to be totally against U.S. military interests there."[8]

The primary vehicle to legitimize the process was the UN, which voted in 1950 for Eritrea and Ethiopia to form a federal union "under the sovereignty of the Ethiopian crown," which Eritreans saw as a thinly veiled annexation. Subsequent steps taken by Ethiopia proved that suspicion right. As soon as Ethiopia set foot in Eritrea in 1952 under the UN arrangement, Emperor Haile Selassie proceeded to strip the territory of all symbols of independent identity as well as the few safeguards the UN had put in place to protect the people. The press was muzzled, labor unions were banned, and the people's rights of assembly and association were abrogated. Finally, the Eritrean National Assembly was forced to vote itself out of existence, thereby finalizing and formalizing the annexation process, and establishing a new political identity of the nation. It became Ethiopia's fourteenth province.

But for every Ethiopian action to annex the territory, there was Eritrean reaction to stop it. The Eritrean press made an effort to maintain the freedom it had enjoyed before, but many editors were jailed or forced into exile. The major labor union vehemently protested Ethiopia's annexationist designs. When it became clear open political actions were impossible without risking jail or death, the movement went underground. In 1961, this sparked what came to be known as "Africa's longest armed struggle" until it ended in 1991 with the collapse of the 500,000-strong Ethiopian army. This also triggered a major transformation within Ethiopia as well as creating a new political order.

However, the economic, political, and social impact of the conflict was unprecedented in the history of this Red Sea territory. When the UN voted to federate Eritrea with Ethiopia, its economy was highly developed by the standards of other African nations, especially Ethiopia. Firebrace and Holland note that:

> although the British sold off and dismantled much machinery and equipment—thereby serving to justify their argument against independence—Eritrea still had a greater industrial capacity in the 1950s than the whole of the Ethiopian empire which, with 10 times the population, was hampered by archaic feudal structures. . . . By the standards of other African colonies of the period, industry in Eritrea was highly developed. In 1939, there were over 846 registered transport companies, 624 construction works, 2,198 trade companies, and 728 light industrial concerns.[9]

However, Ethiopia embarked on a policy of dismantling the Eritrean economy to facilitate its annexation and weaken Eritrean nationalism by forcing the migration of the large and skilled workforce south to Ethiopia. The 30-year armed conflict for the liberation of Eritrea also contributed to the devastation of the industrial base. Sherman,[10] Pateman,[11] and Connell[12] all have chronicled in varying degrees Ethiopia's systematic effort to deindustrialize the territory, partly as a way of subduing it. However, the destruction of the communications and telecommunications sectors may have been greater than in any other sectors of the Eritrean economy. The successive Ethiopian rulers isolated Eritrea from the rest of the world, with almost all international links rerouted through the Ethiopian capital, Addis Ababa.

Eritrea's struggle for independence ended at about the same time as the Cold War did, following the breakup of the Soviet Union and thus ending superpower rivalry in the Horn of Africa and elsewhere in the world. The end of the Ethiopian-Eritrean war marked the dawn of peace and development for this troubled territory and the rest of the region. The Eritrean government began to resuscitate an economy destroyed by decades of war. The rehabilitation of the telecommunications sector, an important source of foreign exchange for the government, was given a top priority on the national economic macropolicy.

This situation did not last long. In May 1998, yet another conflict between Eritrea and Ethiopia erupted, ostensibly over unmarked borders. However, many suspect that the new conflict was about old issues concerning Ethiopia's landlocked status, at least partially. Tens of thousands have died on both sides. Mediation efforts by the Organization of African Unity (OAU) to peacefully resolve the conflict were launched almost immediately, but two years later at the time of this writing, peace still seemed elusive. However, lack of adequate and sustained international attention to the war, which has rightly been called Africa's most murderous conflict, has revived among Eritreans the feeling that they are the only ones who can tell their own story—a logical extension of the national identity of self-reliance. As in the past, this has led to attempts to maximize the resources of communication channels available, especially the Internet. The feeling that there was no one out there who could listen to their pleas forced the Eritreans to turn inward, look deep into their own resources, and develop their strengths. In turn, this has fueled the growth of Virtual Eritrea both in the Diaspora and on home soil.

STATUS IN CYBERSPACE

A recent report from an international conference on the status of Africa's connectivity to cyberspace concluded that "Africa remains the least connected region in the world." The conference, held in Addis Ababa, Ethiopia, June 2–4, 1998, was to serve as an "objective forum in which to analyze the options and projects, their implications for African countries, and, the policy, regulatory, economic, and institutional issues they raised."[13] At the time of the conference, which was held when the Eritrean and Ethiopian border conflict was breaking out, Eritrea was among the very last, small group of African nations that had not achieved full connectivity to the Internet. In fact, Eritrean representatives were unable to attend the conference owing to the conflict that had erupted a few weeks before. However, Eritrea has had e-mail service since 1996 through store-and-forward systems, an arrangement that involved calling Asmara, the Eritrean capital, three to four times a day to send up and collect messages from across the world. Among the receiving sites has been the Energy Research and Training Center within the Department of Energy, which in turn redistributed e-mail messages to key governmental agencies.

The reasons why Eritrea has been so slow in achieving full Internet connectivity have external and internal roots. One external factor that may continue to impact the country's overall future development strategy emanates from Ethiopia's constant attempt to secure access to the Red Sea through Eritrean ports. The slowness of Eritrea's march to cyberspace also is rooted in several internal factors, the most obvious being poverty, low literacy rate—estimated at 20 percent—and a small market. There is also what the San Francisco–based Eritrea Technical Exchange called the "cautious nationalist development style" of the government. Although Eritrea's development strategy, which is based on the same principle of self-reliance that guided the 30-year armed struggle, is rather unique, the rest of the internal factors are the same problems plaguing most of the rest of Africa.

After two years of debate on the Internet's place and cost in the Eritrean macroeconomic program as well as about its potential social impact, the telecommunications unit of the Ministry of Transport and Telecommunications was given the green light at the beginning of 1999 to offer full Internet services. This historic move toward cyberspace was preceded by the "Commercial Proclamation," which was promulgated in March 1998, setting the regulatory parameters for commercial communication services. During 1999, several developments helped facilitate the process. In March, the Telecommunications Agency, which regulates Internet-related services and products, solicited bids for internet service provider (ISP) licenses with a May 30, 1999, deadline. However, the deadline was extended to June 30 of that year to allow investors from outside of Eritrea, especially Eritreans from North America, to participate in the competition for ISP licenses, which indicates how much the government expects Eritreans in the Diaspora to invest in this new venture. As will be discussed, Eritreans in the Diaspora also seem eager to see full Internet connectivity and growth in their homeland, for which many of them have sacrificed so much.

On August 6, 1999, Eritrea and the United States signed a memorandum of understanding "to cooperate in a mutual effort to establish a national Internet gateway in Eritrea" under the Leland Initiative, which was launched in 1996 to help "African countries come into the electronic fold," writes William Jackson, who also argues that the United States believes "Interconnectivity is a powerful force for democracy" and helps create allies.[14]

The initiative is named for the late Congressman Mickey Leland of Texas, who died in 1989 during a mission to the troubled Horn of Africa. The agreement was signed in the Eritrean capital, Asmara, by Estifanos Afeworki, head of the nation's telecommunications regulatory agency, the Telecommunications Service of Eritrea, and Jeffrey H. Allen, acting director of USAID in Asmara. The Telecommunications Service is a component of the Ministry of Transport and Communications.

According to a statement issued following the signing of the agreement, the two parties believe "the goals of using Internet to contribute to the Eritrean national development requires an active policy and a growing and sustainable global information and communication infrastructure." The agreement also is expected to "create a conducive regulatory environment for new Internet Service Providers in the Eritrean market and will ensure the growing access of the Eritrean public to communications and global information [and will] . . . assist national education development and electronic commerce within Eritrea through the use of the Internet network and services."[15]

This long-awaited development also came in the middle of the Eritrean-Ethiopian border conflict, which has devastated these two nations. As in the previous conflict, the current war has had a double-edged effect. Although it has had an adverse effect on all sectors of the economy by diverting material and human resources away from developmental programs, the need for information about the conflict has accelerated the effort to achieve full cyberspace connectivity. The conflict is being fought along the 600-mile border between the two countries as well as in the international media, including in cyberspace; the war is still raging not only in the foxholes and trenches along the disputed area, but also on official, semiofficial, and private web pages. Some of these predate the war, but some were created in response to the surge in demand for information created by the conflict.

Eritrea's Virtual Community as well as the store-and-forward e-mail systems to and from Eritrea are believed to have played a critical role in making the Eritrean case abroad. Among the key e-mail service providers have been the Eritrean Information Systems Agency (EISA), HealthNet, the Eritrean Technical Exchange, Tfanus Enterprises, and EWAN Technology Solutions. In this lineup of providers, it is easy to see the role of Eritreans in the Diaspora, especially those in North America. The U.S. connection is evident in the private enterprises EWAN and Tfanus, which are run by Eritreans returning from the United States; the Eritrea Technical Exchange is a California-based nongovernmental organization.

Some of those who spearheaded these efforts to open cyberspace to Eritreans are among the pioneers who created Virtual Eritrea, which in early 2000 had a membership of more than 5,000 Eritreans and friends of Eritrea from across the world. The strong sense of Eritrean national identity and cohesiveness led to the creation of an Eritrean virtual community in the Diaspora early in the Internet era. This, in turn, has no doubt spurred the introduction of the Internet to Eritrea. One year after the end of the armed struggle in May 1991, a small group of Eritreans in the United States started talking about setting up a newsgroup, which came about with the help of a German graduate student, Martin Roscheiser, and was aptly called Dehai ("news from home") because its creation was essentially driven by the desire to exchange news and information from and about Eritrea and Eritreans.

The membership of this virtual community includes practically all voices from across the East African country and those of non-Eritreans with interest in Eritrea in particular and Africa in general. There are many Eritreans who found each other in cyberspace as members of this community, and discussions revolve around Eritrea and its people. Even those subgroups that initially come together in cyberspace for professional and other personal reasons eventually steer their discussions and activities toward Eritrea and Eritreans. Writing about the composition of the membership, Rude notes, "Each member has a dual identity—Eritrean first, and American, British, Canadian, Swedish, or German second—and many have dual citizenship as well. English is the primary language of the network, but many Dehaiers (as they call themselves) use idiosyncratic English. Dauntless, they plunge into the Net with heartfelt poems, complex arguments, and stories full of twists and puns."[16]

Furthermore, Virtual Eritrea is growing fast. There are more than 750,000 Eritreans still scattered all over the world, most of whom still languish in refugee camps in the Sudan. The rest are in the Middle East, Europe, and North America. In the United States, Eritreans represent one of the three largest immigrant communities from Africa, the other two being Ethiopians and Somalis. Eritreans and Ethiopians were the first Africans to enter the United States as refugees in large numbers as a result of the Refugee Act of 1980. Although Eritrean migration started long before that, the United States did not have a refugee policy for Africa until 1980. Somali influx started a decade later. The Eritreans were forced to start their lives from scratch away from their homeland as a result of the Ethiopian occupation.

QUANTITY AND QUALITY OF CYBERSPACE

When the Eritrean Peoples Liberation Front marched into the Eritrean capital on May 24, 1991, bringing to an end 30 years of armed struggle against two brutal Ethiopian regimes that destroyed the local economy and stripped this former colony of a great deal of its technological infrastructure, there were no computers in Eritrea to speak of. Even the few that were there in the computer laboratory at the University of Asmara were transplanted to southern Ethiopia, partly as a continuation of a standing Ethiopian policy of weakening the Eritrean economy, and partly as a sign of growing recognition that it was a lost cause. It was not until two years later that computers were introduced in significant numbers, and the country then saw a surge in interest in computers. At the time of writing, estimates made by the Eritrea Technical Exchange show that there are about 20,000 computers for a population of 3.5 million—i.e., less than one for everyone 100 people. Although it is difficult to determine with certainty the number of computers in the country, the number of customers who signed up for e-mail services during 1999 increased sevenfold. One of the service providers, EWAN Technology Solutions, reports that it tripled the number of subscribers after the start of the war.

Now that full connectivity has been achieved, the number of end users is expected to increase substantially. Judging by the rate of growth in many African countries in the wake of full Internet wiring, the number of Eritreans in cyberspace is likely to show significant increase in the coming years, a reflection of the new opportunities the Internet offers. Jensen argues that the number of users per Internet host in Africa is much more than double the world average. More specifically, he says, "Each Internet host in Africa has an average of 7.3 users—compared to a world average of about 3.5 users/host."[17]

Similar trends were evident in Dehai web traffic. Data compiled by Abraham Bushra for a presentation at the 1999 Dehai annual retreat shows that more than 60 million pieces of e-mail were distributed in 1998. Total hits in all Dehai-related web pages for 1998 numbered 3,067,908. These numbers—e-mail as well as hits/views—are much higher compared to that of the previous years, and were expected to soar even higher in 1999. Web traffic flowed from around the world, most of it from North America and Europe. Most of the traffic from African countries came from Ethiopia and South Africa. The other African countries with subscribers to Dehai were from Zimbabwe, Kenya, Uganda, Swaziland, Egypt, Tanzania, Namibia, and Botswana. With full connectivity, Eritrea was expected to top the list in volume in 2000.

CYBERSPACE CONTENT

Before the recent Eritrean-Ethiopian conflict erupted, the content in Dehai traffic was dominated by issues that ranged from the making of the Eritrean constitution, which was debated vigorously during the three years the topic was on the national agenda, to female circumcision, which is practiced in some sectors of the Eritrean population. The duration of each topic on the agenda depended on its impact on Eritrea and its people, as well as on the Virtual Community. Here are some of the issues that seemed to linger on the discussion agenda before the current war: secularism, fundamentalism, women's rights, female circumcision, and constitution making—with the last being the most enduring. John Rude, a member of this community, like this writer, since 1997, says, "Blessed with democratic traditions matched only by the Swiss, it is understandable that the 'citizens' of Dehai face the drafting of their nation's first constitution with the utmost gravity."[18] The same issues also dominated the e-mail traffic to and from Eritrea. However, none of these topics came close to stirring the more than 5,000 membership worldwide as the current Eritrean-Ethiopian conflict has done. Issues surrounding the conflict have completely dominated both the Eritrean and the Ethiopian web pages since the war broke out. Dehai also has been instrumental in the development and implementation of programs and projects for Eritrea and Eritrean institutions, including fundraising efforts to reconstruct the war-ravaged economy, and to help those orphaned by the liberation struggle.

Generally speaking, this Virtual Community is like a worldwide town hall where all issues of concern to Eritrea and Eritreans are raised, no matter how popular or unpopular they are. This is how one of its members, Omer Mohammed Kekia, sums up what this medium means to the average Eritrean: "As a friend once said, Dehai is a second home. Living in the industrialized world where life moves in the fast lane, there is little room for socialization and personalized contact, like a relaxed evening in a friend's house or in a local bar or tea room or in the shop of a friend, like people do in places like Eritrea. Dehai gives us that atmosphere."[19]

ACCESS AND CENSORSHIP

Among the key developments following the end of the independence struggle in 1991 was the rebirth of many mass media institutions, some of which had their roots in the national liberation war. Others were resurrected from near death after they were almost destroyed or left bare-bones. Still others were to be recreated after they were completely destroyed by the Ethiopian government. The growing presence of the mass media led to demands to strike down censorship restrictions that were left on the books from the period of Ethiopian occupation. The Eritrean transitional government, set up immediately after the end of the war, struck down the prepublication restrictions. A year later, the people's right of access to public information was recognized in the governmental structural proclamation issued to form the second transitional government. This provision was formalized when it was included in the Eritrean Constitution, which also grants freedom of expression and of the press. Although the constitutional provision fails to specify the type or source of the information the people have access to, it is viewed as a good first step in the effort to give the people access and voice through the mass media. However, although it was expected to energize the Eritrean media, the long-awaited press law enacted in June 1996 came out more restrictive than was expected.

Three factors that will determine full access to cyberspace are the ongoing effort to privatize the telecommunications sector of the Eritrean economy, appropriate legislative and regulatory measures, and, of course, cost. The effort to privatize the telecommunications sector will have an impact on the nature and extent of access that Eritrean users have to cyberspace. The effort to let market forces guide the growth of telecommunications in the country also will determine the growth of the Internet there. The march toward privatization seems to be supported by those in high-level government positions. "The problem is at the level of those who implement the policies [and] are in direct contact with the people," Internet pioneer Menghis Samuel notes. "They see running any sector of the industry as government's job, and no one else's."[20] The same mood was reflected at a 1997 communication policy-making conference, when many of the top-level officials who participated said they wanted to see the growth of the private sphere of the communications sector. Many of the scholars who presented papers at the conference advocated a free-market approach to the communications sector in general and the Internet in particular. It was noted that how Eritrea handles the information superhighway will have profound implications for free speech, for Eritrea's effort to integrate its economy with the world economy, and for the new nation's survival. "The superhighway, which is expanding the frontiers of communication to levels and degrees never anticipated until a decade ago, has started to play a critical role in the world economy and is expected to generate up to a trillion dollars in business per year by 2010."[21]

The legislative and regulatory measures that are necessary for such growth also have taken root. Article 19 of the Eritrean Constitution, which was ratified in

1997 but not yet fully implemented, grants the Eritrean people "the right of access to information." Because the telecommunications sector is an important source of foreign exchange, some midlevel officials or consultants, especially those holdovers from the era of Ethiopian administration, seem to find it hard to visualize the private sector as the dominant force in the country. The Ethiopian model is one of public-sector monopoly with very little private investment. That approach still lingers in the struggle to reform the sector, which also has important implications for the nature and extent of access to cyberspace. One of the pubic-sector advocates and pioneers in this area said, however, that it should not be looked at merely as a source of revenue. "It is like the lifeblood of the economy— like a road which links all sectors of the economy."[22]

In terms of cost, there has to be a fairly good balance between quality, quantity, and cost of service to satisfy the different categories of subscribers. So far, according to the Eritrea Technical Exchange, the existing pricing system for the store-and-forward service was designed to give selected governmental institutions "a low service-level connection for free and other customers receiving services for about $15 to $20 a month from private service providers."[23] In-depth interviews with providers and government information technology officials show that the model being followed in Ethiopia satisfies neither the high-end users nor low-end subscribers, and the cost is less than what the former can afford, but more than the latter can afford. Unless the cost is low enough for enough subscribers, it cannot be spread widely enough to have economic and informational impact on the society.

ISSUES OF CONTROL

As in every society, there is in Eritrea today the expected institutional resistance to technological innovation, despite the enthusiasm of many of the high- and midlevel officials. This should not be surprising, especially when it comes to the Internet, which is transforming societies at a dizzying speed.

One dimension to this resistance can be seen in the persistent questions coming from some government officials as well as members in the Diaspora community about the level of priority and attention the new medium should receive in the macroeconomic policy of the country, and the cost-effectiveness of achieving full Internet connectivity. The hesitation also has to do with who controls cyberspace, since the Internet puts the individual or end user in charge of the process. It breaks down hierarchy. The power at all levels of mass media institutions emanates from the authority that gatekeepers exercise—the power to select what goes in and what is left out, what gets aired or printed and what is not, the power to determine the time, place, and extent of coverage. The Internet to a large extent bypasses the gatekeepers and puts the power in the hands of the individual computer user. This is also a reflection of the culture of monopoly developed during the 40 years that Ethiopia occupied the territory with the blessing of the superpowers. The culture the Eritreans brought with them from the war front, which favored centralization of power and institutions, also reinforced the organizational culture they found when they took power in 1991.

There are also the known Internet-related problems with which every society is trying to grapple, relating to the protection of the children and the rest of the society from this unregulated digital freedom. Andrew Shapiro writes, "What makes this shift [to the end user] so unsettling . . . is its volatility and potential for unforeseen consequences" and that this information revolution "could be pushed to excess, straining the bonds of society."[24]

IMPACT AND POTENTIAL

It is too early to say with any degree of certainty what impact the new technology has had so far on Eritrea and Eritrean society. However, exploratory interviews and studies show that the Internet has already had some discernible effect. One recent study, which used the Internet "as the primary space to observe the discursive interactions of Eritreans with one another and to engage in structured communication with individuals," found that the new medium and its technological basis has played a significant role in the intensification of Eritrean nationalism in response to the threat posed by the current border conflict. Tricia Hepner writes:

> A central medium in this process [of intensification of nationalism] has been the Internet, as battles over the definition of nationhood and the defense of sacrosanct land are waged and resources mobilized via the disembodied, imaginary terrain of cyberspace. . . . Using the Internet as a medium to communicate news from home and engage in vigorous debates over authority, loyalty, responding, and the causes and consequences of the current border war Eritrean transmigrants have effectively contributed to a dramatic intensification of nationalism in the past year.[25]

She argues that "the consolidation of Eritrean national identity resulting from the border war is actively shaped by those who are physically separated from the territory itself, and that issues of identity negotiation are a fundamental current in the explosion of the war."[26]

Despite the fact that cyberspace is mostly an individual encounter with the computer, the Internet has a great deal of integrative capacity, and can be a vehicle for popular participation in national development or national integration. By exposing individuals and groups to diverse modes of thought, customs, cultural patterns, and linguistic varieties, communication can significantly contribute to the integration of different ethnic, cultural, and religious communities. By identifying those factors that divide and bind different groups, communication can build on those points of cultural intersections. More communication is likely to widen and broaden the boundaries of integration.

Its potential in this regard can be seen in Dehai. A cursory look at the effect of Dehai and the limited e-mail service in Eritrea shows that the Internet, like—or maybe more than—other mass communication media, facilitates national integration, strengthens national unity and national identity, and promotes issues of nation building and development. This is becoming evident among Eritreans at home and abroad. For example, it played a measurable role in the year-long effort to raise funds for victims of the war, selling savings bonds and mobilizing people to financially support the war.[27] Eritreans in the Diaspora raised tens of millions of dollars to support the latest war with Ethiopia. Some of that is attributed to cyberspace-based campaigns conducted mostly by Dehai-affiliated groups, but also by the Eritrean government.

In-depth interviews with some of the country's Internet pioneers as well as end users also support such exploratory findings on the impact of the new technology on Eritrean nationalism. The new medium was popularized among Eritreans in the summer of 1998 when it was badly needed to fill a news void; it also provided access to Virtual Eritrea abroad and its Internet-related services. In fact, according to Menghis Samuel, one of the pioneers both in the United States and in Eritrea, the Internet has come to be viewed as a reliable source of information. "People, when passing on news, hasten to add 'This came from e-mail [Internet],' to ascertain the veracity of the news piece," he said. "Today, the words 'e-mail' and 'Internet' are used interchangeably."[28]

As in the rest of Africa and indeed in the world, the Internet's potential as an economic force is still too distant and too abstract for most Eritreans. In the area of development, the Internet can play a critical role by facilitating participation. There can be no development without the full participation of the people because it is an all-encompassing and human-centered process. But such participation cannot take place without the full utilization of the communication media to mobilize the people. Melkote notes that communication theorists who advocate new approaches to development view "participation by itself as central to the development process" and equate increased participation—through the different modes of communication—"with individual and social development."[29] Robert Stevenson says the communication media do more than just serve as vehicles of participation. "Communication as a factor in social change—the magic multiplier of national development—is a major theme in the literature of the adolescent science of human communication but for some reason is rarely mentioned in the broader literature of development in economic and political science."[30]

As noted, one characteristic that separates Eritrea from many nations is its strong belief in and practice of economic self-reliance. The national macroeconomic policy is fully anchored on this concept. This too has its roots in the armed struggle when Eritreans had to fight for such a long time without outside help. International neglect through the long war also led to strict prioritizing of the society's meager resources. Therefore, it was not surprising to hear the persistent questions from government officials at the 1997 communication policy conference and during private interviews about the level of attention the technology should get from the government. Although there was a general feeling among the policy makers that the new medium is a potential agent of change, discussion focused on its potential impact on the Eritrean society, especially as it relates to religion, ethnicity, and national unity. The government views the guarding of the religious, cultural, and ethnic diversity of the Eritrean society as a top national priority. Eritrea, which is home to nine different nationalities, half of whom are Christians and the other half Muslims, goes to extreme lengths to guard the relationships among the ethnic communities and religions. The Eritrean national identity is being cultivated carefully and forged in the struggle for independence. The delicate balance between the two major religious communities is also enviously guarded by the society and the government. The unity of the Eritrean people was seen as indispensable to achieve Eritrean independence; so it is today for its maintenance. Adding to its significance are the policies of its neighbors. On the one hand, there is Sudan, now viewed as the hub of Islamic fundamentalism. On the other, there is ethnically divided Ethiopia, which traditionally portrayed itself as a Christian island surrounded by hostile Muslims. However, in sharp contrast to the practices and history of its neighbors, Eritrea historically practiced religious pluralism.

In the area of governance, the new technology is also either forcing or making it easier for governments in the developing nations to open up their political systems to broader participation. One can see this in the way the new medium is making available information that would not be acceptable in the Eritrean mainstream media. A cursory look at Dehai, which is an unregulated and unmoderated medium, shows how difficult it would be for governments to control cyberspace content. Much information that could be classified as objectionable to the majority of the Dehai membership was made available on many Dehai web pages covering a broad area of topics. Even ideas that were characterized as treasonous by some members were widely discussed on practically all Eritrean web pages. Hepner's study indicates that:

> news stories about opposition groups have recently proliferated on the Eritrean networks, and while almost uniformly dismissed, the information nevertheless exists and can be easily accessed. [There is no question that cyberspace] exists as a more democratic (and potentially democratizing) arena that cannot be successfully censored, averted, or silenced. It is a powerful tool that has multiple uses in different contexts, acting at once as a facilitator and mediating link between exiles who support and maintain the nation-state and its projects, and as a potential site for subversion and perhaps even resistance.[31]

Generally speaking, the new medium has so far had some discernible effect on Eritreans as well as Eritrean institutions at home and abroad. In his general assessment of Virtual Eritrea, Rude notes: "One cheer for technology, then save the other two for the resourcefulness and sense of community of the Eritrean people. In this case, it is the messengers rather than the medium who provide the message."[32] However, it will be a while before a broader assessment can be made on its impact with an acceptable degree of scientific accuracy.

CONCLUSIONS

The marginalization of Africa is evident in cyberspace more than in any other area. This is more so for Africa's newest nation just entering cyberspace. With Eritrea still at the starting gate in the race for full Internet connectivity, it is too early to say how the new technology is going to affect this Red Sea territory and its people. But how Eritrea deals with the Internet and the rest of the communications sectors will greatly determine its development programs as well as its competitiveness in the region and, to some extent, globally.

The challenges Eritrea is facing are multifaceted, but so are the opportunities the Internet offers. The solutions to some of the problems and challenges could be in the higher technology the Internet represents. Fortunately, among the encouraging signs in Eritrea today is a growing recognition of the centrality of information to developmental strategies. That wasn't the case in the past in Africa. During the last four decades, African leaders viewed information not as an important national need, but as a luxury that the fragile and diverse societies could ill afford not to control to preserve national unity. However, history has shown that a free flow of information can and does strengthen the bonds of diverse communities.

Among the challenges small, developing nations like Eritrea have to grapple with in this race toward and in cyberspace include high poverty level, low literacy rate, and small market. And all of these have a direct bearing on how much access the average Eritrean will have to the new technology. The problem of a "digital divide" has implications for almost every aspect of Eritrea's national life. When one talks about the Internet in Africa, sometimes it is easy to forget that one is talking about a small percentage of the population in the respective nations. In the case of Eritrea, the discussion automatically leaves out the 80 percent in the rural sector, almost all of whom cannot read or write, who live outside of the global information village, where there are no computers, modems, or telephones. Addressing the danger of the digital divide, one Internet service provider puts it this way: "Information access must not become the monopoly domain of a few affluent foreigners. The Internet is a public resource, and the public in every country and at every income level should have the right and the means to access it."[33] Fortunately, bridging this rural-urban divide is a top priority in the Eritrean macroeconomic policy.

There are also the usual concerns about and implications of what the new digital freedom means with regard to the protection of the innocent. Efforts should be made on several fronts—including legislative, technological, and educational—to protect the innocent and the rest of the population from aspects of the Internet that can be harmful. The legislative approach can prevent that aspect of the information that poses danger to children in particular and the society in general. For example, the transmission of pornographic materials over this global computer network should be criminalized. The technological side to this effort should encourage users to adopt screening and filtering software. Instead of regulating the Internet, let us support "the use of technology that allows users to screen what children, for instance, can access on the global computer network."[34] But the best protection comes from what the schools will do to prepare the young to use this technology. To take the maximum out of this technology and the information that flows through it, the appropriate training is required.

However, security issues will continue to represent the biggest challenge to this young nation and the rest of the region for some time to come. How the current conflict with neighboring Ethiopia is concluded will determine how much of the national resources can be invested in Internet and Internet-related programs and infrastructure. As was stated earlier, such conflicts seem to have a paralyzing effect especially on small nations. For example, at the center of the Eritrean macroeconomic policy is the development and expansion of the country's telecommunications infrastructure. However, a public program designed to substantially expand and improve the telephone infrastructure was put on hold partly owing to the ongoing conflict. Another plan that has been adversely affected by the Eritrean-Ethiopian and other regional conflicts is an economic regional cooperation program among the nations of the Horn of Africa. Speaking about how regional conflicts are frustrating Africa's desires to use new communication technologies to advance the continent's development plans, an Organization of African Unity official warned that "if Africa drags its feet in the introduction of modern information and telecommunication technologies, it will deepen the information gap between it and the developed countries, to the detriment of its economic survival." Addressing African transport and communication ministers, the official reiterated that the desire to benefit from the same technologies that are transforming the economies of the rest of the world would be thwarted "because of the way conflicts and civil strife are raging across the continent."[35]

NOTES

1. Hagos 1998, 76.
2. Kaplan 1991, 17.
3. Rude 1996, 17.
4. Connell 1993, inside front jacket.
5. Vick 1999, A29.
6. "In Defense of the Eritrean Revolution," 1976, 64.
7. Connell 1993, 21.
8. Yohannes 1988, 68.
9. Firebrace and Holland 1985, 70.
10. Sherman 1980.
11. Pateman 1990.
12. Connell 1993.

13. World Bank 1999, ix.
14. Jackson 1997, 43.
15. "Eritrea and USA Sign Agreement," 1999.
16. Rude 1996, 18.
17. Jensen 1999, 1.
18. Rude 1996, 19.
19. Rude 1996, 22.
20. Author's interview with Menghis Samuel on June 20, 1999, in Washington, D.C.
21. Baker 1997, A6.
22. Interview with Menghis Samuel, 1999.
23. Eritrea Technical Exchange, "An Optimal," 1999, 5.
24. Shapiro, 1999, B5.
25. Hepner 1999, 8.
26. Ibid., 2–3.
27. *Haddas Eritrea*, June 21, 1999, 1.
28. Interview with Menghis Samuel, 1999.
29. Melkote 1991, 247.
30. Stevenson 1993, 97.
31. Hepner 1999, 27.
32. Rude 1996, 22.
33. Eritrea Technical Exchange, 1999, 11.
34. Baker 1997, A6.
35. Associated Press, "OAU Official Warns Ministers," Aug. 25, 1999.

REFERENCES

Anderson, Benedict (1983). *Imagined Communities: Reflections on the Origins and Spread of Nationalism*. London: Verso Bank.
Associated Press (1999). "OAU Official Warns Ministers." August 25, 1999.
Baker, Peter (1997). "Clinton Calls a Summit on Internet Smut," *Washington Post*, July 2, A26.
Bourgault, Louise (1995). *Mass Media in Sub-Sahara Africa*. Bloomington: Indiana University Press.
Connell, Dan (1993). *Against All Odds: A Chronicle of the Eritrean Revolution*. Trenton, N.J.: The Red Sea Press.
Dunn, Hopeton S. (ed.) (1995). *Globalization, Communications and Caribbean Identity.* New York: St. Martin's Press.
Eritrea Technical Exchange (1999). "An Optimal Eritrean Internet: How to Do an Internet Connection That Is Right for Eritrea." Unpublished manuscript.
"Eritrea and USA Sign Agreement." Press statement Issued by the Eritrean Ministry of Transportation and Communication, Aug. 6, 1999.
Firebrace, James, and Stuart Holland (1985). *Never Kneel Down*. Trenton, N.J.: Red Sea Press.
Gaye, Sidey (1999). "South Africa—Internet Usage Slowing Down in South Africa," Pan African News Agency (PANA), July 7, 1999.
Hagos, Asgede (1993). "Indigenous Channels of Communication, Development and Governance in Africa." Prepared for the World Bank. Unpublished.

—— (1998). "Mass Communication and Nation Building: Policy Implications for Eritrea." *Eritrean Studies Review, 2* (2). Lawrenceville, N.J.: The Red Sea Press.

Hepner, Tricia Redeker (1999). "Contested Terrain and Transnational Borders." Unpublished manuscript.

"In Defense of the Eritrean Revolution." Association of Eritrean Students in North America and Association of Eritrean Women in North America, New York, February, 1976.

Jackson, William (1997). "U.S. Will Help Africa Establish a Commercial Net Presence." *Government Computer News*, Oct. 27, *16* (33), 42–43.

Jensen, Mike (1999). "The 'In' Thing." *The News*, Africa News Online, July 6, 1999.

Kaplan, Robert D. (1991). "Eritrea's Sudden Rebirth: New World Orphan." *New Republic*, June 24, 16–18.

Melkote, Srinivas R. (1991). *Communication for Development in the Third World: Theory and Practice.* New Delhi: Sage Publications.

Ministry of Transport and Communications, Communications Department (1999). Press statement, issued Aug. 6.

Pateman, Roy (1990). *Eritrea: Even the Stones Are Burning.* Trenton, N.J.: The Red Sea Press.

Rota, Joseph, and Tatiana Galvan (1987). "Information Technology and National Development in Latin America," in *Political Communication Research: Approaches, Studies and Assessments.* Vol. 1, by David L. Puletz (ed.). Norwood, N.J.: Ablex Publishing.

Rude, John C. (1996). "Birth of a Nation in Cyberspace." *The Humanist*, March/April, 17–22.

Shapiro, Andrew (1999). "Internet's Gain, Society's Loss." *Washington Post*, June 27, B1–B5.

Sherman, Richard (1980). *Eritrea: The Unfinished Revolution.* New York: Praeger.

Stevenson, Robert L. (1993). "Communication and Development: Lessons from and for Africa," in *Window on Africa: Democratization and Media Exposure*, Festus Eribo, Oyeleye Oyediran, Mulatu Wubneh, and Leo Zonn (eds.). Greenville, N.C.: Center for International Programs.

Vick, Karl. 1999. "African Leaders Turn on Each Other," *Washington Post*, September 2, 1999, A29.

World Bank (1999). "Global Connectivity for Africa: Issues and Options." Conference Report on Global Connectivity for Africa, Addis Ababa, Ethiopia, June 2–4, 1998. Washington, D.C.: The International Bank for Reconstruction and Development/The World Bank.

Yohannes, Okbazghi (1988). "Behind the Ethio-Eritrean Federation: The Conspiracy Thesis." *Journal of Eritrean Studies* III (2), 67–75.

6

Ethiopia in Cyberspace

Robert G. White

Ethiopia is not the brightest star in African cyberspace. There are good reasons why that is so as well as a number of factors that suggest that changes are under way. The star is rising and getting brighter. This chapter will examine some of the reasons Ethiopia has lagged behind other African countries in the development of information and communication technologies (ICTs), and suggest reasons why that may be changing at the dawn of the twenty-first century. What are some of the factors favoring the growth of ICTs in Ethiopia? How can they be useful in the social and economic development of the country? What are the barriers to ICT growth? What can we expect for the future? How will ICTs benefit the peasant coffee farmer?

Ethiopia is located in the northeastern Horn of Africa, bordered on the west by Sudan, the northeast by Djibouti, the east by Somalia, and the south by Kenya. Eritrea, the former northern province of Ethiopia, is now an independent country, and separates Ethiopia from the Red Sea to the north, thus making it a landlocked country. In Europe and North America, Ethiopia is often associated with the long reign of Emperor Haile Selassie, believed by some to be the descendent of King Solomon and the Queen of Sheba. For others, perhaps, it is associated with the ancient northern city of Axum, the legendary resting place of the Arc of the Covenant, the original Ten Commandments given to Moses by God. For still others, it is the location of "Lucy," the oldest hominid fossil. Everyone remembers the grim images of famine and feeding camps that filled television screens in the West in the mid-1980s, evoking an outpouring of sympathy and aid, but contributing little to our understanding of Ethiopia.

Why has Ethiopia lagged behind many other African countries in the development of ICTs? Its recent history is one good reason. Ethiopia has only recently emerged from 17 years of a bloody military dictatorship and civil war. After a short interlude of peace and rebuilding, it found itself engaged in a new war, this time with its northern neighbor, Eritrea. Eritrea became independent from Ethiopia peacefully after a referendum in 1993, although this peaceful dissolution had been preceded by decades of Eritrean armed struggle. After more than a year and a half of fighting between the two countries, a cease-fire was brokered by the Organization of African Unity (OAU). This period of turmoil and war has consumed a huge proportion of resources that might otherwise have been directed to development, and has inevitably handicapped Ethiopia's emergence into the information age. With lasting peace in the offing, there is good reason for hope.

A second reason Ethiopia has lagged behind in ICT development is the state-owned Ethiopian Telecommunications Corporation (ETC). Established over 100 years ago, the ETC is one of the oldest telecommunications companies in Africa. Although the economy as a whole has been liberalized in specific ways, and private investors are clearly welcome in a number of areas, there seems to be strong resistance on the part of the government to privatizing telecommunications. Just how strong this resistance is was made clear in 1999, when the U.S. Agency for International Development (U.S. AID) refused to fund expansion of the Global One (Sprint) link to double its capacity from 256 kbps to 512 kbps, unless the government agreed to liberalize some of the telecommunications business. U.S. AID was said to have insisted that the ETC allow additional Internet service providers to set up operations. The Ethiopian government refused, however, and turned to the United Nations Development Program for the money, which agreed to provide it under its Internet Initiative for Africa program. The tender for this project, which includes additional information on ETC's plans, is available on the ETC site.[1]

In late 1999, the government seemed to have reconsidered its opposition to telecommunications privatization. This may be due to widespread public criticism in the lively free press that has flowered since the end of the dictatorship in 1991, or from the pressure from international donors like the International Monetary Fund (IMF) and the World Bank. One newspaper characterized the ETC as "a graphic example of a big corporation in a developing country suffering from overweight and threatened with what we might call a 'bureaucratic cardiac arrest.' The symptom is widespread corruption and inefficiency."[2] The president of the Ethiopian Information Technology Professionals Association noted that "in addition to creating the necessary awareness among the top management of institutions, the government will have to help expedite the dissemination of modern information technology by encouraging joint venture or partial privatization of the Ethiopian Telecommunications Corporation (ETC)."[3] In April 1999, the government formally issued regulations permitting privatization of telecommunications.[4] However, the regulations are seen as too vague and general to be attractive to most foreign investors. Six months after the regulations were issued, the Ethiopian Privatization Agency announced that it was looking for "an internationally recognized consultancy firm for technical and financial guidance in preparation to privatize the Ethiopian Telecommunications Corporation (ETC)."[5] Meanwhile, encouraging statements continued to come from the government. Girma Birru, Minister for Economic Development and Cooperation, for example, said in October 1999 that "measures will be taken soon to allow investors to play a role in the expansion and development of telecommunication services."[6] Therefore, the government does appear to be slowly moving toward privatization of telecommunications, although it is unclear how much of it is to placate international donors, and how much of it is for real change in the telecommunications sector.

This question of monopoly versus privatization requires some discussion. The argument is usually made, especially by the United States, that the private sector is more efficient and has the capital and management skills to provide better service. Therefore, it is better to have the telecommunications operated by a private business than a government monopoly. But Ethiopia's decision was made in the middle of a war, a situation that often causes governments to make conservative decisions based on control of telecommunications. Sometimes, governments even resort to censorship. Ethiopia seems to have resisted this predicament.

One argument against privatization, at least from the government's point of view, is that telecommunications are, and will increasingly be, very good business. If so, why sell them to a private corporation and perhaps see the profits go out of the country and into the pockets of shareholders in the industrialized countries? Moreover, a private, for-profit company is less likely to invest in the costly extension of telecommunications to rural areas, since these are unlikely to generate very high revenues in the short term. From this point of view, it might be better in the long run to charge slightly higher rates for the urban business sector and others who can afford to pay, and then use the profits to bring telecommunications to the rural masses. For this to work, there must be a government monopoly. There is, after all, no inherent reason that it could not become an efficient monopoly, especially if it received sufficient infusions of capital.

Whoever owns and operates it, it is clear that the most of the basic telecommunications infrastructure is minimal, and much of it is not in very good condition. There are about 300,000 telephones for a population of around 60 million. Fewer than 1 percent of the people have a telephone. At the same time, the waiting list for new connections is 150,000, indicating enormous demand. Whether telecommunications remains a government monopoly or becomes all or partially privatized, extensive infrastructure must be provided. For Internet service, dial-up PPP, 900 are on the waiting list. Perhaps only about half of these can be accommodated even with the proposed increase in Global One bandwidth.[7] Repair rates—the number of repairs per line—also are very high, indicating an aging and poorly maintained infrastructure.[8]

Although the border war with Eritrea and the inefficiency of the Ethiopian Telecommunications Corporation represent significant barriers to ICT development, there are some hopeful signs. First among these is the location in Addis Ababa, the capital, of the UN Economic Commission for Africa.[9] The UN ECA is the headquarters of the African Information Society Initiative (AISI) and has sponsored a number of conferences on information and communications. One such conference sponsored by the ECA's African Development Forum, "The Challenge to Africa of Globalization and the Information Age," was held in Addis Ababa in October 1999.[10] Because so many conferences take place in Addis Ababa, there is an inevitable and substantial spillover of information and awareness of ICTs in the country, at least in the capital. Addis is also the site of the African School of Information Studies[11] and the headquarters of the Organization of African Unity (OAU). Ethiopia is thus fortunate to be the locus for so much activity focused on information and communications. Resolution of the Eritrean war could permit it to take much greater advantage of this unique situation.

A second factor favoring ICT development in Ethiopia is that there are a number of initiatives under way to promote Internet connectivity and increase the presence of Ethiopia in cyberspace. For example, Ethiopia is included in two U.S. AID projects to promote ICTs: the Leland Initiative and the AfricaLink project. The Leland Initiative is described as: "a five-year, $15 million U.S. government effort to extend full Internet connectivity to approximately twenty African countries in order to promote sustainable development. [It] seeks to bring the benefits of the global information revolution to people of Africa, through connection to the Internet and other Global Information Infrastructure (GII) technologies."

The Leland Initiative has three primary objectives. First, to create an "enabling policy environment" that will provide low-cost and widely available Internet services, free from government interference. Second, it hopes through technical and entrepreneurial training to create a sustainable supply of Internet services, including service providers, with special attention to countrywide access, including in rural areas. Third, the Leland Initiative seeks to build capacity for the Internet to be used for "sustainable development in manufacturing, business, the environment, health, democracy, education and other sectors."[12] A number of conferences, surveys, and training workshops have been sponsored in Ethiopia; their value, in terms of Internet education and application as well as generally increased awareness, is substantial but hard to measure.

The AfricaLink project is perhaps more promising. It is designed specifically for "the end users of information technologies, in particular the scientists and policy makers . . . in the agricultural, environmental, and natural resource management sectors."[13] For example, AfricaLink seeks to train and connect to the Internet scientists from the various agriculture research centers in Ethiopia. These research scientists say it is very helpful in their work, especially their collaboration with others inside and outside the country, and greatly reduces their sense of isolation. Other AfricaLink projects include working with the Bureau for Trade, Industry, and Tourism "to automate their process of business registration and licensing."[14] This project appears promising because the target audiences have a direct link to the country's economic development.

One of the most interesting cyberspace developments from an historical and cultural perspective is the Ethiopian Art and Architecture database project. This collaboration between Harvard University's Afro-American Studies Program and the Institute of Ethiopian Studies aims to digitize Ethiopian art and architecture and make it available on the Internet. The project will include Christian, Islamic, and pre-Christian art and architecture both within Ethiopia and around the world, including private collections.[15]

Finally, Noah Samara, the Ethiopian-born chair and CEO of WorldSpace, Inc., in 1999 launched the AfriStar satellite. WorldSpace plans to have 80 digital radio channels available to anyone on the continent who has a special digital radio. Several contracts have been signed with broadcasters in several African countries and in North America and Europe. Data services and web pages will be transmitted. Uplinking and reception tests were completed in 1999.[16]

These initiatives and projects suggest that Ethiopia's presence in cyberspace is likely to expand. But will this really make much difference in people's lives? One place it might make a very welcome difference is in the Ethiopian economy.

How can the Ethiopian economy benefit from the increased Internet connectivity that these and other initiatives promise? Business-to-business transactions will benefit and become increasingly important, especially with the liberalized economy, the open market, and the increasing privatization that is taking place in many sectors. It is worth noting that Ethiopia already has a tradepoint on the web[17] although it has not been updated, and UNCTAD also has a site specifically directed to further privatization and economic investment in Ethiopia.[18] In addition to business-to-business e-commerce, the retail level also holds some promise, and there are already a few pioneer sites, like EthioGift, making their way onto the Internet, although their server is located outside the country.[19]

Coffee, Ethiopia's largest export, accounts for about 60 percent of its foreign exchange earnings. Coffee was first discovered in Ethiopia, and the quality beans grown there, particularly *sidamo, yergacheffe,* and *harrar,* are widely regarded as the finest coffee in the world. A substantial reward awaits the person who figures out how to market fine Ethiopian coffee over the Internet. But before the reward can be collected, there are a few "potholes" on the road to cyberspace that will have to be filled.

For example, if an entrepreneur needs a server for Ethiopia, or if one has a large database, it is advised to locate it outside the country. Ethiopian Airlines, for example, keeps its server in Atlanta, and the Ethiopian Chamber of Commerce has its server in Vancouver.

In late 1999, the ETC was the only Internet Service Provider (ISP) permitted to operate in the country. The UN ECA's Pan African Document and Information System (PADIS) provided low-cost e-mail service with a FiDonet system (store and forward), but was discouraged from continuing when the ETC introduced Internet connectivity. The ETC wanted to be the only service provider in the country and PADIS, therefore, had to go. While PADIS was not providing the highest-quality service, it was inexpensive, and thus attractive to many nongovernmental organizations.

Public access to the Internet is neither widespread nor inexpensive. The British Council in Addis Ababa has a cyber café, but use is restricted to Ethiopian residents and a membership and monthly fee are required. In collaboration with the Ethiopian Science and Technology Commission and the Wolisso City Council, the British Council opened a multipurpose community telecenter in Wolisso, south of Addis Ababa.[20] The two top hotels in Addis, the Hilton and the Sheraton, have business centers with Internet access, but the cost is prohibitive for most people, except those who can afford to stay in such places. Another hotel, the Meridian, also opened a cyber café. The university is connected, but use is limited to faculty and graduate students. The ETC provides Internet training and access but not for the casual public user. With only one domain and one ISP, it may be some time before there is widespread public access and use. Indeed, Fanta Adane of the ETC expects the number of Internet subscribers to decrease after the expansion of the international gateway because "we will provide service only to those who can afford it."[21]

There has been much interest in the potential of ICTs to enhance transparency in government, to make information more widely available, and thus to promote good governance. Many believe this is very important, for many of Africa's difficulties are a result of the lack of good governance. In terms of availability of government information on-line, few countries in Africa are as advanced as South Africa, but many are moving in that direction. Both Tanzania and Uganda, for example, have their parliaments on-line. The Ethiopian parliament maintains a web site, but it contains little useful information. Many of the links do not work, including those to "general information," which contains the constitution and list of bills adopted. The links to the House of Peoples' Representatives, the House of the Federation, and "current developments" also rarely work. The latter link is said to contain "a wealth of information . . . on what is currently happening in parliament, what the committees are doing and the day to day schedules of various activities of the two houses." Therefore, while Ethiopia clearly is taking steps to make its legislative activities more open and transparent, it still has a way to go.

One area that would contribute to greater transparency is greater freedom for the press. How has the arrival of the Internet affected journalism and the mass media in Ethiopia? There are several factors to consider in answering this question. Historically, under the emperor (1930–1974), the press was restricted. The first printing press was not set up until 1930, and radio and television broadcasting did not come until the 1960s. Today there are only about three million radio sets and about one million television sets among the 60 million people. When the emperor was overthrown in 1974, press freedom was severely restricted and became very tightly controlled. With the end of the Mengistu dictatorship (1974–

1991), there was a flourishing of independent media. For 18 months, until October 1992, there was a period of euphoria. This came to an end with the passage of the Press Law of 1992.

The 1992 Press Law says freedom of the press is recognized and respected in Ethiopia. This is reiterated in the 1995 constitution. The ambiguity comes from provisions that prohibit the dissemination of information deemed dangerous by the government including incitement of ethnic hatred. The law also provides that journalists and newspapers must be licensed by the government. In the six years after 1992, journalists were often harassed, intimidated, and arrested for crossing the invisible line defining what the government would tolerate. Many were jailed without trial, unable to pay the high bail required by the government. Many others fled into exile. According to Amnesty International, over 200 editors and reporters from the independent press have been arrested at various times, several of them many times over.[22]

Government attacks on the media intensified near the end of 1997 and the first part of 1998 with more than 31 new arrests. January 1998 saw an unprecedented attack on one newspaper alone, *Tobia,* where four of its journalists were arrested, the office burnt down by unidentified arsonists, and six staff members detained on suspicion of setting fire to their own office.[23] The end of 1998 saw at least 16 reporters in jail and another dozen in exile. The government still refused to recognize the legality of the Ethiopian Free Press Journalists' Association, whose application had been pending for seven years.

Thus, by spring 1998, there was little cause for optimism about freedom of the press in Ethiopia. Then two things happened. First, the Internet, which came to Ethiopia in 1997, became available to those who could afford it, including many reporters and newspapers. The second factor was that tensions increased with Eritrea, resulting in war in May 1998. Generally, one would expect that war would bring greater restrictions on press freedom. In this case, however, the government appears to have liberalized its attitude toward the press. The end of 1999 saw the number of journalists in jail decline dramatically from the previous year. March 2000 saw the Ministry of Justice legally recognize the Ethiopian Free Press Journalists' Association. EFJA president Kifle Mulat said, "After seven years of bitter and relentless struggle, this is a major victory for Ethiopian journalists."[24] Previously, Mulat himself had been arrested and held without charge for two months for publishing a list of journalists detained by the government. Nevertheless, the watchdog organization Reporters sans Frontiers on April 28, 2000 called for the release of the eight journalists still in prison, referring to Ethiopia as the biggest prison on the African continent for journalists.[25]

Do these events signify a genuine change for freedom of the press in Ethiopia? Did the introduction of the Internet have anything to do with it? I believe so. I think these changes should be seen in the larger context of the liberalization of the economy, and the run up to the May 2000 elections. As U.S. President Clinton noted in his opening remarks to the National Summit on Africa, now we can go on-line and read the *Addis Tribune*. Although the *Addis Tribune* is currently the only Ethiopian newspaper available on-line, stories and editorials from others, including the *Reporter*, the *Mirror*, the *Sun*, and the *Ethiopian Herald*, are frequently posted by Africa News Online and the Walta Information Center. The *Tribune* web site has links to the official Ethiopian News Agency and the *Government Spokesperson*, both of which give the government's point of view.

How has the Internet affected the government? A number of sites have been created that will be useful to the press. One of these is the government page maintained by the ETC.[26] It contains links explaining the political process, including electoral laws, the economy, including banking, finance, investment, and tourism. It also has a link to the telecom page with information on tariffs and services. While it is better maintained than the parliament page, it still leaves one underwhelmed at the amount of available information. It remains to be seen what kind of democracy Ethiopia would have if every village had a computer with Internet access to their Member of Parliament, and to the proceedings of Parliament.

In addition to economic development and good government, potentially one of the most important applications of the Internet in Ethiopia is for distance education. The government's interest in distance education is twofold. First, in some cases distance education can be less expensive, especially for specialized courses; it also can help prevent "brain drain." It is very costly to send students abroad for education. There are the expenses of travel, tuition, books, equipment, and living expenses. If the student does not return after completing the course of study, all the investment may be lost. Educating students at home is desirable. There is already a clear indication of interest in distance education in the country. There is, for example, an Ethiopian Distance Education Association, although it is not very active.[27]

The African Virtual University, funded by the World Bank, includes Ethiopia among the dozen or so countries participating in this ambitious distance education project.[28] In its pilot phase, completed in 1999, several courses in science and technology were sent to the participating African universities from the United States and Ireland. Mostly they were video-based courses sent by satellite, but they had some Internet content, and there are plans for much more intensive use of the Internet.

Largely overlooked in discussions of distance education, not just in Ethiopia but elsewhere in Africa, is the potential for exporting distance education courses to the industrialized countries. The same technology that permits knowledge and information to flow from Ireland and the United States to Ethiopia, Kenya, and Uganda, or from Tanzania to Nigeria, also permits knowledge and information to flow from Africa to the north. In other words, the Internet and distance education via the Internet are not a one-way street. Students in Ireland and the United States could be receiving courses originating in Africa, based on knowledge generated in Africa, and taught by African professors from an African perspective.

Courses originating in Ethiopia or elsewhere in Africa, ranging from art and archeology to agriculture and soil science, might find their way into universities outside the continent that otherwise are not able to offer them. In many cases, such courses are particularly well suited to asynchronous distance education because the enrollment is spread so thinly across a vast geographical area. That is, there may not be enough students at any one university in North America or Europe to support a course on the history of Axum, or the political economy of coffee. But, as O'Donald has pointed out, if there are two students in Washington, three in Florida, and one in Ireland, then there are enough to make a class.[29]

Can Ethiopia become an exporter of information in the twenty-first century? Only training, equipment, access, and initiative stand in the way. Also, fees generated from Ethiopian-originated courses would represent a major supplement for the earnings of almost all Ethiopian professors.

It is clear that Ethiopia has a modest presence in cyberspace. One good example of this is that there are more than five dozen web sites listed on the well-respected Stanford University Library's Ethiopia page.[30] Some of these sites contain little and fairly esoteric information, but others have vast content with many additional links. Most of this material, however, is hosted on servers located outside the country. Therefore, while Ethiopia has a clear and substantial presence in cyberspace, it is only a small portion of what it could and should have given its size as the third most populous country in Africa, and its significant historical and cultural importance.

Finally, as connectivity and access improve, a stronger Ethiopian presence in cyberspace would likely incorporate the enormous Ethiopian Diaspora in Europe and North America into the country's social and economic development.

One might well ask, however, how the cyber revolution in Ethiopia will affect the peasant coffee farmer. Will the improvement of ICTs make any difference to those hard-working farmers who pick the red coffee cherries from the trees in Keffa province? After they wash the coffee, dry it, and transport it to Addis Ababa, how could ICTs help them? Consider this imagined scenario:

Because of improvements in information and communication technologies, a union of coffee cooperatives near the provincial capital of Jimma has decided to venture into the world of electronic commerce, and sell roasted coffee over the Internet. The goal is to capture a greater share of the profits, most of which are "downstream" from the grower. They install a coffee roaster and learn to roast their coffee to American tastes. They set up a web page displaying their varieties of coffee and tell the story of how they grow and process it. Since fine Ethiopian coffee is already available on the web at $11.95 per pound, they, on the advice of their marketing consultant, decide to undercut the market and sell theirs at $9 per pound. After paying for roasting, packaging (including the new one-way valve bags that keep roasted coffee fresh longer), and advertising, all of which cost them almost a dollar per pound, and shipping it by air to the United States ($2 per pound), they net about $6 per pound. Since they previously sold their coffee at auction in Addis for about $1 per pound, their net profit has increased sixfold. That first year they sell only 10,000 pounds—enough to pay for the coffee roaster, the marketing consultant, and other expenses associated with the new business venture, and still earn more from their coffee than usual.

The next year, they package the coffee in handmade Ethiopian baskets produced by a women's cooperative, and launch a large advertising effort for the U.S. holidays of Kwanza, Christmas, and Hanukah. They are very successful, and many of those who received coffee for holiday gifts become regular customers. The following year, they expand the business to include wholesale roasted coffee to restaurants and coffee shops in five-pound bags.

The next year, they expand the market to Japan and Europe. By now, the cooperative's coffee has been certified as organic and fair-traded so they are able to increase the price slightly, giving them an even better financial return. Their next step is to add a line of coffee accessories including handmade Ethiopian coffeepots and cups, and an instructional video about how to conduct the Ethiopian coffee ceremony. In cooperation with Ethiopian Airlines and a farsighted tourist agency in Addis, they explore the idea of coffee tourism.

By the fourth year, they are selling their entire crop of 300,000 pounds over the Internet. There was so much work associated with the coffee roasting and packaging that everyone connected with the cooperative is employed. The profits are used for school fees, uniforms, improving existing schools, and building new ones. In conclusion, the future for Ethiopian information and telecommunications is still open and waiting to be created. Clearly, there is not likely to be much improvement as long as the war with Eritrea continues, and the government retains its monopoly ownership of the Ethiopian Telecommunications Corporation. The fact that both of these barriers show hopeful signs of change leads to the conclusion that Ethiopia, while it may not be the brightest star in African cyberspace, is a rising star, and we can expect it to get brighter as the century unfolds.

NOTES

1. telecom.net.et/bid.htm.
2. B. Estifanos, *Capital*, Oct. 17, 1999, 2.
3. Brehanu 1999, 11.
4. "Telecommunications Services Council" 1999.
5. *Addis Tribune*, Oct. 15, 1999, 4.
6. *Capital*, Oct. 3, 1999, 5.
7. Cochrane to AFRIK-IT list.
8. telecom.net.et/services.htm.
9. un.org/Depts/eca/.

10. un.org/Depts/eca/adf99m.htm.
11. lucy.tele.pitt.edu/SISA/.
12. info.usaid.gov/regions/afr/leland/
13. info.usaid.gov/regions/afr/alnk.
14. Cochrane, June 18, 1999.
15. Gates, AFRIK-IT.
16. worldspace.com.
17. telecom.net.et/~et.
18. ipanet.net/unctad/investmentguide/ethiopia.htm.
19. ethiolink.com/EthioGift/.
20. britcoun.org/ethiopia.
21. *The Reporter*, April 2000.
22. amnesty.org.
23. amnesty.org/ailib/aipub/1998/AFR/12501098.htm.
24. Committee to Protect Journalists March 2000.
25. www.rsf.fr.
26. telecom.net.et.
27. unicorn.ncat.edu/~michael/vses/index.html.
28. avu.org.
29. O'Donald, ccat.sas.upenn.edu/jod/teachdemo/teachdemo.html.
30. sul.stanford.edu/depts/ssrg/africa/ethio.html.

REFERENCES

African Development Forum. un.org/Depts/eca/adf99m.htm.
African School of Information Studies. http://lucy.tele.pitt.edu/SISA.
African Virtual University. avu.org.
"Attacks on the Press 1999." Committee to Protect Journalists. cpj.org/attacks99/frameset_att99/frameset_att99.html.
Bird, Girma, quoted in "Foreign Investors Invited to Hold Shares in ETC." *Capital* (Oct. 3, 1999), 5.
Brehanu, Soloman, quoted in "Privatization of Telecom Vital for IT Development, Expert Says." *Capital* (October 17, 1999), 11.
Cochrane, Jeff. AfricaLink advisor, in a message to the AFRIK-IT listserv, June 18, 1999. AFRIK-IT messages are archived at: http://193.1.198.5/afrik-it.html.
Estifanos, Biniam (Oct. 17, 1999). "Why Does Government Hesitate to Swallow Own Pill?" *Capital*, 2.
EthioGift. ethiolink.com/EthioGift.
Ethiopian Distance Education Association. http://unicorn.ncat.edu/~michael/vses/index.html.
Ethiopian Government. telecom.net.et.
Ethiopian Parliament. ethiopar.net.
"Ethiopian Privatization Agency Seeks a Consulting Firm to Privatize the Ethiopian Telecommunication Corporation." *Addis Tribune* (Oct. 15, 1999), 4.
Ethiopian Telecommunications Corporation, Bids. telecom.net.et/bid.htm.
Ethiopian Telecommunications Corporation, Services. telecom.net.et/services.htm.
Ethiopian Tradepoint. telecom.net.et/~etp.
Gates, Henry Louis, Jr. http://193.1.198.5/afrik-it.html.

Keller, Edmond J. (1988). *Revolutionary Ethiopia: From Empire to People's Republic.* Bloomington: Indiana University Press.

Marcus, Harold G. (1983). *Ethiopia, Great Britain, and the United States 1941–1974: The Politics of Empire.* Berkeley: University of California Press.

O'Donald, J. J. ccat.sas.upenn.edu/jod/teachdemo/teachdemo.html.

Oromo Liberation Front. oromoliberationfront.org.

Pankhurst, Richard (1998). *The Ethiopians.* Oxford: Blackwell Publishers.

Stanford University Library Africa South of the Sahara: Ethiopia. sul.stanford.edu/depts/ssrg/africa/ethio.html.

"Telecommunications Services Council of Ministers Regulations No. 47/1999." *Federal Negarit Gazeta* (April 27, 1999).

United Nations Conference on Trade and Development (UNCTAD). *Ethiopia Investment.* ipanet.net/unctad/investmentguide/ethiopia.htm.

United Nations Economic Commission for Africa (UNECA). http://www.un.org/Depts/eca.

United States Agency for International Development AfricaLink. info.usaid.gov/regions/afr/alnk.

United States Agency for International Development Leland Initiative. info.usaid.gov/regions/afr/leland/index.html.

WorldSpace. worldspace.com.

Web sites:

  Ethiopian Weekly Press Digest. newsdirectory.com/news/magazine/af/et/.

  Addis Tribune. addistribune.ethiopiaonline.net/.

  Ethiopian News Headlines. enh.ethiopiaonline.net.

  Tobia. tobia.ethiopiaonline.net/G.pl/Selamta/.

7

The Internet: Triumphs and Trials for Kenyan Journalism

Okoth F. Mudhai

Optimists argue that "the computer revolution . . . will have an overwhelming and comprehensive impact, affecting every human being on earth in every aspect of his or her life."[1] Much has been written about how the Internet will change the ways people live, work, and do business. This chapter discusses the status and potential of the Internet in Kenya, particularly its possible impact on journalism. It takes a broad approach based on the premise that journalism cannot be practiced in a vacuum; that the Internet is part of a string of inventions in communications in the Briggsian sense;[2] and that Kenya does not exist in isolation. Consequently, before assessing the place of Kenya in the world of the Internet, this chapter highlights interrelated factors that determine access and connectivity.

Research findings suggest that up to 23 percent of Kenya's population of 28.7 million[3] reads a newspaper daily, although other findings indicate just more than 350,000 Kenyans, about 11 percent, read newspapers daily. Kenya has six million registered radios and 650,000 TV sets, according to the global advertising firm McCann Erickson.[4] In 1994, 13 out of 1,000 people read daily newspapers, compared to an African average of 11/1,000 and world average of 98/1,000. In 1996, there were 19 TV sets per 1,000 people. There were no mobile phones in 1996. The same year, there were only 1.6 personal computers per 1,000 people, compared to a world average of 50/1000.[5] John Onunga of the University of Nairobi estimates that Kenya had between 200,000 and 400,000 computers in 1999. At that time, pundits generally agreed that Kenya's computer density was at 100 people per computer.

These statistics indicate that very few Kenyans have access to or use media channels; this illustrates that talking about the Internet without addressing the larger informational scene is putting the cart before the horse.[6]

JOURNALISM AND THE INTERNET

Guy Berger, head of Journalism and Media Studies at Rhodes University in South Africa, notes: "Journalism is a critical element in any society. In Africa, this is probably more so than in most other places. These are people who wrestle on a daily basis with a multitude of problems, but who still successfully communicate despite the difficulties."[7]

With the advent of the Internet, it is of interest to explore the place of journalism in this new media landscape. Much has been said and written about how the Internet could engender novel ways of living, working, and doing business. Despite myriad problems, the impact of the global information superhighway—the fastest-growing communications tool[8]—is advancing slowly but surely in Kenya.

Journalism is one area of society that has embraced the Internet culture in this East African nation. Like their counterparts in other African countries, including Tanzania, Ghana, Ivory Coast, Zambia, Zimbabwe, and South Africa, Kenyan newspapers and magazines post editions on the Internet. The oldest (since 1997) and most dependable web site for daily Kenyan news is *The Nation on the Web*,[9] run by the Nation Media Group. Updated daily, it hosts the *Daily Nation* and the *Sunday Nation*. It is also hyperlinked to the group's regional weekly, the *East African*, and its radio station, Nation 96.4 FM radio.

While the *Nation* claimed in mid-November 1999 that it was Kenya's most popular site, with eight million hits a month, Jensen[10] estimated the *Nation*'s hits at an average of 50,000 a day—translating into about 1.5 million hits a month. During the Aug. 7, 1998, U.S. embassy bombing that killed at least 250 people in Nairobi, the *Nation* site hit its peak, winning prizes for its daily updates. At that time, the *Nation* was the only Kenyan newspaper on-line. Its closest competitor,[11] the Standard Group, waited until the last quarter of 1999 to post on the web its brand, the *East African Standard*, the oldest newspaper in the region, and the *Sunday Standard*.[12]

Having adopted the tabloid format with the latest printing and reproduction technology, the *Standard* was expected to be the first newspaper to go on-line. This was more so because of its appeal to the elite, mainly urban middle- and high-income households leading Western life-styles and commanding high purchasing power. This allowed the paper to earn more from advertising than the *Nation*, which had higher circulation penetrating even the rural areas. However, the owners were reluctant to put the *Standard* on-line owing to uncertainty about the benefits of investing in the Internet coupled with lack of understanding of, and interest in, the new medium. These same reasons explain the Internet-cautious stance of the other two national newspapers, the *People Daily* and the *People on Sunday*, owned by leading opposition politician Kenneth Matiba; and the ruling-party mouthpiece, the *Kenya Times*. The *People*, owned by Matiba's Kalamka Ltd., has provided e-mail-only facilities for all editorial staff. In 1999 the paper's top editors were toying with the idea of putting the paper on-line. However, the

People and the *Kenya Times*, which changed its Sunday edition to the *Herald* from the *Sunday Times*, must first assure its investors that its print editions are doing well.[13]

Because of low teledensity, high failure rate, and prohibitive telecommunications costs resulting in a limited number of local Internet host computers and web users, many media managers do not find it sensible to invest in the Internet. Even when the *Nation* went on-line in 1997, it was seen mainly as a marketing strategy to make its presence felt. This paid off when the publication achieved record hits during the terrorist bombings in Nairobi and Dar es Salaam in 1998. "Kenyan papers are not making money on the Net. They just want its presence felt, especially in those areas that are not in their distribution network," one participant said at a session on technology and African media held in Nairobi in November 1997, one of a Freedom Forum series on new media in Africa. Part of the problem has been the task of convincing advertisers to divest from the traditional advertising forums and invest part of their marketing budgets in banners on the web editions of newspapers. Gradually, advertisers are becoming convinced, but it is the early bird that is catching the worm. Sources at the *Nation's* finance division indicate that in the 1998/99 financial year, the company substantially exceeded its Internet advertising revenue target of Ksh1.8 million ($25,000). On its part, the *Standard* has yet to make an impression on advertisers. However, it may not be long before they catch up with the *Nation*, if local Internet penetration improves significantly.

For the moment, the target audiences of the on-line newspapers are mainly Diaspora Kenyans as well as a variety of international Kenya watchers. Although the U.S.-based Kenya Community Abroad (KCA) estimates the numbers of Kenyans living outside the country's borders at 300,000,[14] other estimates put the number at between 100,000 and 150,000, with students comprising at least a quarter.[15] The Diaspora Kenyans could number anywhere between 50,000 and 60,000, with students comprising more than half. This perhaps explains Jensen's estimation of the *Nation's* hits at 50,000 a day, with a majority of the visitors based outside the country. Not many of Kenya's 30,000 Internet users read daily newspapers on-line because the web editions are scarcely different in news content from the print editions. Kenyans outside the country mostly rely entirely on the on-line editions, which they read long before the print editions hit the streets back home. In contrast, local on-line readers only take a "glimpse" and wait for the print edition. Locally, those with access to the Internet also have easy access to the traditional newspapers. It is believed that Kenya watchers who read the country's on-line newspapers are officials of intergovernmental organizations, like the Bretton Woods institutions (the World Bank and the International Monetary Fund), foreign intelligence groups, and foreign government officers. On its Feb. 21–27, 2000, web edition, the *East African* reported that "American President Bill Clinton has singled out the *East African* as one of the newspapers in Africa that are enhancing globalization through promoting openness of societies and borders." In an article hyperbolically titled "I Read the *East African*—Says Clinton," the paper quoted President Clinton as saying: "We can go online and read the *Addis Tribune*, the *Mirror* of Ghana, the *East African*, or dozens of other African newspapers." The U.S. president made his remarks at the start of a four-day National Summit on Africa, attended by 2,000 guests including President Daniel arap Moi, Kenya's head of state since 1978.

It is worth noting that Moi previously has expressed disappointment at the way on-line editions of newspapers spread unpleasant news about Kenya, thus "spoiling the country's good image."[16] Once, as soon as he arrived at the Nairobi airport from a foreign country where he had read Kenyan news on the *Nation on the Web* site, Moi condemned the *Nation* for the kind of news it disseminated worldwide. A few days later, some of the staff on the *Nation* Internet section claimed they were being followed by people they suspected to be government security intelligence. They expressed their fear to their bosses and the newspaper carried a news report of the incident. Moi and other senior government officials have repeatedly accused the local press of being antigovernment and unpatriotic, bent on serving "foreign masters." He also has been suspicious of foreign publications. Before the world's newspapers went on-line, Kenyan security officers would sometimes confiscate the consignment of imported foreign newspapers at the airport.[17] Though the situation is changing, repressive laws on libel, contempt, and sedition, as well as lack of a constitutional guarantee to press freedom, has made it possible for the government to destroy, confiscate, or damage printing facilities. Press proprietors have been arrested and publications banned, while journalists have been intimidated, threatened, harassed, or imprisoned. This has caused fear and despondency among journalists and resulted in self-censorship by editors.[18]

Since Kenyan on-line newspapers are updated only once a day, and are, in terms of content, simply partial reproductions of the print editions, the self-censorship evident in the print editions is reflected on the Internet. Shapshack may be right in saying, "The growth of the Internet seems to be having an effect on and challenging the prevalence of state control in many African states."[19] That is, if a print newspaper is banned from publishing or is suppressed for printing views contrary to the government, the same information can be published on the World Wide Web, "making it accessible anywhere in the world and bypassing any country's internal censorship." However, a Kenyan example is hard to come by, because the web editions are just brief versions of print editions. Delany gives the example of edition 401 of the *Post of Zambia*, whose print edition was banned while the on-line version was published. In South Africa, the web edition of the *Star*, one of the leading dailies, is updated several times a day, and is not necessarily a reflection of the print edition. The best Kenyan journalists can do for now is send via e-mail articles that cannot be published by local newspapers to publications in neighboring Uganda or even to the United Kingdom and the United States. Local Kenyan newspapers often pick up such articles and attribute them to those foreign publications—a lesser crime in case of any repercussions.

All the same, Kenya has not recorded any known direct attempt by the government to censure access to, or use of, the Internet. Members of a task force on media law appointed in 1993 by the Attorney General's office confessed that by the time they finished their work five years later, their report did not address the regulation of the Internet and related forms of new information and communications technologies (ICTs). However, observers are convinced there are calculated indirect strategies, including restricted offering of bandwidth through the state-owned Internet backbone. This puts Internet Service Providers (ISPs) at the mercy of the government, forcing them to go by its demands. For instance, media practitioner Lynne Muthoni Wanyeki notes, in response to a questionnaire sent out to inform this chapter, that the government sometimes demands that ISPs produce their subscriber lists. As a result, ISPs engage in self-censorship. In one case, she recalls, an ISP shut down a list created to discuss the 1997 general election out of fear about what was being expressed.

Other than the daily news updates through on-line newspapers, there are other sites for both general and specialized news and analysis. An example is the *Expression Today*'s web site, or on-line edition, dubbed Kenyanews, which specializes in the coverage and analysis of issues related to the media, democracy, and human rights. Aware of the importance of Kenyan news to visitors of sites with Kenyan content, ISPs have made news a vital part of their service. Africa's most successful ISP, AfricaOnline (AfOL), created in 1994 by three (then U.K.-based) Kenyan students and in early 2000 taken over by London-based investment group Africa Lakes, has several links in their News and Information section. These include the *Daily Nation, Sunday Nation,* and *East African.* In addition, AfOL distributes stories by Nairobi-based Features Africa Network (FAN) through which a team led by a leading journalist summarizes national news, business news, sports news, and travel information gathered from 24 African countries. Other sites are *Coastweek* (carrying news about Kenya's coastal town of Mombasa), and *Karengata Chronicle* (for Karen-Lang'ata, a middle- and high-income residential district in Nairobi). AfOL also distributes the *Kenya Engineer* and *PC World East Africa.* Other Kenyan AfOL clients include the state broadcaster, the Kenya Broadcasting Corporation (KBC), and the Nairobi-based private radio station, Capital FM 98.4.

AfOL, which has home pages for other countries as well, also provides general information services. Besides banners from the Organisation of African Unity (OAU) and similar advertisers, AfOL hosts the Central Bank of Kenya and the on-line Kenyan Business Directory. AfOL's closest rival, Form-net Africa, also provides information on weather, currency exchange rates, the economy, travel, education, history, sports, people, and entertainment. It lists agencies (nongovernmental organizations, United Nations agencies, and diplomatic missions) as well as basic information on Kenya government offices and a link to the national anthem, perhaps as a mark of patriotism.

Despite such attempts, analysts believe one of the greatest drawbacks to the popularity of the Internet is the lack of substantial Kenyan content on the web.

Because of the government's reluctance to embrace the Internet, it has not found it necessary to take advantage of this technology for information dissemination and communication. This can be attributed partly to Kenya's history of putting tight state controls on the instruments of communications. Even postapartheid South Africa has done better with the ruling party, the Africa National Congress (ANC), having a web site with links to the sites of former president Nelson Mandela and incumbent Thabo Mbeki.

Currently, Kenya has no policies on government use of the Internet to disseminate official information.[20] Mureithi[21] cites the low Internet customer base and the "psychological barrier" created by the government's reluctance to use the medium and integrate it with economic development. As a result of the government's indifference, if not prohibition, many ordinary Kenyans, professionals, organizations, and businesses bear the brunt of denied access to the information superhighway.[22]

The frustrations of access are, of course, not limited to journalists. *Daily Nation* Education Editor David Aduda cites poor infrastructure—frequent power disruptions, poor telephone connectivity, high phone charges and subscription bills—as some of the problems. Others are a lack of political will to liberalize the information technology sector and allow many players to join in. Aduda also mentions low literacy levels and negative attitudes toward technology.

For most of Kenya's journalists, even if newspapers go on-line, "thereby disseminating critical information world wide and providing a direct line to African communities abroad,"[23] the Internet remains a rare, if not alien, technology. It also is a luxury. Chaacha Mwita, Internet publications subeditor for the *Nation*, says: "Many journalists I have met and spoken to are bewildered about the Internet." The editor of Nairobi-based African Women and Child Feature Service, Rose Kasiala Lukalo-Owino, says that although many journalists are aware of the Internet and e-mail, "those with access to these facilities are far fewer and almost all are concentrated in [the capital city of] Nairobi." David Makali, the executive director of the Nairobi-based Media Institute, which publishes *Expression Today,* notes: "There is no access to the Internet by rural correspondents. Only those in main towns and working for newspapers like the *Nation* have some limited access to the Net." Not even the *Nation* and the *Standard* have Internet host computers in every bureau outside Nairobi. In general, Makali says, "Internet use by Kenyan journalists is especially poor. Many journalists do not even have e-mail addresses, and those with addresses limit their Internet use to e-mailing only."

This is mainly due to the frustrations of logging in as a result of phone failure or line congestion as well as the crowding and queuing for the only newsroom Internet host computer shared by several journalists—often up to 20. Most journalists blame their media houses, especially the national newspapers that can afford the cost. "Media organisations do not recognize the power of the computer and most still use it as an up-market typewriter and restrict the use of the Net by junior journalists," Lukalo-Owino says. Makali concurs: "In most media houses,

Internet use is restricted to a few top editors, and access by the rest is not easy." This is not surprising, according to Dutton,[24] who notes that the new media tend to be implemented in ways that follow and reinforce prevailing structures of power and influence within organizations.

Understaffing is another problem that stems from the view that the Internet edition is a lesser component of the paper. The *Nation* and the *Standard* have only editorial staffers on the on-line desk, working on daily and weekly publications, assisted by a handful of technicians. This is one reason why the newspapers rarely update their web editions more than once a day. Take the case of South Africa's *Daily Mail and Guardian*, which employed 12 journalists and received 500 to 700 e-mails daily in 1999, according to the paper's editor Irwin Manoin, speaking at a seminar in South Africa.

Anecdotal evidence indicates that the existence of on-line newspapers does not reduce the sale of the traditional newspaper, and that the Internet may not necessarily make journalists lazy—the same way it cannot make mediocre journalists better. However, Makali points out that even where journalists have access, they are not too enthusiastic about the Internet. The older generation of Kenyan journalists, in particular, is not interested in the Internet. "Even in Denmark, most journalists are inward-looking and do not even use the Internet much although it is usually accessible, cheaper and efficient," says Makali, whose organization provides free Internet access for all staff. As for the younger generation, the only barrier is the cost or absence of computer, modem, and telephone line.

Apart from the prohibitive costs, lack of basic knowledge and skills on computing and the Internet also hinders access by many journalists. This is why media houses were invited to nominate journalists to apply for a three-month training program on electronic subediting to be held in mid-2000. Kenya does not have such initiatives as MISAnet, the basic e-mail communications system set up in the 1990s by the media watchdog organization, the Media Institute of Southern Africa (MISA). Rural journalists in Kenya are not as lucky as their counterparts in Nigeria, who were delighted to learn about computers. There are neither training programs nor facilities. So when the African Women's Media Center in Senegal wanted to train East African women journalists on the use of the Internet, it was not easy to find 20 computers logged on to the World Wide Web. However, the situation may change when MISA finalizes plans for a media resource center in Nairobi. It will include Internet facilities, a computerized library, and an auditorium for training, research, and media discourse. The U.S.-based Freedom Forum was interested in the project, which was expected to take three years (from 1999) to launch. Because of perceived higher standards, recent funding for journalism training has bypassed Kenya. This means the country's journalists are also left out of programs with the Internet as a component. An example is the African Journalist/Media Ethics Talking Point[25] discussion list that resulted from a recent seminar in West Africa.

All the same, a handful of Kenyan journalists—mostly the urban-based well-educated and widely traveled editors, subeditors, and senior reporters—are at home with the Internet. They surf the Internet regularly each week and keep in touch via e-mail with their peers. Some even interview via e-mail their more technology-minded sources, especially those in the private sector but also including a few senior government officials like conservationist-turned-civil-servant Dr. Richard Leakey. Freelancers as well as staffers doing private work but lacking Internet connection at home use cyber cafés to send their stories around the world via e-mail, without being censored by their bosses or by government officials. They contribute to foreign media houses that pay in hard currencies (mainly dollars and pounds sterling), which, when converted into local currency, amount to up to 10 times more than what local publications would pay for a single story. To this extent, one would say the Internet and e-mail have turned out to be a gold mine, financially empowering poorly paid African journalists. Berger notes that new markets have been opened for African journalists, and they can now act as foreign correspondents for overseas publications, writing African news stories and sending them abroad via e-mail.[26] However, the number of such journalists is very few. It would be much better if the Internet allowed local correspondents to file stories and communicate fast and freely within the country.

The Internet is a gold mine for information and resources not only for African journalists, who have to keep abreast of current affairs, but also for other consumers of the media in Africa. Many Kenyan journalists who have access to the Internet write articles based on web research—though with little effort to acknowledge their sources. For Delany,[27] the fact that journalists can now access news and information much more easily on the Internet results in better reporting of international (as well as local) politics and economics, in addition to such issues as gender equity and the environment. One hazard is that some of those sources cannot be authenticated, and this raises questions of accuracy and credibility. Shapshack points out that the Internet provides a journalist in the poorest, most remote village in Africa the same access to information and resources as journalists in more developed areas of the world.[28] However, this is a typical exaggeration of the impact of the Internet, even as many more African newspapers are going on-line. While Delany argues that it is much easier to search on-line newspapers and their archives, Kenyan on-line newspapers are slow and poorly archived. The *Nation*'s archive is searchable only by publication dates rather than by subject. Apart from newspapers, other on-line databases provide a wealth of information that used to be completely inaccessible, or at the very least extremely difficult, to access by journalists in Africa. Kenyan journalist David Aduda explains: "Yes, the Internet has empowered me a great deal. I am able to get some information that I would otherwise not get without the Internet. Most importantly, it serves as a data base for me, especially when I am doing research on areas that have not been documented in books and journals, or information that is not available locally." There are very few journalists in Aduda's position.

POLITICAL CHANGE AND THE INTERNET

On the political scene, the concepts of teledemocracy, cyberdemocracy, or digital democracy have yet to be fully developed in the country, but political participation through the Internet is taking shape. If well developed, the new medium may fill a huge communications vacuum for ordinary Kenyans. In 1998, the Britain-based press freedom watchdog Article 19 issued a report on the political violence after the 1997 general election. Kanyongolo and Lunn wrote, "There is a problem all over Kenya with [regard to] access to accurate and affordable information, particularly in rural areas. Rumours and misinformation thrived because there was so little independent and impartial information available to act as a counter balance. Virtually all newspapers were perceived to be biased, and the KBC (the state-owned broadcasting corporation) was perceived to favour the government."[29]

One may argue that the Internet is a rumor channel and a recipe for chaos, but it could turn out to be the medium for ordinary people to talk directly to each other, thus sharing experiences and mediating propagandist reports. It also could boost attempts at people-driven, people-owned constitutional review with special focus on gender equity and articulation of women's issues, and issues affecting the disabled and the poor. Children comprise another vulnerable group that could be protected through Internet networking within Kenya. The Kenya chapter of the African Network for the Prevention and Protection Against Child Abuse and Neglect cited "the culture of silence and apathy around children's rights" as one of the country's greatest challenges. The Internet just may give voice to the voiceless not just in politics but also in such social realms.

The Internet has given a voice to many African dissidents, as well as providing on-line contact services for exiles,[30] thus fostering democracy on the continent despite dictatorial governments. Apart from local Internet discussion lists, Kenyans network through lists and web sites established outside the country. One popular list, U.S.-based KenyaOnline (KOL), openly discusses Kenyan politics, economy, and sociocultural issues. By coincidence, in February 2000, KOL suffered a disruption just as some list members suggested a demonstration be held against President Moi during his visit to the United States and Canada that month. A few weeks earlier, some list members had suggested a coup as the only way to get rid of the long-serving president who, it was suspected, wanted to renew his term beyond year 2000 in spite of a constitutional provision barring him from doing so. For this reason, although the list's shutdown was attributed to a technical error, some list members suspected it was the machinations of Moi's sympathizers among them.

Popular among web sites serving mainly Diaspora Kenyans are Kenyan Community Abroad and the Kenyan Community Worldwide.[31] The latter has links to KCA and other Kenyan associations, including one for Kenyan students at Cambridge University, Kenyan Students Society Malaysia, the Union of Kenyan Students Abroad, the National Association of Kenyan Americans, and the Kenyan-American Chamber of Commerce. Another popular site is the *Spear*,[32] which carries news on Kenya and Africa, originating mainly from the United States and Canada. Through such lists and web sites, Diaspora Kenyans often join their counterparts back home not only in feeding on news updates but also in such fund-raising ventures as the Bomb Blast Fund, following the 1998 terrorist bombing, and the *Nation* Famine Relief Fund of 1999. The KCA also uses its electronic network to nominate and award Kenyan role models. The sites have links to Kenyan on-line newspapers and other sites of interest to Diaspora Kenyans.

In contrast, most Kenyans in the rural areas are excluded from the Internet network. However, some of them have Internet access through community telecommunications access centers, or telecenters. Most telecenter initiatives target women in organized groups. Kenya has more than 30,000 women's groups, with membership exceeding one million. So it is not surprising that a women's craft cooperative learns through its use of Internet advertising that it can charge $15 for units it was intending to sell for $1.[33] A number of telecenter initiatives use the Internet to disseminate information on health, education, business, farming, and politics.[34]

KENYA IN THE "GLOBAL VILLAGE"

Kenya, a former British protectorate, was one of those countries expected to be among the first in Africa to obtain full Internet status. However, it was not until late 1995 that Nairobi, the capital city, obtained (albeit illegally) a large concentration of dial-up e-mail services.[35] After the launch of the first full Internet service by the African Regional Computing Centre in 1995, other ISPs were started as the points of presence increased and Internet awareness rose.[36] Since then, Internet connectivity in Kenya has expanded rapidly, although the technology still serves only a very small percentage of the population, mainly in the urban areas.

Still, Kenya now boasts one of the largest Internet communities in sub-Saharan Africa;[37] there were about 30,000 users at the beginning of year 2000. In 1998, Mureithi and Shaw[38] claimed that the country, then with 20,000 e-mail accounts, had the highest number of Internet hosts (458) in sub-Saharan Africa. By July 1997, when Kenya had 0.16 Internet hosts per 10,000 people, it was surpassed only by the Ivory Coast (0.17), Morocco (0.32), Namibia (2.16), Zimbabwe (0.24), Zambia (0.27), and South Africa (30.67). Kenya's ratio compared favorably with the sub-Saharan Africa average of 2.03, and low-income-countries' average of 0.06, but it compared poorly with the world average of 34.75, the United Kingdom's 149.06, and the United States' 442.11.

However, communications experts and investors believe Kenya's telecommunications and Internet landscape is far below expectation, and that the country needs to exploit its potential and play "its rightful role as the hub of telecommunications services in the region."[39] At this point, it is useful to examine the obstacles to better connectivity in Kenya, and explore measures to improve the situation. Studies have shown that socioeconomic factors such as income, literacy, age, and gender greatly determine Internet access. The typical Internet user is a medium- or high-income earner, well educated (mostly to college or university level), young, and male.[40] About 70 percent of the 29 million multiethnic, multireligious Kenyan population lives in rural areas. Most urban dwellers are poor, without access to electricity and telephone facilities. Nearly 80 percent of Kenyans survive on less than $2 a day, while more than half the population lives below the international poverty line, surviving on less than $1 a day.[41] Consumption statistics indicate a wide gap between the rich and the poor.

Poverty has a female face. Although women constitute 50 percent of the population, and contribute significantly to the gross domestic product (GDP), they are more constrained from participating in key economic, electoral, and governance decisions and activities.[42] The tendency also is reflected in education, where, for those aged 15 and older, the illiteracy rate is 30 percent for females compared to 14 percent for males. The adult illiteracy rate for those aged 25 and older is 54.2 percent for females, compared to 26 percent for males.[43]

For both the individual and the state, there are other priorities competing for attention alongside the Internet, such as the roads network (only 14 percent paved or sealed with asphalt in 1996), education, food, and health care, including access to sanitation and safe water. With the introduction of cost sharing, public expenditure on health and education has gone down—from 5 percent of the gross national product in 1989 to 1.9 percent in 1995. This policy has made the situation worse for the poor. In the last quarter of 1999, for example, a woman from western Kenya and her baby died while she was giving birth outside a rural hospital as her helpless husband watched. They were barred from entering the premises because they did not carry their own surgical gloves to be used during her delivery.

In medical emergencies, the Internet would be of little or no use. However, the telephone, on which the Internet relies for connectivity, is crucial. Unfortunately, 1996 statistics indicate this country of seven million households has only 1.7 main phone lines per 100 households. There are only 0.8 main lines per 100 inhabitants, and 0.2 pay phones per 1,000 inhabitants. The waiting time for telephone hookup is at least six years. Consequently, one way of delivering the Internet is through universal access to basic telephone services, especially in hitherto unserved and underserved areas. Another is through the expansion of the public service telecommunications network (PSTN). At the cost of U.S. $5.4 billion, to be met largely by the private sector, the government hopes to improve penetration per 100 population by the year 2015 from 0.16 to 1 in the rural areas and from 4 to 20 in urban areas.[44]

All of these factors, socioeconomic, technological, and political-regulatory, are interrelated and important. They boil down to the affordability of the Internet for individuals and groups. Access to the Internet, like any other form of modern media, is not only dictated by the nature of political economy, which defines the workings of an industrial and commercial system. It is also a matter of the structured inequalities of life within contemporary society.[45] These inequalities reinforce economic and cultural disadvantages by progressively denying the disadvantaged full political and cultural participation. They increase and magnify traditional levels of disadvantage in an increasingly market-led world, which offers greater choice, but at a price and only for those who can afford it. The result is disparity between the rich and the poor.[46]

CONCLUSION

In the foreword to the World Development Report 1999, World Bank President James Wolfensohn wrote:

> The information revolution makes understanding knowledge and development more urgent than ever before but, with these opportunities come tremendous risks. In our enthusiasm for the information superhighway, we must not forget the villages and slums without telephones, electricity, or safe water, or the primary schools without pencils, paper, or books. For the poor, the promise of the new information age—knowledge for all—can seem as remote as a distant star.

In response to questionnaires sent out for this chapter, a number of Kenyans—mostly journalists—agree the Internet could be a powerful development tool. However, the respondents concur that the gap between the Internet haves and have-nots, which virtually all of them describe as "extremely wide," greatly diminishes the Internet's expected potential. Access to the Internet runs along the fault lines of national societies, dividing the educated from the illiterate, the rich from the poor.[47]

Lack of equipment (computers, modems, telephone cables, and other facilities), a poorly developed infrastructure, and lack of power and frequent power cuts inhibit access. These, together with computer breakdowns, lack of relevant education and training, low disposable income, poverty, and starvation, make the Internet accessible to only a negligible proportion of the population. Indeed, Mowlana[48] views this alienation of some individuals as "the detrimental effect of modern technological society and its monstrous institutions."

Petersen notes[49] that although the Internet and e-mail have significantly benefited African journalists by attempting to reverse the historical flow of information, the region's media professionals remain vulnerable because they work in difficult environments. Apart from the repressive laws, weak judiciaries, and government officials who target journalists with impunity, the poor state of the communications infrastructure is a major obstacle.

Groups like the East African Internet Association and the Association of Telecommunications Service Providers have put the government under pressure when it has been unreasonably slow or indecisive. Kenya has been slow to take advantage of the fiber-optic necklace partnerships going on in the rest of the continent. As Richard Vincent[50] suggests, the existing African Internet services could "form a mutual organization to share information, co-ordinate services and collaborate on service extension."

The Internet cannot be expected to radically change Kenyan society in general or journalism in particular, but It may help if Kenya factors informational needs into its ambitious development goals, which include health for all and water for all, and universal quality basic education.

NOTES

1. Webster 1999, 140–141.
2. Briggs 1966.
3. 1999 census.
4. mind-advertising.com/us/mccann_us.htm.
5. World Bank 1999. Africa statistics (1996): Gabon, 6.3 PCs per 1,000; Ghana, 1.2; Lebanon, 24.3; Morocco, 1.7; Mozambique, 0.8; Namibia, 12.7; Nigeria, 4.1; Senegal, 7.2; SA, 37.7; Tunisia, 6.7; Uganda, 0.5; Zimbabwe, 6.7. At that time, the United States had 362.4 per 1,000 while Great Britain had 192.6 per 1,000.
6. This chapter is neither a comprehensive impact survey nor an empirical media effects study. Data have been drawn from secondary sources, as well as anecdotal evidence and responses to questionnaires sent to Kenyan journalists. Where necessary and appropriate, a comparison has been drawn between Kenya and other countries, but this chapter is in no way intended to take a fully comparative approach.
7. journ.ru.ac.za/amd.
8. According to UNDP 1999, the Internet reached 50 million people in only four years, compared to the 13 and 38 years that TV and radio, respectively, took to diffuse to that extent.
9. www.nation.co.ke or www.nationaudio.com.
10. Jensen 1999.
11. Circulation figures are guarded secrets, but the *Daily Nation* has an estimated average circulation of 100,000 compared to the *East African Standard*'s 60,000. The *Sunday Nation* sells 150,000 on average compared to *Sunday Standard*'s 80,000. Both firms have subsidiary companies owning TV stations.
12. www.eastandard.net.
13. *The People*, formerly a popular weekly, has an average daily circulation of 40,000. *Kenya Times*' circulation is 6,000 to 10,000.

14. The KCA gave this "conservative" figure when they wrote to the Minister for National Planning and Development on March 9, 1999, asking him to facilitate the enumeration of Kenyans abroad. See www.welcome.to/kca or www.kenyanabroad.org.

15. The Ministry of Education estimates that the number of Kenyan students abroad averages 20,000, but the figure is higher because many students travel abroad without government clearance.

16. See *Sunday Nation*, Oct. 10, 1999 and *Sunday Standard*, Oct. 10, 1999. Moi criticized the *Nation* for "sensationalizing" a parliamentary report that the country had lost $8 billion through fraud and corruption. He said such news could destroy the country. Kenya was then under the scrutiny of the World Bank and the IMF over aid suspended in 1997 as a result of graft and bad governance.

17. Sinkala 1997 in Delany 1999.

18. Okoth 1998, 123–126; Richardson 1999.

19. Delany 1999.

20. Jensen 1999.

21. Mureithi 1999, 2.

22. Whether mere access is beneficial is another matter.

23. Petersen in JMS 1999.

24. Dutton 1996, 5.

25. Contact Chudi Ukpabi at Chudi Communication Consult, cukpabi@worldonline.nl.

26. Delany 1999.

27. Ibid.

28. Ibid.

29. Richardson 1999.

30. Delany 1999.

31. www.welcome.to/kca or kenyanabroad.org and www.kenya.8m.com/kencom.htm. Hits to KCA's site reached 4,100 within a year of startup.

32. www.mshale.com, which publisher Tom Gitaa says began in 1996 and in 1999 received 15,000 to 20,000 hits a day mainly from the United States, Canada, Europe, Asia, and Africa. Also see www.kenyanews.com/eXpression/february/diaspora.html.

33. Wilson 1996.

34. Khasiani 1999; Mureithi 1999.

35. Jensen 1999.

36. Mureithi 1998, 183; Mureithi 1999.

37. Jensen 1999.

38. Mureithi 1998, 184.

39. News story on the African Information Technology Exhibitions and Conferences (AITEC) in Nairobi.Nation/23022000/Business2.html. Studies by Tyler et al. (in Gatheru and Shaw 1998, 186) indicate Kenya is foregoing over Ksh600 million ($8.2 million) annually in foreign exchange earnings due to poor telecommunications.

40. UNDP 1999, 62–63.

41. World Bank 1999, 187–248.

42. Khasiani 1999.

43. World Bank 1999; Healthnet Kenya 1999.

44. Mureithi 1999, 1.

45. Dutton 1996, 229.

46. Dutton 1996, 230–231; Mowlana 1997, 219.

47. UNDP 1999, 62–63.
48. Mowlana 1997, 235.
49. JMS 1999.
50. Delany 1999.

REFERENCES

Briggs, Asa (1966). *The Communications Revolution*, Mansbridge Memorial Lecture 3, delivered at the University of Leeds. Oct. 16, 1965.

Delany, Caitriona (1999). "Internet Journalism: Is the Internet a Gold Mine for African Journalists?" African Media Debates: Seminar Paper. http://www.journ.ru.ac.za/amd/intern.htm.

Dutton, H. William (Ed.) (1996). *Information and Communication Technologies: Visions and Realities*. Oxford: Oxford University Press.

Healthnet Kenya (1999). Statistics from the World Health Organisation's World Health Report 1998. www.healthnet.org/hnet/ken.html.

Jensen, Mike (1999). "Kenya Statistics: Internet Status, ICT Developments, Policies and Strategies." http://www3.wn.apc.org/africa/kenya.htm.

JMS. (1999). Journalism and Media Studies Dept., Rhodes University, South Africa. "Contemporary Debates on African Media." www.journ.ru.ac.za/amd.

Khasiani, Shanyisa Anota (1999). "Gender, Civic Education, and ICTs: Use of Telecentres by Rural Women in Communities in Kakamega and Makueni Districts of Kenya to Access Information, for Training, for Trade, and for Life-long Learning," BICA-Kenya workshop paper, 13–14 Oct. 1999, Nairobi: Family Support Initiative.

Mowlana, Hamid (1997). *Global Information and World Communication: New Frontiers in International Relations*. London: Sage.

Mureithi, Muriuki (1998). "Creating an Environment for Economic Growth." In *Our problems, our solutions*. Nairobi: Institute of Economic Affairs. 180–191. Published online at www.iea.or.ke.

Mureithi, Muriuki (1999). "Empowerment for Sustainable Development: Opportunities for a Telecentre Strategy in Kenya" (Preliminary discussion paper), prepared for the British Council, Nairobi: Summit Strategies.

Okoth, F. Mudhai (1998). "The Need to Centre-Stage Culture: The Media and Cultural Identity in Kenya." In Mumma, Opiyo, et al. (Eds.). *Orientations of Drama, Theatre and Culture: Cultural Identity and Community Development*. Nairobi: Kenya Drama and Theatre in Education Association, 116–136.

Richardson, Vicky (1999). "Kenya Media Report." In *African Media Debates*. Grahamstown, South Africa: Rhodes University. Published online at journ.ru.ac.za/amd/.

UNDP (1999). United Nations Development Program. *Human Development Report 1999*. New York: Oxford University Press.

Webster, Frank (1999). "What Information Society?" In Hugh Mackay and Tim O'Sullivan (Eds.). *The Media Reader: Continuity and Transformation*. London: Sage.

Wilson, Ernest J., III (1996). "The Information Revolution Comes to Africa." CSIS Africa Notes, No. 185. Centre for International Development and Conflict Management, University of Maryland, USA. http://www.bsos.umd.edu.cidcm/papers/wilson/CSIS2.pdf.

World Bank (1999). *World Development Report 1998/99: Knowledge for Development.* New York: Oxford University Press.

Web sites:

Africa News. www.africanews.org/media/stories.

AfricaOnline (Kenya). www.africaonline.co.ke.

Daily Nation on the Web. www.nationaudio.com or www.nation.co.ke.

The *Star.* www.thestar.co.za.

Sunday Times of South Africa. www.suntimes.co.za.

8

The Internet in Namibia

Protasius Ndauendapo
and Chris Paterson

Namibia demonstrates how a new nation may be best positioned to embrace a new technology. By some measures, Namibia has the third-greatest Internet usage in Africa, behind South Africa and Egypt.[1] This chapter traces the rapid development of the Internet in Namibia and projects its growth in the new millennium. We address the following aspects of the Internet in Namibia: its introduction, its popularity and accessibility, who the providers are and how they see their role, the regulatory framework governing the Internet, and prospects for future growth.

Rapid change in both the political and telecommunications environment set the scene for Namibia's enthusiastic acceptance of the Internet. Namibia gained its independence from more than 100 years of colonial and apartheid rule in 1990. South Africa turned control of the country over to President Sam Nujoma in March of that year. Since then, the nation of 1.7 million people has experienced strong growth in the economy generally and the telecommunications sector in particular.[2] These developments cleared the way for enthusiastic Internet development.

ADVENT OF INTERNET IN NAMIBIA

As a result of the changes in the regulatory environment, coupled with massive investments by Telecom Namibia in telecommunications infrastructure development,[3] local Internet growth began in 1994 with the establishment of the Namibia Internet Development Foundation (NAMIDEF), whose aim was to provide Internet services to Namibians on a noncommercial basis.[4] Lacking funds as well as skilled and dedicated personnel, NAMIDEF ceased to exist in early 1996. Commercial Internet services started that same year with the establishment of Internet World Wide Namibia (IWWN), followed by UUNET Internet Africa Namibia in October 1996.

The advent of the Internet in Namibia also should be viewed in light of changes in the global geopolitical situation in the late 1980s and early 1990s that resulted in the disintegration of the former USSR and paved the way for Namibia's independence from South Africa in 1990.[5] These changes necessitated the restructuring of the regulatory framework governing the telecommunications and broadcasting sectors in order to address the challenges and opportunities the new political, economic, and global environments offered to Namibians.

The Namibian constitution specifically encourages a mixed economy, which, according to Namibia's minister of information, led to an information policy that "allows for the mixed ownership of the media by both the public and the private sectors."[6] It took the new Namibian government two years to embark on restructuring the legal and policy frameworks,[7] resulting in the enactment of the Namibian Communications Commission Act of 1992, as well as the Posts and Telecommunications Establishment Act of 1992. These laws were designed to regulate the telecommunications and broadcasting sectors and to respond to the demands, challenges, and opportunities of globalization and the free market economic system, which Namibia adopted at independence.

Deregulation was spurred by changes in 1992 to the framework governing the telecommunications and broadcasting sectors with the establishment of the Namibian Communications Commission (NCC), as well as the incorporation of the Department of Post and Telecommunications into three companies—Namibia Post and Telecom Holdings Limited, Namibia Post Limited, and Telecom Namibia Limited.[8] The NCC represents Namibia in the International Telecommunications Union.[9]

In view of these developments, the Internet in Namibia became possible through the establishment of the Namibia Internet Development Foundation (NAMIDEF) in 1994. This organization sought to provide Internet services to Namibians on a noncommercial basis.[10] The founders of NAMIDEF attempted to generate enough funds to enable them to spread Internet services, mostly e-mail, to schools, resource centers, and rural areas.

However, as a result of a lack of funds, unskilled personnel, and poor telecommunications infrastructure at that time (particularly telephone lines), the foundation collapsed in 1995.[11] The foundation laid by NAMIDEF was instrumental in the establishment of UUNET Internet Africa Namibia, a commercial Internet service provider (ISP) that took over NAMIDEF in October 1996.[12] That, with the establishment in early 1996 of another ISP, Internet World Wide Namibia (IWWN), heralded the beginning of commercial Internet service provision in Namibia. However, this development was characterized by a number of problems, including the lack of adequate technology, financial resources, and skilled manpower, and unfamiliarity with the Internet by most Namibians. Other commercial ISPs also were established in Namibia's capital, Windhoek.[13] In these early stages, the commercial Internet industry provided only services such as e-mail and web surfing to mostly Windhoek-based private and corporate clients. However, some ISPs in late 1999 began to provide value-added services such as web development and design, and audio and video connectivity and networking.

As with most African countries, the early days of the Internet in Namibia were frustrated by insufficient access to bandwidth linking Namibia to South Africa. According to one analyst,[14] several of Africa's international connections to the Internet still operate on analog circuits rated at 9.6 Kbps, often pushed to 14 Kbps and sometimes to 24 Kbps. Namibia had a similar problem of analog circuits and low bandwidth at the initial stage of Internet development in the country in 1994–1996. This has changed with the introduction of digital circuits and higher bandwidth capacities, which Namibia has been gradually introducing since 1995.[15] With the 1999 switch to a new fiber-optic link to South Africa, private ISPs may obtain up to 1 Mbps of international bandwidth.[16]

ACCEPTANCE OF THE INTERNET

The lack of reliable data on the Internet in Namibia makes it difficult to ascertain its popularity five years after introduction. However, interviews with more than half of the country's ISPs suggest that approximately 7,000 Namibians had access to the Internet in late 1999.[17] According to one provider, most Internet users in Namibia are pulling in information. By contrast, the interactive potential of the Internet—e-commerce, security, and the Intranet—is starting very slowly. It is forecast that, before the year 2003, Namibia will experience a dramatic change in the Internet industry from an environment based on pulling in information to one based on "pushing" information.[18]

In the media, the *Namibian*, the country's premier newspaper, has had great success as an international information provider for the Internet, with its web site receiving 220,000 hits from around the world during the week of Namibia's elections in November 1999.[19]

By 1999, only three of six national newspapers had started their own web sites. Joining the *Namibian,* an English-language publication, were the German language *Die Republikein* and the journal the *Namibian Economist.* The German language *Allegemeine Zeitung* newspaper also was going on-line at the time of this writing, and, unlike most of the other publications, plans to sell advertising for its web site.[20] The *Namibian* also had started very limited web advertising. Ndauendapo[21] concluded that the Internet is popular with most Namibian journalists, but that to date they have used it as little more than a supplementary research tool.

A Namibian Internet site has played a vital role in monitoring press freedom throughout southern Africa. The Windhoek-based Media Institute for Southern

Africa[22] distributes its magazine to subscribers by e-mail, saving over $1,000 in printing and mailing costs for each issue.[23] It also posts news of any regional attacks on the press on its web site and relays these to the International Freedom of Expression Exchange, providing extensive and instant international exposure and substantially increasing pressure on local governments.

QUESTIONS OF ACCESS

It is clear that the Internet in Namibia is not yet popular among the majority who resides in the rural areas. More than 70 percent of the population[24] does not have access to the Internet. This is due to insufficient telecommunications infrastructure in rural areas, which makes connectivity impossible, coupled with the underdeveloped stage of the Internet in the country. The cost of getting connected to the Internet—approximately $2,000—can be exorbitant for rural people in particular and for urban residents in general. It can cost a corporate user about $9,000 to acquire both hardware and software, and nearly $900 per month to lease a telephone line.[25] However, one analyst[26] puts the monthly cost of access in Namibia (as of 1998) at about $250 per year, well below the $704 average he estimates for Africa as a whole. Another factor contributing to lack of popularity of the Internet in Namibia is the high level of illiteracy, particularly in the rural areas. Illiteracy was estimated at 80 percent one year after Namibia's independence.[27]

The monopoly given by the Posts and Telecommunications Establishment Act of 1992 to Telecom Namibia to provide telecommunications services to the public[28] makes it difficult to create competition among ISPs, thereby resulting in high costs. This monopolistic state of affairs might be linked to the market segmentation of the sector, having resulted in the concentration of the Internet market among the urban, middle- and upper-income earners, as well as literate users.

While the Internet industry is relatively young and underdeveloped in Namibia and not yet popular among Namibians, it has taken hold as a corporate and information tool. According to Gorelick, the popularity of the Internet among Namibians will increase once it becomes an integral part of the school curriculum, enabling more people to have access to and increasing understanding of the new technology.[29]

INTERNET SERVICE PROVIDERS

In late 1999, there were six Internet service providers (ISPs) offering commercial services to both private and corporate clients in Namibia. All are based in the country's capital of Windhoek, with branches in some of the country's 13 regions.[30] The government of Namibia, the University of Namibia (UNAM), and the Polytechnic of Namibia each has its own web page. A 1999 directory of southern African media[31] lists the Namibian ISPs as UUNET Internet Africa

Namibia; Club Internet; Internet World Wide Namibia (IWWN); Internet Solution; Creative Computer Connections CC; Namibia Web Services (M-Web). In terms of the Posts and Telecommunications Establishment Act of 1992, Telecom Namibia Limited has the monopoly over the provision of telecommunications services in the country and therefore provides the backbone for ISP infrastructure.

Since its inception in 1996, UUNET Internet Africa Namibia has provided Internet services to both private and corporate clients in nearly all the major towns, and claims to have most of the dial-up subscribers of all ISPs (5,500) and about 40 leased/corporate clients. The company also claims to have the largest bandwidth (1.5 megabits), linking its Internet services in Namibia with South Africa, as well as providing access to the 32-megabit bandwidth channel between South Africa and Europe.

UUNET Internet Africa claims to provide 70 percent of the country with Internet connectivity, but states the majority of Namibians are not using the technology at present, and that the poor-quality rural telephone lines provided by Telecom Namibia make universal access difficult. UUNET offers normal Internet connectivity (dial-up), leased line connectivity, international roaming, web page design, and hosting, as well as data services such as e-mail to private and corporate clients.

M-Web does not see the Internet industry as a great revenue maker in Namibia because of the limited number of subscribers. But there is hope it will take hold as a corporate and information tool, moving beyond its introductory period as the "private toy" of a few Namibians who had earlier experience in use of the Internet in Europe and the United States. They claim that when the Internet started proving itself, corporate Namibia began using it more extensively because companies with head offices in other countries were under pressure to use the Internet for better communication and to transfer prices, technical data, and product information.

While M-Web is a relative newcomer to the Namibian Internet industry, having begun operation in Namibia in June 1999, it claims it has made inroads in the industry with the support it is getting from the South African W-Web company, in terms of branding, technology, and development.[32]

As far as Club Internet is concerned,[33] the growth of the Internet in Namibia has a long way to go before it reaches an acceptable level as in South Africa, which is ranked number one on the African continent in terms of the number of Internet users. Since its inception in 1997, Club Internet has established nine branches across the country. The company claims to be the only ISP in the country that can offer "value-added" services such as web design and web development for e-commerce.[34]

Club Internet has protested a Telecom Namibia policy that permits ISPs to receive Internet data by satellite but not to send data by the same means. For Namibia's ISPs to survive with the high cost and low international bandwidth availability in many African countries,[35] they must begin to use satellites for

Internet services, such as very small aperture terminals (VSATs). This is the wish of all the ISPs in the country, and so may be permitted under new legislation. Telecom Namibia obtained its own international satellite facilities only in 1995, finally freeing it from dependence on South Africa's international links.[36]

PROSPECTS FOR INTERNET DEVELOPMENT

Initiatives taken in 1999 by the Namibian government, the University of Namibia (UNAM), and the Polytechnic of Namibia to develop their own web pages and facilitate communication links among government offices, agencies, educational institutions, and the regions augur well for the future development of the Internet among the Namibian population.[37] In order to realize its objective of expanding access to the Internet to the majority of Namibians, the government signed a memorandum of understanding with the United Nations Development Programme (UNDP) so that the country can benefit from UNDP's Internet Initiative for Africa program aimed at improving and enhancing Internet access in Africa.[38]

Under the Initiative, UNDP was to provide about $500,000 over a three-year period, as well as the necessary coordination and logistical support, while the Namibian government would provide approximately $500,000 for the project and create an enabling policy environment to provide for the greatest access to the Internet.[39]

In line with this initiative, the Namibian government produced a document entitled *Telecommunications Policy and Regulatory Framework for Namibia*. The initiative, along with envisaged changes in the regulatory framework governing the telecommunications sector, is intended to provide the vast majority of Namibians with easy access to the Internet. The cooperation between the government and UNDP has the following key objectives:[40]

Implementation of an Internet Gateway in Namibia: The establishment of a national Internet gateway by Telecom Namibia should increase access for the vast majority of Namibians, particularly the rural dwellers. Telecom Namibia has pledged to ensure access to the Internet is provided to all sections of society on a nondiscriminatory basis and at a reasonable price. A particular effort will be made to ensure that all students, especially in rural areas, have access to the Internet.

Integration of the ministries' Intranet/Internet: The necessary equipment for integrating the government's existing Intranet/Internet is being procured, and regional government headquarters are to be connected to the national Internet gateway in order to facilitate information flow within government. The project also aims to enhance Internet connectivity for the University of Namibia (UNAM) campuses around the country.

Training: Capacity building is to be facilitated through the provision of training programs.

Promotion of an enabling regulatory and policy environment: Finally, this umbrella project seeks to promote an enabling regulatory environment for Internet use and growth within Namibia. This includes facilitating the purchase, importation, ownership, use, and private installation of equipment and supplies for computer-based communications; promoting fair competition, which includes entrusting the responsibility for regulating the telecommunications industry to an independent regulatory authority; encouraging universal service through deployment of the Internet infrastructure, particularly in the rural areas and in schools; encouraging the adoption of a reasonable fee structure to use the national network, including leased lines and dial-up service to access the Internet; and ensuring a significant role for the private sector that complements government efforts to achieve universal access.

Correspondingly, the Namibian government's formulation of a new telecommunications policy and regulatory framework, which was adopted by Parliament in October 1999, epitomizes the government's commitment to the Internet. ISPs in Namibia waited long (with skepticism and optimism) for the new regulatory framework governing the telecommunications sector. The framework enables the Namibian government to formulate and enact new telecommunications policies, although this process had not begun at the time of writing in late 1999.

This new policy and regulatory framework spells out the Namibian government's views on market development, competition, regulation, transparency, ownership, licensing, tariffs, and human resources development in telecommunications and broadcasting. The legislation promises to dramatically quicken the pace of liberalization, with a fully open telecommunications market envisioned by 2004. In addition, the establishment of the Internet Service Providers Association of Namibia (ISPAN) in 1999 appears to encourage the development, growth, and accessibility of the Internet in the country, through lobbying on policy and strategizing on making the Internet viable to more Namibians.

As described in the government framework, the new Namibian Information and Communications Regulatory Authority (NICRA) will ensure the development of the telecommunications market, overseeing standards and ensuring competition. It is intended to be independent from ministries, and to be financed by license fees and levies. A fund is to be provided by the regulator to assist with projects promoting local participation, attaining universal service goals, and providing education and training. Key goals targeted for 2004 include:

- Access (within walking distance) to telecommunications services for 80 percent to 90 percent of Namibians.
- Every community with more than 100 people should have at least one telephone connection or business center.
- Every telephone connection and business center should have the capacity of accessing "the information society."

It was expected that in the year 2000 Telecom Namibia would enter the Internet market as a service provider, although regulatory controls will prevent it from exploiting its inbuilt advantage over existing commercial players. ISPs will carefully monitor Telecom Namibia's plans for the provision of Internet services to ensure that the company does not use cross-subsidies for its own benefits, and to ensure that the pricing Telecom Namibia offers is fair. Telecom Namibia is striving to digitize its network, and make general improvements in telecommunications infrastructure including the automation of all manual and farm telephone lines.[41]

Hopefully, these government, private sector, and civil society efforts will pay dividends in coming years in terms of an increase in the number of users, revenue enhancement to ISPs, and increasing the popular understanding of the potentially extensive socioeconomic benefits Namibians stand to derive from the Internet.

CONCLUSION

The global geopolitical shifts that saw the collapse of Communism and resulted in the independence of Namibia in 1990 allowed the newly independent state to become a full and equal member of the international community, ensuring the country's access to new telecommunications technologies such as the Internet. However, the growth of the Internet has been a painstaking process, characterized by lack of financial resources, lack of expertise, lack of buying power among the previously disadvantaged black majority, and a lack of access to the Internet in rural areas and in schools.

Efforts are under way to improve the state of the Internet in the country through programs such as the UNDP Internet Initiative for Africa, which seeks to provide universal access to the Internet in the new millennium. Good cooperation has been evident among the state, the private sector, and civil society. The future growth and development of the Internet in Namibia will be determined by a number of factors. Foremost among these is the provision of an enabling regulatory and policy framework, of which the new telecommunication policy is a key component and a hopeful signpost marking Namibia's on-ramp to the information superhighway.

NOTES

1. Gorelick 1999a. This statistic is based on a count of registered Internet domains by country ("na" for Namibia). This data is available from Network Wizards at http://www.nw.com/zone/WWW/dist-bynum.html. Jensen's (1999) survey of ISPs puts Namibia in eleventh place in Africa for number of Internet subscribers.

2. Telecom Namibia, for example, added 50,000 customers from 1993 to 1998, and saw large increases in revenue. Interview with H. Oberprieler of Telecom Namibia Limited.

3. In 1999 and 2000, totaling N$41,414,153, which is about US$6.7 million (Oberprieler 1999).

4. Gorelick 1998; Gorelick 1999a; Wessels 1999; Southern Africa Telecommunications Restructuring Program's Study Report on Internet 1998. N. Gorelick is the founder of Internet World Wide Namibia and currently the General Manager of M-Web; U. Wessels is the customer support manager at UUNET Internet Africa Namibia.

5. Ndauendapo 1999.

6. Amathila 1996.

7. Barnes 1998.

8. 6 Interviews: B. Barnes; V. Kandetu; J. Kruger. B. Barnes was the former Chairperson of the Namibian Communications Commission (NCC); V. Kandetu is the current Chairperson of NCC; J. Kruger is the Deputy Director of the NCC. Telecom Namibia is in turn a subsidiary of the government-owned Namibia Post and Telecom Holding Limited (NPTH).

9. Amathila 1996.

10. Gorelick 1998; Gorelick 1999a; Wessels 1999; Southern Africa Telecommunications Restructuring Program's Study Report on Internet 1998.

11. Gorelick 1999b.

12. Wessels 1999b.

13. Gorelick 1999b; Wessels 1999; Megenis 1999. C. Megenis is the Web Developer at Club Internet Namibia.

14. Jensen 1998.

15. Amathila 1996.

16. Jensen 1999.

17. Jensen (1999) puts the figure at 3,000, as of May 1999. His data are also based on contact with local ISPs.

18. Gorelick 1999b.

19. *Namibian* (1999), "Web Site Tops polls," Dec. 9, via Africa Online.

20. Hofmann 1999.

21. Ndauendapo 1999.

22. misanet.org.

23. Lush 1996.

24. NEPRU 1996.

25. Gorelicks 1998; Steinmann 1999; Hofmann 1999; Amupadhi 1999; Prinsloo 1999; Panos 1995.

26. Jensen 1999.

27. This figure is taken from a document entitled "Proposals for a National Literacy Programme in Namibia," a consultation document by Edwin K. Townsend Coles and Ulla Kann, submitted to the Ministry of Education and Culture, and funded by the Swedish International Development Authority (SIDA), March 1991.

28. Barnes 1998.

29. Gorelick 1998, 1999a.

30. Namibia's 13 regions are: Ohangwena, Omusati, Oshana, Oshikoto, Kunene, Kavango, Otjozondjupa, Khomas, Erongo, Omaheke, Hardap, Karas, and Caprivi.

31. MISA 1999.

32. Gorelick 1999b.

33. Mengenis 1999.

34. Ibid.
35. Jensen 1998.
36. Amathila 1996.
37. Asino 1999; Gorelick 1999b; Megenis 1999. E. Asino is the Chief Systems Analyst in the Directorate of Public Service Information Technology Management, in the Office of the Prime Minister of Namibia.
38. Jakobsen 1999. O. Jakobsen is the Deputy Resident Representative of UNDP in Namibia.
39. Jakobsen 1999.
40. As per the Memorandum of Understanding (MOU) signed between the Namibian Government and UNDP. Jakobsen 1999.
41. Oberprieler 1999.

REFERENCES

Amathila, Ben (1996). "Namibia Shifts into High Gear." *Africa Communications* 7 (4).
Amupadhi, T. (1999). Interview with P. Ndauendapo.
Asino, E. (1999). "The Development of Government Web Content in Namibia: The Public Sector Policy and Experience." Paper delivered at the National Information and Communication Initiative Workshop, Sept. 28–29, Windhoek, Namibia.
Barnes, B. (1998). "Legal, Regulatory and Policy Management Issues in Namibia." Address to the workshop on a National Information and Communication Infrastructure Strategy for Namibia, May 11–13, Windhoek, Namibia.
Fouche, B. (1997) "Knowledge Networks: A New Paradigm for Promoting Information Access and Exchange." Paper delivered at the IUCN Workshop on Environmental Documentation and Resource Centre Network, Nov. 24–26, Windhoek, Namibia.
Gorelick, N. (1998). "The Internet Industry in Namibia." Paper presented at the workshop on a National Information and Communication Infrastructure Strategy for Namibia, May 11–13, Windhoek, Namibia.
——— (1999a). "The Development of the Internet Industry in Namibia: Progress and Constraints Hampering Growth." Paper presented to the National Information and Communication Infrastructure Strategy for Namibia, Sept. 28–29, Windhoek, Namibia.
——— (1999b). Interview with P. Ndauendapo.
Hofmann, E. (1999). Interview with P. Ndauendapo.
Jakobsen, O. (1999). Keynote address, National Information and Communication Initiative Workshop, Sept. 28–29, Windhoek, Namibia.
Jensen, M. (1998). "An Overview of Internet Connectivity in Africa," Aug. 5. http://www3.SN.APC.ORG/Afrika/AFSTAT.HTM.
——— (1999). *African Internet Connectivity* web site at http://www3.wn.apc.org/africa/index.html.
Kandetu, V. (1998). "Convergence in the Media, Information and Communications Sectors." Address to the Namibian Press Centenary Conference, Oct. 12–13, Windhoek, Namibia.
Kruger, J. (1999). Interview with P. Ndauendapo.

Lush, D. (1996). "The Advent of the Information Super-Highway and Its Significance to the Media in Southern Africa." Paper Delivered at the Media Institute for Southern Africa general conference, Zanzibar.

Megenis, C. (1999). Interview with P. Ndauendapo.

Namibian Economic Policy Research Unit (NEPRU) (1996). "Focus on Poverty and Government Policy," No. 2/Aug., Windhoek, Namibia.

Ndauendapo, P. (1999). "The Advent of Internet in Namibia: A Study of Its Sociopolitical, Economic and Legal Impact on the Newspaper Industry." Unpublished master's dissertation, Centre for Mass Communication Research, University of Leicester, UK.

Oberprieler, H. (1999). "Taking Telecommunication Services to the Namibian Population." Address to the National Information and Communication Initiative Workshop, Sept. 28–29, Windhoek, Namibia.

Panos (1995). *The Internet and the South: Superhighway or Dirt Track?* London: Media Briefing No. 16, October.

Prinsloo, H. (1999). Interview with P. Ndauendapo.

Southern Africa Telecommunications Restructuring Program (1998). Study Report on Internet in the Southern Africa Development Community (SADC) Region.

Southern African Media Directory (1999). Windhoek, Namibia: Media Institute of Southern Africa (MISA).

Steinmann, D. (1999). Interview with P. Ndauendapo.

Telecommunications Policy and Regulatory Framework for Namibia (1999). Windhoek, Namibia: Ministry of Information and Broadcasting, Government of the Republic of Namibia.

Wessels, U. (1999). Interview with P. Ndauendapo.

9

Dynamics of the Internet in Nigeria

Festus Eribo and Kelly Fudge Albada

The introduction of the Internet in Nigeria has been a milestone in development communication in Africa's most populous country. With 120 million people, Nigeria is home to the highest concentration of black people on Earth. By 2050, Nigeria will have more than 337 million people, making it the world's fourth-largest country in terms of population after India, China, and the United States.[1] While the population increase is good news for business, communication, and market analysts in Nigeria, existing information and communication technologies may be inadequate for the promotion of meaningful development. Communication in Nigeria is largely oral because of the dearth of communication infrastructure. Most Nigerians have never made or received a phone call.

Nigeria has a low technological, educational, and economic support base. As a crucial information technology for social change in the next century, the information superhighway could not have been introduced to Nigerians at a better time. It brings hope to a country that is one of the poorest nations in the world. Nigeria is a major oil-exporting country with oil revenue equaling that of Kuwait. In spite of its rich natural and human resources, Nigeria's developmental status has been abysmal. Much of the wealth of the nation was misappropriated and stolen by various military rulers and their cohorts at a time when Nigeria was being governed without fiscal accountability and political legitimacy. In July 1999, Nigeria's vice president disclosed that the government was gathering information on $55 billion looted from public funds during the military regime.[2] Nigerians welcome the Internet revolution and the potential to unleash meaningful social change. The Internet may be the golden gate to the fountain of knowledge and development for millions of Nigerians. If properly harnessed, the Internet could deliver fundamental freedom of expression, free flow of news and information, distance education, health services, agricultural extension, electronic commerce, and entertainment to millions of Nigerians and other citizens of the developing and developed nations. The Internet offers global reach, easy access to an ocean of information, and the ability of an individual or organization to contribute to the world's wealth of information.

This chapter focuses on the dynamics of the Internet in Nigeria and the potential effects of cyberspace on the social, economic, political, and cultural landscapes. The authors examine the diffusion of Internet accessibility and the efforts by the government and the private sector to accelerate the process. The mass media presence on the Internet also is examined. The constitutional guarantee to freedom of expression, including press freedom and the freedom of the Internet, and the resurgence of democracy in Nigeria are examined. Some of the obstacles to Internet development are highlighted.

DIFFUSION OF INTERNET ACCESSIBILITY

Internet accessibility in Nigeria is at its embryonic stage. The slow diffusion of the Internet to less than 1 percent of the population in Nigeria is not peculiar to the country. The global growth of the Internet has been slow in both the developed countries and the developing countries. For example, only about 150 million people out of a population of 5.7 billion people worldwide have access to the Internet. Although the United States, the cradle of the Internet, leads the world with about 85 million Internet users, or 40 percent of the country's population above the age of 16, Asia with more than two billion people has a mere 24 million Internet users.[3] At the end of 1998, there were 9.75 million Internet users out of a population of 126 million Japanese, and 8.1 million Internet users out of a population of 58 million British. During the same period, there were 7.1 million Internet users out of a population of 82 million Germans, and 6.5 million Internet users out of a population of 31 million Canadians.[4]

It should be pointed out that in 1998, 19 African countries each had more Internet users than Nigeria, while more than 25 countries on the continent had fewer than 900 Internet users. By comparison in 1998, a free South Africa with a population of 45 million people had more than 900,000 Internet users, while more than 99 percent of Nigeria's 120 million people had no access to the Internet under the military regime. During the same period, smaller neighboring African countries such as Benin, Cameroon, and Ghana had several enthusiastic groups of Internet users that were two to four times the number of Internet users in Nigeria. Countries like Libya, Somalia, Congo, and Western Sahara had neither Internet service providers nor Internet users. The number of Internet users in Nigeria rose from 1,000 in 1998 to 10,000 in April 1999.[5] By world standards, the number of Internet users in Nigeria is negligible but the rate of adoption of the Internet and interest in the new technology among the elite and a cross section of the population is on the increase.

As of 1999, there were only 300,000 phone lines in use out of a total 600,000 available lines in Nigeria. The cost of installing a telephone in Lagos was $1,500, or 150,000 *naira*.[6] To the average wage earner in a developing or developed country, this installation fee is prohibitive. Similarly, many of the Internet service providers find it difficult to pay about $130,000 a year for an international 9.6 kilobits per second (Kbps) leased line.[7]

Meanwhile, the basic cost of a personal computer, Internet access fees, and telephone installation fees are the major obstacles to Internet accessibility among the majority of the people. Until a reduction in the price of the leading brands of computers in June 1999, the price of a personal computer in Nigeria was more than 150,000 *naira*, or $1,500. Low-cost Asian-made computers such as Enhance, Samtron, and Studioworks sold for about $100. These cheap computers are popular among low-income end users. However, the computers have to be connected to the local Internet service providers (ISPs). In 1999, there were more than 30 ISPs in Nigeria. In Nigeria, the usefulness and user friendliness of the Internet are the keys to the popularity of e-mail and the World Wide Web among the elite.

A connection to an ISP costs about 75,000 *naira* ($750 in late 1999) to 100,000 *naira* ($1,000) a year. Dedicated dial-up service costs 200,000 *naira* ($2,000) and a yearly fee of 60,000 *naira* ($600). The annual subscription to e-mail without full Internet connectivity costs 15,000 *naira* ($150) to 20,000 *naira* ($200). At these rates, the Internet is clearly beyond the reach of the majority of the people in Nigeria. With the introduction of low-cost Internet services, it is possible to use the new technology at a cost of about 12,000 *naira* ($100) a year at a central Internet service location. The prices vary according to the e-mail account category. The accounts are packaged in time slots of 12 hours, 36 hours, 72 hours, and 144 hours per month. The customer pays top dollar or *naira* for more hours.

In order to increase the adoption rate of the Internet in Nigeria, some of the Internet service providers have created Internet centers known as cyber cafés or cyberville for public use at low cost. The use of a cyber café costs about 700 *naira*, or $7. At the cyber café, a customer can learn how to use the computer and the Internet, and gain access to the World Wide Web and e-mail while enjoying a snack and soda provided by management. After establishing a free e-mail account, the individual or organization pays a few cents or *naira* per minute. Cyberville users are able to access news agency reports, mass media sites, research articles, books, and information on agriculture, business, education, new technologies, international job openings, and new products.[8]

The cost of personal computers and Internet access, and the tentative level of education in Nigeria, are reminders of the American phenomenon. In the United States, the level of education, income, and racial division are predictors of adoption of the Internet. For example, the U.S. Commerce Department reported in July 1999 that people with college degrees are eight times more likely to own a computer and 16 times more likely to have Internet access than people with an elementary school education. The report pointed out that American families with incomes of above $75,000 a year are more than five times as likely to own a computer at home and 10 times more likely to have Internet access than families who earn less than $10,000. Just as more whites have personal computers and Internet access than African-Americans, Asians, and Hispanics, urban dwellers have more access to the Internet than rural dwellers.[9]

As the world becomes increasingly interdependent in cyberspace, the Internet promises to become the global living room, the global university without walls, and the universal marketplace. The Internet offers the people of Nigeria and other nations some victory in space and time on a cyber-planet without frontiers. However, Mansell and Wehn[10] point out that "there are many instances where information and communication technologies (ICTs) are making no difference to the lives of people in developing countries or are even having harmful effects." To avoid this negative impact of the Internet, the Nigerian government actively supports all efforts to bring the Internet to the majority of the people. The governmental Nigerian Communications Commission[11] has redoubled its efforts to promote the development of telecommunication facilities, markets, industries, services, and skills.

The Nigerian Communications Commission (NCC), established in 1992, became operational in 1993. According to its mission statement, the NCC is charged with licensing telecommunications operators, establishing technical and operational standards for telecommunication networks, and ensuring the protection of consumer interests. The commission also promotes the development of the telecommunications sector of the national economy.

The diffusion, development, and regulation of the Internet in Nigeria are at the core of the immediate objectives of the Nigerian Communication Commission. The NCC, in collaboration with the Nigeria Internet Group and the Internet Society of Nigeria, actively promotes and supports the evolution of the Internet in Nigeria. The NCC and Nigeria Internet Group educate the public about the benefits and potentials of the Internet for national development. The NCC encourages several international organizations to support its efforts to promote Internet connectivity, accessibility, and reliability by organizing seminars and workshops in Nigeria.

In May 1999, the NCC organized Afrinet '99, a forum for African countries to meet, discuss, and map out developmental strategies for the spread of information technology and the use of cyberspace on the continent.[12] The summit, hosted in Abuja, Nigeria, was open to a wide range of participants, including ISPs, telecommunication operators, regulators, and consultants. Journalists, educators, researchers, librarians, business leaders, and Internet users attended. At the end of the summit, participants released a communiqué encouraging African leaders in business and government to provide a gateway facility on the information superhighway, to establish sustainable and affordable Internet services, and to engage Africans in research and development relevant to communication technology and infrastructure. The communiqué called for the development of rural and urban communication infrastructure, the establishment of telecenters and cyber cafés, and the promotion of a revenue base for Internet expansion.

To facilitate the diffusion of the Internet at every level of the social strata, the NCC has granted licenses to private telephone operators to acquire state-of-the-art telecommunication technologies. In May 1999, Nigeria signed a contract with Titan Corporation to design and deploy a global network of cost-effective satellite Earth station gateways to offer telephone and Internet services to rural areas. The centrally managed gateways are designed to use Titan wireless's patented Xpress Connection (TM), single channel per carrier (SCPC), very small aperture (VSAT), and demand-assigned multiple access (DAMA) in order to provide voice, data, Internet, virtual private networking (VPN), and facsimile services. These services were to be provided in 1999 to local communities and remote locations using existing conventional geostationary satellites. The services will be provided at low cost in prepaid and conventional customer care arrangements.[13] Another agreement was reached with Simba Technology to provide wireless Ethernet from Breezecom called BreezeNet PRO. The connections of wireless systems to local area networks (LANs) and wide area networks (WANs) were seen as an effective way to provide wireless Ethernet and Internet networking without the constraints of network cabling in Nigeria. Such wireless Internet connectivity is already in operation in the United States, Europe, Kenya, and Tanzania.[14] In addition, Integrated Network Solutions and other companies are providing Nigeria with web page design, web page hosting, domain name registration, and access to the Internet.

Nigeria's determination to catch up with the rest of the world in cyberspace is evident in the acceleration of rural telephone communication. The Federal Ministry of Communication and the Nigerian Telecommunications Limited (NITEL) are the major players in the National Rural Telephone Program (NRTP). The program is aimed at the distribution of telephone lines and possibly Internet access to the rural areas. One of its objectives is to provide telecommunication services in all the local government areas in Nigeria. In May 1999, 14 council headquarters across 14 states (out of the 36 states in Nigeria) participated in the Digital Access Rural Telephone (DART) program. They were Opobo (Rivers state), Odulepani (Cross Rivers), Kaiama (Bayelsa), Achala (Anambra), Akodo (Lagos), Oke-Agbe (Ondo), Fugar (Edo), Iseyin (Oyo), Bwari (FCT), Obarikpe-ito (Benue), Burare (Katsina), Kumo (Gombe), Takum (Taraba), and Kadamari (Borno) (the *Guardian*, May 25, 1999). In June 1999, the Prest Group introduced the Wireless Local Loop (WLL) to Benin City, the capital of Edo state. The loop provides Internet services, cable satellites, broadcasting, and telephony to the residents of Edo and Delta states. The rural telephone program is a part of the quiet revolution within the telecommunications sector directed at linking the remote areas of Nigeria to the global community. The goal is to bring the Internet to the 12.5 million households in more than 700 local governments in Nigeria.

The diffusion of the Internet in Nigeria depends not only on the government but also on the people, the economy, and the infrastructure. Although the model for Internet adoption is top down, it is significant to point out that demand, participation, and availability of telecommunication and computer facilities to a large extent drive the diffusion of cyber-communication. The availability of the new information and communication technologies, and the evidence of mass participation in cyberspace, are interdependent and indispensable in the digital age. Already, there is strong evidence that the Internet has stimulated job creation. The NCC reported in March 1999 that Internet and e-mail addresses are now found on corporate and individual business cards. Early theories of diffusion of innovation appear to support the view that successful innovations for social change more often than not are affected by participatory variables and adoption rates.[15] In many instances, the user friendliness, cost, usefulness, availability, and cultural significance of communication innovations are sine qua non to the rate of adoption and the concomitant social change. Meanwhile, however, the Internet is an urban phenomenon with little impact on the rural dwellers in Nigeria.

INTERNET ADOPTION PROBLEMS

There are many problems confronting the adoption of the Internet in Nigeria. These problems are not unique to the country. The problems of low adoption rate of the Internet and computer technology in Africa, Asia, Australia, Europe, the Middle East, Latin America, and North America are similar. The problems include cost; insufficient number of computers, telephone lines, and peripherals; limited information about software availability; scarcity of software; and inadequate funding. Other problems include the lack of confidence in using computers and handling the software, the lack of time to learn new programs, and the difficulties encountered when integrating computers into teaching practices. Additionally, a feeling of intimidation about computers experienced by government officials, business leaders, students, and teachers is limiting the integration of computer-based Internet resources in offices, classrooms, and libraries.[16]

The activities of hackers, the crippling effects of computer viruses, and the lack of privacy in unsecured or unscrambled Internet communication are not limited to the developed countries. For example, the loss of about 700 million *naira* by a Nigerian bank through electronic fraud in 1998 has yet to be resolved.[17] In Nigeria, the unreliable supply of electricity, the paucity of telephone lines, illiteracy, poverty, and the subsequent low demand for the new information technologies further limit the adoption of the Internet. Military dictatorship, political instability, and the pariah status of Nigeria under the tyrannical regime of General Sani Abacha from 1994 to 1998 were major obstacles to the spread of the Internet.

Other factors such as traditionalism, economic crisis, political turbulence, and war also militate against the adoption of the Internet. These problems are not insurmountable, because the leadership and the lack of accountability in government and society create them. In order to avoid the imbalance of technological diffusion in any given society, the United Nations Educational Scientific and Cultural Organization[18] is assisting many countries, including Nigeria, to build information and communication capacities and ensuring that the new technological applications do not lead to exclusion among and within societies.[19] The computer Association of Nigeria (COAN), Computer Vendors' Association of Nigeria (CoVan), and Computer Professionals Registration Council of Nigeria (CPN) are working with several local and international organizations to bring computers to low-income workers.

To promote the effective use of the Internet at the local level, the acquisition of local top-level domain (TLD) and second-level domain (SLD) international standards was necessary. The management of the Nigerian Top Level Domain (.ng) complies with the international requirements for name structure for all registered domains. Although the Nigerian TLD was registered in March 1995, there was an earlier experimental phase at the Yaba College of Technology in Lagos. The Nigerian TLD (.ng) is hierarchical by organization type and geographical location vis-à-vis interorganization relationship and network service providers. The second-level domains are, however, generic and similar to second-level domains in the Unites States. The second-level domains such as edu, com, gov, net, org, and region are used in Nigeria to represent the appropriate organizations. For example, educational institutions have edu.ng as second-level domain and top-level domain. Similarly, commercial bodies, government agencies, network service providers, and nongovernmental organizations have com.ng, gov.ng, net.ng, and org.ng, respectively.

In Nigeria, domain registration policy requires that a domain name be attributed to a legal entity such as a company, an educational institution, or an organization with administrative and technical contacts. Although a foreign company is not allowed to have a domain under the Nigerian Top Level Domain (.ng), a foreign or international Internet service provider is allowed to register a domain name for a Nigerian customer. Domain names are registered at the Nigerian Registration Authority, where structural changes of domain names and policies are under frequent consideration. However, all first-level domains are registered in Pisa, Italy.[20] With the establishment of the basic infrastructure for Internet usage, web pages and electronic mail addresses are registered in Nigeria with the same ease they are registered in developed countries.

NIGERIAN INTERNET RESOURCES

Internet communication among Nigerians was first developed in the United States with support from Nigerian academics, scientists, and students in the United States. Nigerian Internet resources are the creation of local and external contributors. At the local level, the government, business, and private contributors are the major sources of Internet materials and communication. Outside the Nigerian border, several international organizations, public domain databases, and independent contributions from Nigerians in the Diaspora dominate the vast pool of cyber-information on Nigeria. In the early 1990s, Nigerian discussion groups such as Naijanet, Igbo-net, and naija-woman@gradient were typically lively, boisterous, thought provoking, and entertaining. The Nigerian discussion groups were virtual cyber-market, cyber-news agency, cyber-parliament, and training ground for democratic debates on events in Nigeria as well as on its future. There were some exciting moments of ethnic flames and national aggrandizement, and some enigmatic invasion by annoying, clandestine, or anonymous netsurfers. Generally, the net etiquette was outstanding. A global association of Nigerians abroad was conceived and born on Naijanet as Nigerians in Australia, Europe, America, and Asia found a forum to exchange ideas in cyberspace.

The Internet debates among Nigerians abroad were reminiscent of the great debates among African students overseas in the early part of the twentieth century. The heydays of such African leaders as Nnamdi Azikiwe of Nigeria, Kwame Nkrumah of Ghana, and Leopold Senghor of Senegal, and the great debates on the liberation of Africa from colonialism, were symbolically revisited in cyberspace. The offshore debates in the last decade of the twentieth century witnessed a new crop of highly educated black actors in exile or self-exile debating the liberation of Nigeria or Africa from military tyrants and crushing economic and technological dependency and underdevelopment.

NIGERIA'S MEDIA AND CYBERSPACE

The Internet may bridge the communication gap that has existed in Nigeria for decades. The convergence of the mass media at the doorstep of the Internet is a phenomenon that has virtually erased the communication gap between Nigerians at home and those in the Diaspora. Nigerian media were quick to seize the opportunity to be present on the Internet. (See Table 9.1.) Nigerian newspapers and magazines such as the *Guardian, Vanguard, Abuja Mirror, Abuja Today, Post Express Wired, Africa News Online,* and *African Watch* are accessible globally over the Internet. The presence of Nigerian dailies and some weekly newspapers on the World Wide Web has revolutionized the flow of Nigerian news within the country and abroad. Like many of the world dailies on the Internet, the Nigerian dailies and magazines can be accessed without paid subscription. There is, however, a section for paid subscription for users who wish to search the archives of the *Guardian.*

Nigerian publications on the Internet have been thrown into the global arena to compete with the world's great publications from London, Paris, New York, Washington, Tokyo, Berlin, Moscow, Beijing, and New Delhi. Nigeria, now caught in the web, is able to communicate with the world at the speed of the First World. Although the Nigerian publications are free, the aim is to reach a global

Table 9.1
Selected Media-Related Web Sites

Name	Web address
Abuja Mirror	http://www.ndirect.co.uk/~n.today/mirror.htm
Abuja Today	http://www.ndirect.co.uk/~n.today/
Africa News Online	http://www.africanews.org/west/nigeria/
African Watch	www.africanwatch.com
NCC	http://www.ncc.gov.ng
News Watch	http://www.afbis.com.newswatch/default.htm
Nigerian Resources	http://www.asaba.com/nigeria.html
NigeriaWeb	http://odili.net/nigeria.html
PANA	http://www.africanews.org/PANA/index.html
Post Express Wired	http://www.postexpresswired.com
The Guardian	http://www.ngrguardiannews.com/
Vanguard	http://www.afbis.com/vanguard/

audience and attract advertisers, just as it is in the United States. For example, the *New York Times'* on-line edition, which has two million registered users, indicates the potential of such a rich database of readers for advertisers and the direct marketing industry. The *Times* plans to boost its advertising strategy, since it can electronically reach a worldwide audience through the Internet.[21]

In addition to the presence of Nigerian media web sites, the Pan African News Agency (PANA) and two major web sites, Nigerian Resources and NigeriaWeb, carry news items on Nigeria. They serve as a gateway for Nigerian web resources and have links to important web pages on Nigerian events, statistical information, and news. The sites provide direct links to Nigerian government home pages, embassy and consular home pages, sports outlets, university home pages, corporate and private web sites, research centers, interest groups, media home pages, and a digest of media news from Nigerian and international sources. Designed by a Nigerian in Charlotte, North Carolina, Nigerian Resources and NigeriaWeb are professionally edited and managed in the United States. These information delivery sites have contributed to Nigerian Internet development and mass communication in cyberspace.

However, in adopting Internet resources, the media should be wary of its dependency on the developed countries that control the central net system. Critics of the Internet in Nigeria cite national security as a deterrent to the adoption of the Internet, because the Lagos Internet Gateway is linked to Global One in the United States. However, it is counterproductive to shy away from the Internet, since the advantages of the Internet outweigh any disadvantages. For example, Nigeria's 37 public universities and four private universities are beneficiaries of the Internet revolution and the concomitant access to the global knowledge pool.

The same benefits will trickle down to primary and postprimary education sooner than later.

THE INTERNET AND PRESS FREEDOM

The Internet has become a great facilitator of individual freedom in a non-threatening way. It is a dependable vehicle of unfettered expression in writing, painting, video, and multimedia. It is a tool for stimulation and production of knowledge.[22] The ability to provide content from remote or immediate sources empowers the journalist as well as the individual in search of objective, timely, and uncensored news and information. Friedman, Baron, and Addison[23] note that the Internet redefines what we mean by remote acquisition of data from distant sites and from multiple locations around the world. For example, a Nigerian journalist in Abuja, Lagos, Benin City, Enugu, Ibadan, Jos, or Kaduna may write a feature or news story on American exploration of Mars by accessing without censorship any of the existing Mars web sites via the Internet from a personal computer.

There is no doubt that the Internet has empowered privileged Nigerian journalists and others as active participants in the realm of uncensored information. The ability of a Nigerian to access information from the leading libraries and databases around the world using a personal computer is a major contribution to the advancement of a free press system in the country. Reddick and King[24] point out that the Internet is at the same level of development as the telephone system was in the 1890s because of the lack of universal access at the early stage. They argue that although only a select number of reporters currently use the Internet, it is, nevertheless, "very useful because it allows reporters to perform their fundamental tasks of collecting and communicating information in a much more comprehensive," efficient, and timely fashion. It should be noted that the media are only some of the social and economic institutions being shaped by the new Internet technology.[25] UNESCO, recognizing the significance of the free flow of communication and information on the Internet, is committed to promoting the application of information and communication technologies for the free flow of information, innovation, and effective management in education, science, culture, and the media.[26]

Nigeria's 29-year ordeal under military dictatorship is an indelible chapter in any analysis of mass communication, economic, and political developments in the country. The checkered military oligarchy and the concomitant political instability, tyranny, economic malaise, and social crisis since the first military coup in 1966 culminated in the stunted growth of meaningful development in virtually all walks of life in Nigeria. From one military junta to another, there was a gradual decimation of the country's political, economic, educational, and technological dynamics. Even the basic infrastructure was in disrepair and there was avoidable delay in the development and diffusion of the Internet. Until the inauguration of a democratically elected government in Nigeria on May 29, 1999, the military oligarchy paid less attention to the popularization of the Internet because the flow of news and information via the Internet could not be censored. There are, of course, other reasons for the late introduction of the Internet in Nigeria, including the mass exodus of Nigerian intellectuals and flight of capital under the dictatorships. In addition, many multinational corporations and investors shied away from Nigeria because of the political risks and instability unleashed on the nation by the military officers and coup mongers.

The new constitution of the Federal Republic of Nigeria that took effect on the inauguration of the Fourth Republic in May 1999 guarantees press freedom and fundamental human rights to freedom of expression and democratic governance. Chapter 2, Article 22, of the 1999 constitution states: "The press, radio, television and other agencies of the mass media shall at all times be free to uphold the fundamental objectives contained in this Chapter and uphold the responsibility and accountability of the Government to the people." In addition, Chapter 4, Article 39, of the constitution states: "(1) Every person shall be entitled to freedom of expression, including freedom to hold opinions and to receive and impart ideas and information without interference. (2) Without prejudice to the generality of subsection (1) of this section, every person shall be entitled to own, establish and operate any medium for the dissemination of information, ideas and opinions."[27]

The 1999 constitution is believed to have several internal contradictions, but the sections on press freedom are explicit. Never in the history of Nigeria has the constitution so clearly guaranteed freedom of the press. The democratic government in Nigeria recognizes the potentials of the mass media, including the Internet, for the general development of the country. The emergence of Nigeria's Fourth Republic in 1999 will facilitate new democratic opportunities, press freedom, societal emancipation, and technological development in the country. Nigeria, in the postmilitary rule era, is embarking on a deliberate policy to catch up with the rest of the world in cyberspace. It should be pointed out that before the constitutional guarantee for press freedom was enacted, Nigerian journalists were known for their heroic struggle for press freedom under military rule.[28]

CONCLUSIONS

As a new information delivery system, the information superhighway is already a part of the free-press cultural legacy from the twentieth century to the twenty-first century. The Internet is growing at a geometrical rate of progression with the assistance of the Nigerian Communications Commission, local Internet groups and organizations, and international organizations. The growth is driven by the ability of the Internet user to access or contribute information in cyberspace from remote or immediate locations. The Internet in Nigeria, as in other countries, has opened a new world of information gathering, processing, dissemination, and retrieval in an unexpected fashion. Nigerians in business, education, communication, and other sectors continue to develop a strong appetite for the e-mail system and the World Wide Web.

Despite the adoption problems of the Internet, this major breakthrough in global communication promises to revolutionize and invigorate the knowledge pool, communication, and information resources in time and space. In Nigeria, as in many African countries, the adoption of the Internet faces serious infrastructural, technological, educational, and financial problems. A major obstacle to Internet diffusion in Nigeria is the cost of computers and Internet connectivity. Thirty years of military dictatorship set back freedom of the press and cyber-communication. However, the role of international organizations and indigenous efforts in the development and expansion of the Internet in Nigeria appear to be successful since the inauguration of a democratically elected government.

Since physical proximity no longer limits the ability to access the rich pool of information on the Web, the use of the Internet in Nigeria will create a flood of information for journalists and ordinary citizens. The world has become a global village for the Nigerian on the Internet. The full potentials of the Internet are, however, still limited to those with access.

NOTES

1. U.S. Census Bureau 1999.
2. *Africa News Online*, July 5, 1999.
3. The *Guardian*, May 18, 1999.
4. *Internet Daily*, Feb. 10, 1999; U.S. Census Bureau 1998.
5. The *Guardian*, April 13, 1999.
6. Reuters, June 25, 1999.
7. The *Guardian*, April 22, 1999.
8. The *Guardian*, June 6, 1999.
9. Associated Press, July 8, 1999.
10. Mansell and Wehn 1998.
11. ncc.gov.ng.
12. The *Guardian*, May 11, 1999.
13. *America Online*, May 17, 1999.
14. *Tanzania America Online*, May 26, 1999.
15. Rogers 1976; Hedebro 1982.
16. Charp 1996; Lee and Fleming 1995; Singer et al. 1996.
17. The *Guardian*, June 1, 1999.
18. firewall.unesco.org.
19. Khvilon and Patru 1997.
20. *ISOC Nigeria Chapter*, Feb. 18, 1999.
21. *Internet Daily*, July 24, 1997.
22. Charp 1996; Gaines et al. 1996; Partee 1996.
23. Friedman et al. 1996.
24. Reddick and King 1995, 71.
25. Dizard 1994, 21.

26. Khvilon and Patru 1997.
27. *NigeriaWeb*, June 1999.
28. Eribo 1997.

REFERENCES

Africa News Online, July 5, 1999.

America Online, May 17 and 26, 1999.

Associated Press, July 8, 1999.

Charp, Sylvia (1996). "Curriculum Integration." *Technological Horizons in Education 23* (10), 4.

Dizard, Wilson, Jr. (1994). *Old Media/New Media: Mass Communications in the Information Age.* New York: Longman.

Eribo, Festus (1997). "Internal and External Factors Affecting Press Freedom in Nigeria," in Festus Eribo and William Jong-Ebot (Eds.). *Press Freedom and Communication in Africa.* Trenton, N.J.: Africa World Press.

Friedman, Edward A., Joshua D. Baron, and Cynthia J. Addison (1996). "Universal Access to Science Study via Internet." *Technological Horizons in Education 23* (11), 83–86.

Gaines, Curman L., Willie Johnson, and Thomas D. King (1996). "Achieving Technological Equity and Equal Access to the Learning Tools of the 21st Century." *Technological Horizons in Education 23* (11), 74–78.

The *Guardian* Internet editions, April–July 1999.

Hedebro, Goran (1982). *Communication and Social Change in Developing Nations: A Critical View.* Ames: Iowa State University Press.

Internet Daily. Washington, D.C.: Data Broadcast Corp., July 1997.

ISOC Nigeria Chapter, February 18, 1999.

Khvilon, Evgueni A., and Mariana Patru (1997). "UNESCO's Mission in the Promotion of International Cooperation." *Technological Horizons in Education 24* (6), 58–60.

Lee, Kevin C., and Charles A. Fleming (1995). "Problems of Introducing Courses in Computer-Assisted Reporting." *Journalism and Mass Communication Educator 50* (3), 23–34.

Mansell, Robin, and Uta Wehn (1998). *Knowledge Societies: Information Technology for Sustainable Development.* Oxford: Oxford University Press, 1.

Partee, Morriss Henry (1996). "Using E-Mail, Web Sites and Newsgroups to Enhance Traditional Classroom Instruction." *Technological Horizons in Education 23* (11), 79–82.

Reddick, Randy, and Elliot King (1995). *The Online Journalist: Using the Internet and Other Electronic Resources.* Orlando: Harcourt Brace.

Rogers, Everett (1976). *Communication and Development: Critical Perspectives.* Beverly Hills, Calif.: Sage Publications.

Singer, Jane B., David Craig, Chris W. Allen, Virginia Whitehouse, Anelia Dimitrova, and Keith P. Sanders (1996). "Attitudes of Professors and Students about New Media Technology." *Journalism and Mass Communication Educator 51* (2), 36–45.

10

Senegal and the Internet

Alain Just Coly

Senegal, a country of nine million people on the West African coast, achieved Internet connectivity in March 1996. The origin of the Internet in Senegal can be traced to the 1980s, when research organizations trying to access scientific information created extraterritorial networks to permit e-mail and access to the World Wide Web. Among these networks was the Regional Informatic Network for Africa; ProMed, a network for medicine doctors created in 1993 by the World Health Organization; and the Sustainable Development Network. The coming of the Internet was advanced by the Institut de Recherche et de Développement, Cheikh Anta Diop University of Dakar (through its polytechnical college), and Sonatel, the sole telecommunications operator.

Senegal is predominantly agricultural, with about 70 percent of the labor force engaged in farming. More than half of its population is made up of people younger than 20, most of whom live in rural areas.

The situation in Senegal as regards the information and communication technologies (ICTs) is in many ways similar to that found throughout Africa, although there also are some differences. This chapter will detail the country's status regarding connectivity, and examine how the Senegalese, including journalists, are adapting to and using the Internet.

THE INTERNET AND THE PRESS

The Committee to Protect Journalists[1] cites Senegal's media climate as one of the most tolerant in Africa, although a 1997 press code may have caused some self-censorship by reporters, editors, and publishers. Coverage of the continuing rebel activity in the Casamance area also has been seen as problematic to the press. Even so, there have been no attempts to curb the growth of the Internet in that country, and none are expected.

Senegal's constitution provides for freedom of speech and of the press, and the government generally respects these rights in practice, according to a 1999 U.S. State Department report on human rights.[2] Laws prohibit the press from the expression of views that "discredit" the state, incite the population to disorder, or disseminate "false news." A broad spectrum of thought and opinion is available to the public through regularly published magazines and newspapers, including foreign publications. Political and economic views expressed in the independent press often are critical of the government and its programs. While publishers are required to register prior to starting publication, the government routinely approves such registrations.

Radio, being relatively inexpensive, remains the most important medium of mass information and the main source of news for citizens outside urban areas. Five privately owned radio stations broadcast within the country; of these, four are owned by Senegalese citizens. There are also three international stations that rebroadcast within the country. In January 1999, a new independent station in Dakar, 7 FM, began broadcasting nationwide. Another independent and locally owned station, Diamono, began broadcasting in the Dakar region only, along with two community-owned radio stations in Pikine and Keur Momar Sarr. All of the locally owned stations broadcast national news and political commentary. Some of them have been critical of the government, but no harassment has been reported. Throughout 1999, the state radio and television company retained a monopoly in the allocation of frequencies and licensing of private radio stations, and independent stations had to pay fees to the state company, which infringed on the principle of free competition. However, at the end of the year, the government transferred this authority from the state company to an independent agency.

A government monopoly controls local television, which is an important source of news. While there are no privately owned domestic television stations, French-owned pay television is available but offers no local news.

Senegal's media naturally were interested in the coming of the Internet in 1996. Sud Communication, a multimedia group, created the first press web site, where people could read the daily newspaper, *Sud Quotidien*, or listen to Sud FM. Since 1997, the Walfadjri Group, which publishes a daily newspaper and owns a radio station, also has a web presence. State radio (RTS) has had a site since 1997. *Le Soleil*, the state newspaper, launched its site in 1998; that same year, it was classified as among the 10 best world press web sites by the French weekly *Le Courrier International*. The Senegalese Press Agency (APS) also is on the web.

At the end of 1998, the first Senegalese magazine went on-line. *Afrique-Initiative* covers political, economic, and cultural topics. It is intended to be updated every two weeks.

Sud Communication Group organizes training seminars for journalists, where they can improve their multimedia skills, and exchange ideas with African and international professors.

Readers both inside Senegal and elsewhere seem to appreciate the web sites. Senegalese living abroad can actively send e-mails to editors, when before they had to subscribe to publications that took weeks to arrive by mail. *Le Soleil*, for example, can be read on-line anywhere in the world before printed copies are sold in Senegal. SUD FM's programming can be heard live.

However, uneven site maintenance is a chronic problem in the media. Some publishers and station managers, proud at having their media on-line, don't seem to understand the importance of regularly updating content and design. In late 1999, for example, *Le Soleil*'s web site had not had a face lift since its creation in 1996. At times, some issues are still on-line after a week. Facts often are not accurate. At the end of 1999, the state radio site still showed its last update as December 29, 1997.

Also lacking is sufficient content about the new information and communication technologies (ICTs). Multimedia stories and sections are few and irregular. The newspaper *Wal Fadjri* published the country's first multimedia section, but it lasted only one or two editions. *Le Soleil* has published its multimedia edition every two weeks during one year, while *Wafta*, a magazine on new technologies, soon folded. Another magazine, *Tendances informatiques*, publishes only irregularly.

Dakar is the headquarters of the Pan African News Agency (PANA), which was set up 17 years ago by the Organisation of African Unity (OAU) as the continent's news distribution organization for state-run news agencies. It was hoped that PANA would become the leading news source in Africa, but demand for its services was lower than expected, it was often seen as a mouthpiece for governments, and it has had many financial problems. In 1999, the OAU decided to sell the operation to private interests.

HISTORY OF SENEGAL'S PRESS

The Internet in Senegal is not an isolated medium. Understanding the birth and evolution of the print media in Senegal helps to create a framework in which to understand Senegal's ongoing attempt to become a full member in global cyberspace.

Formerly a French colony, Senegal was one of the first African countries to publish newspapers. In Saint-Louis, in the northern part of the country, the first printing house was born in 1856. The journals *Le Bulletin administratif du Sénégal* and *Le Moniteur du Sénégal et dépendances* soon followed. Both were read mainly by colonial government employees. News was composed primarily of local and international information, including reports on military campaigns against dissidents, world news, and scientific literature.

Other newspapers appeared during legislative elections, influenced by the fact that, since 1880, people from Saint-Louis, Goree, and Rufisque, and, in 1887, from Dakar, were able to become French nationals. Those who were not natives of these towns were merely *subjects*. Those born in the four areas were able to gain almost the same rights as French people, sparing them from most colonial oppression. People from these *quatre communes* could study and get jobs in the colonial administration.

In this context, the press began to develop. *L'Eveil du Sénégal* was founded in 1885, and *Le Petit Sénégalais* one year later. However, both began to attack the colonial administration, and both were closed down within two years. French colonists had their own publications, including *L'Afrique occidentale* and *L'Unité africaine*. Other papers emerged after 1910. *L'aof* (1907) was published by the French socialists. Other publications of that time included *La Démocratie du Sénégal*, *L'Ouest africain français*, and *La France coloniale*. All were managed by entrepreneur Blaise Diagne, a prominent member of Parliament. These controversial and opinionated newspapers focused on the troubled relationship between the half-caste community and the African community, and on problems between the administration and Europeans colonists.

An economic press started with *Le Bulletin mensuel de la Chambre de Commerce de Saint-Louis* (1885), and another publication in Dakar that had the same name in 1910. Neither, however, was able to gain the same circulation as those publications that covered politics and society. Other newspapers included Galandou Diouf's satirical *Le Périscope africain*, and the weekly magazine *Sénégal*.

By the 1930s, Senegal had 17 official publications, 52 political or general information newspapers, and 13 various other publications.[3] *Paris-Dakar*, the ancestor of the present governmental daily *Le Soleil*, was founded as a weekly in 1933 by the Frenchman Charles de Breteuil. After several years, it became the first daily newspaper in French-speaking black Africa and was one of the several newspapers published by the de Breteuil family based in Côte d'Ivoire (*Abidjan-Matin*), Cameroon (*La Presse du Cameroun*), and Madagascar (*Paris-Tana*).

From 1945 to 1960, 170 newspapers or other publications were published, even if they had little circulation and ephemeral existence. *Afrique nouvelle*, a Roman Catholic weekly, began publishing in 1947. It was very influential until independence, and closed down in 1987.

When Senegal gained independence in 1960, the single government party did not favor the development of an independent and private press. *Le Soleil*, the first daily, took the place of *Dakar-Matin* in 1970, managed by the De Breteuil group.

In the 1970s, publications covering politics and social news were created. *Lettre fermée* published stories attacking the political system courtesy of letters written by the readers. It was closed down by the government after only a few issues. The satirical newspaper *Le Politicien* appeared in the mid-1970s. Many kinds of publications managed by private entreprises or single persons emerged in that decade.

In 1999, Senegal had eight daily newspapers (*Le Soleil, Sud Quotidien, Wal Fadjri, Le Matin, L'Info 7, Le Populaire, Dakar-Soir,* and *Le Tract*); many private FM radio stations; and one national TV station (*Radio-Télévision sénégalaise*), controlled by the government.

GAINING ACCESS

To use the Internet, electricity must be widely available, there must be adequate telephone infrastructure, and people must have both training and access to computers. Where does Senegal stand on these necessities?

Electricity

Power, produced and distributed by Senelec, is not available all day long throughout the country. Many rural areas still do not have power lines. In the cities, power cuts—especially during the rainy-season months of July, August, and September—are common. For example, during the summer of 1999, the citizens of Dakar, the capital city, often went for 12 hours or more without electricity at home or in the office.

Senelec, formerly a public enterprise, was sold in 1999 to Canadian and French interests headed by Hydro-Quebec Canada. New management announced the end of power cuts, and $1.3 million (CK) to upgrade the network.[4] Even so, given the low incomes in Senegal ($517/year, according to 1998 estimates), electricity is relatively expensive. Senegal is not an oil-producing country.

Equipment and Connectivity

Both are easily found. Even so, most companies do not have enough computers owing to the high cost; when factoring in income, a computer bought in Dakar is more expensive than one sold in New York. A computer with monitor, keyboard, and mouse cost more than $1,600 in 1999. A modem and printer are extra, and a $72 fee is charged for connection. Therefore, only a handful of people can afford having the Internet at home. Locally assembled computers are somewhat cheaper, but the cost differential is too low to attract buyers. However, a new plant in Dakar was to produce 100,000 units by the end of 2000. Another similar project was announced in spring 2000.

Telephone Infrastructure

As in most African countries, the telephone system is inadequate. Senegal, with a population of about 9 million,[5] has only 140,000 phone connections. Disparities in urban and rural connectivity are wide. However, this is still a vast improvement since 1985, when Sonatel was created. In 1998, the cost for a home phone line was halved from $144 to $72, still expensive for most people.

Competition in the telecommunications field may help improve the situation. Sentel, a division of Milicom International, had 10,000 subscribers in 1999, one year after start-up. A third firm, Irridium Africa, in late 1999 had just begun to offer access to 66 satellites.

One alternative has been a boon to the Senegalese. Public telecenters owned by private entrepreneurs offer phone and copy service, faxing, and sometimes Internet connection. In 1998, there were 6,800 telecenters, 57 percent of them in Dakar.

Language and Training

Using the new media requires literacy. More than 35.5 percent of Senegal's nine million people can neither read nor write. Even for those who can, training to use computer and software is nearly nonexistent. Although the situation is improving, most intellectuals and businesspeople do not know how to use computers. When they are used, they more often than not are used to type letters. Computers rarely are integrated into daily work.

Training, therefore, is imperative. However, it too is prohibitively expensive. Even for the self-motivated, books and magazines cost too much. Computer magazines cost about $5, while books cost $40 and more.

Despite these problems, the Internet still is developing in Senegal. Many improvements have been made since its initiation in 1996.

CYBERCAFÉS AND *INTERNAUTS*

After the Internet came to Senegal in 1996, the Metissacana became the first cybercafé in West Africa. Since then, many others have sprung up. In addition, some cybercenters also have been initiated in Dakar—among them Telecomplus, a division of Sonatel; the Pyramide Culturelle; XS 321-Internet and World Voyages Cybercenter. Outside of the capital, the Futurix cybercenter can be found in the tourist area of Saly Portudal, 100 km from Dakar. Saint-Louis, in the north, got its first cybercafé in 1999. Sud Informatique, a company in Ziguinchor in the south, opened a cybercafé in 1997. Such facilities are not available in the other regions.

Cybercafés and cybercenters have greatly advanced Internet use in Senegal. Customers can access the Internet for a $2 or $3 connection fee and eight cents for 15 minutes. A personal account with unlimited access time costs about $18 per month.

It is difficult to know how many Internet users there are in Senegal. Providers estimate there are perhaps 10,000, although the figure may be much higher as businesses become more computer dependent and new cybercafés open. In May 1999, one commercial survey indicated there were 7,500 users.[6]

Senegal has hundreds of sites, coming from a half-dozen commercial service providers, all in Dakar, and various noncommercial servers. Unfortunately, many of these sites are not regularly updated, rendering the information obsolete. For example, one political party's web site in 1999 contained the names of influential members who had resigned months previously.

Web sites are maintained by commercial companies, ministries, nongovernmental organizations, public companies, banks, political parties, and individuals. Fashion designers like the French-Senegalese Claire Kane, who makes clothes for such famous people as singers Youssou N'dour and Peter Gabriel, have their own web sites. It is possible to place an order on-line, although payment by credit card on-line was not available in 1999. This will open the door to e-commerce.

INTERNET ASSOCIATIONS AND INITIATIVES

In 1999, the Internet Society (ISOC), a worldwide private association promoting the Internet, opened a regional section in Senegal. ISOC Senegal is not the only association participating in the development of the new media. Osiris was created in 1998 to gather data, inform decision makers, and encourage regional networking. International initiatives such as Acacia from Canada and the U.S. Leland Initiative also are being accessed, which work to upgrade infrastructure and democratize access to individuals, communities, and service organizations. Another important project is telemedicine, in which the sick can receive distance consultation by doctors; other projects target women, youth, and educational institutions.

INTERNET EDUCATION INITIATIVES

The World Bank's World Links for Development program intends to connect 40 schools by 2001. Twelve had been linked in 1999. The intent is to provide access to educators and pupils to strengthen curricula. Globally, the project is expected to connect 1,200 in 40 developing countries.

One interesting project, Malick Sy On Line (MSOL), was created by a Senegalese student in France. MSOL attempts to popularize computer science to students from the Malick Sy Avenue neighborhood, a famous street in the heart of Dakar. Today, there is a library and a computer room. Pupils from primary and secondary schools receive free training and access.

In higher education, the Internet is seen as having great potential. Cheikh Anta Diop University in Dakar is participating in two projects: the African Virtual University (UVA), sponsored by the World Bank; and the French Virtual University (UVF). Both involve global video conferencing, simultaneous classes held live via satellite, and hyperlinks to further content.

CONCLUSION

Since its implementation in 1996, Internet connectivity, access, and use have greatly expanded in Senegal. The country's engineers and computer science technicians have put the country on a par with others in West Africa. According to UNESCO, Senegal has 809 technical agents per millon people, compared to more-developed South Africa's 625 per million. Thus, the availability of human resources is a reality, even if Senegal is a poor country.

To sum up the situation, a 1999 report by Osiris notes:[7]

- The use of the new technologies is quickly developng, even if the phenomenon is still largely urban.

- Users are becoming more sophisticated and organized, as is evidenced by the proliferation of new associations.

- The development of the new technologies is hindered by cost of equipment and connectivity; a feeble telephonic network, especially in rural areas; a lack of Internet service providers; a lack of training; and a need for documentation.

Finding solutions to these problems is imperative if the Internet is to spread in Senegal. Besides easing cost restrictions, another focus should be the implementation of the new technologies in education, at both the secondary and tertiary levels. The new technologies should be available to all, which is not the case at present.

NOTES

1. cpj.org.
2. Bureau of Democracy 2000.
3. Tudesq 1998.
4. $1US = 625 FCFA.
5. 1998 estimate.
6. NUA 1999.
7. Sagna 1999.

REFERENCES

African Internet Society Initiative. *African Internet Connectivity: Senegal.* www2.sn.apc.org/africa/countdet.CFM?countries__ISO_Code=SN.

Bureau of Democracy, Human Rights and Labor. U.S. Dept. of State (2000). *1999 Country Reports on Human Rights Practices,* Feb. 25. state.gov/www/global/human_rights/1999_hrp_report/senegal.html.

NUA Internet Surveys. nua.ie/surveys/how_many_online/africa.html.

Sagna, Olivier (1999). *Bref aperçu sur l'usage des TIC au Sénégal.* Report presented at Osiris seminar in Dakar, July.

Tudesq, Andre-Jean (1998). *Journaux et radio en Afrique noire aux XIXème et Xxème siècles.* Paris: GRET, Agence de la Francophonie.

11

Togo and the Internet

Victor Louassi and Melinda B. Robins

Although Togo lagged behind its neighbors Benin and Ghana in introducing the Internet to the public in 1995,[1] it since has overcome the lag and made dramatic progress. In fact, it is one of the few countries in the region to have two Internet nodes. This chapter will examine the status of the current situation of Internet access and use in Togo. It also will look at how the media in this politically troubled country are using the new technologies.

Togo is a small West African country with a population of 4.5 million people,[2] 60 percent of whom live in the capital city of Lome. From 1884 until World War I, Togo was a German colony, then was divided between France and Great Britain. West Togo became the nation of Ghana, and the east gained its independence from France as the country of Togo in 1960.

Continuing political instability is one reason for Togo's late introduction to the Internet. The democratic process has stumbled owing mainly to the reluctance of the ruling party to share power. The political crisis culminated in 1991 with a military coup against the elected Prime Minister, Joseph Kokou Koffigoh. He was sequestered in a military barracks by army mutineers, then released and reappointed as head of a state dominated by cabinet members with allegiance to the former one-party system. Former President Gnassingbe Eyadema, who had been stripped of all essential powers, regained control over all the institutions with backing from the army. Throughout 1992, opposition leaders were continually threatened with assassination. They responded by exhorting the population to go on strike, which lasted nine months and had a profound impact on the country's fragile economy. In 1993, a rally by opposition forces was bloodily suppressed even as visiting German and French ministers attempted to negotiate a peaceful transition of power. The subsequent Ouagadougou Agreement between the ruling party and a coalition of opposition parties led to a presidential election in 1998, which was boycotted by the opposition. Eyadema won with 96.5 percent of the vote.

The years 1996–1998 were characterized by terrible violence across the country. It climaxed in 1999 when an Amnesty International report charged that state security forces had executed 100 people after the presidential elections. The charge was corroborated a week later by the Human Rights League in neighboring Benin, where more than 60 corpses had washed up. Togo's government threatened the human-rights activists with legal action.[3] The country has yet to regain its political stability or economic health. Key foreign aid was suspended after the coup. As a result of the situation, the country lost many opportunities that could have speeded its connection to the Internet. Many neighboring countries such as Benin and Burkina Faso benefited from the resources diverted from Togo.

Togo was one of the last countries in the subregion to open up the Internet to the general public in 1995, even though a digital transmission network has been available since 1991. According to government telecommunications officials, Togo Telecom, the national telecommunications authority, could have offered Internet access four years earlier, but it was not identified as a top commercial priority. However, observers say the lag has been conquered, and significant development has been made to facilitate the use of the new media. In addition, many cybercafés have recently opened up to further the advances in access.

Despite continuing political suppression, no law addresses the Internet. Ange Dokoué, Togo's "Mister Internet" at Togo Telecom, notes this is due "either to a lack of interest or laxity. I believe that those who might have anything to say do not see the importance of the new technology. Whenever I discuss the issue with [government officials], I make sure not to stress the dark side of the medium. Above all, we are mainly concerned about making the Internet available for the great majority of the Togolese."[4] Another official from Café Informatique, the country's first private Internet provider, shares the same opinion. "There is no censorship, and it has been so from the beginning. It is due to lack of knowledge on the part of the authorities."

Togo's 1998 press and communication codes do not mention the term "Internet," and there are few allusions to the new technology.[5] No license is needed for those who intend to become an Internet Service Provider (ISP). No authorization is required for the marketing of Internet services. No private or public organizations protect users or promote the Internet. This lack of government oversight is encouraging. But one wonders whether the absence of law translates into a real desire not to rule over this technology. Rather, there is a lack of awareness of the challenges posed by the Internet. In a country where the government is very sensitive to criticism, especially that from the independent press, it remains to be seen what will happen if an on-line publication, available for viewing outside Togo's borders, contains negative coverage of government.

One may guess, however, if current government-press relations are any indication. In early 2000, Togo's Parliament passed a controversial press code that included a six-month jail sentence without parole and heavy fines for "insulting the head of state."[6] Independent journalists have been warned about their coverage of government, and several have been beaten up or arrested. Under current law, journalists may not be incarcerated before trial. In 1999, however, police arrested the editor of an independent weekly for publishing an account of an opposition activist who claimed to have been tortured by security forces. Copies of another paper that contained a critical account of the same incident were seized from newsstands.[7]

THE INTERNET AND THE MEDIA

Internet use is in its infancy for Togo's media. The few journalists trained to use it have access mainly through the cybercafés, and then primarily for e-mail. The introduction of the Internet into newsrooms has been slow in coming. The journalists' association has had an e-mail address only since 1997. At the time of writing, almost all of the country's newspapers had an e-mail connection, but most did not yet have permanent access to the Internet.

Lack of means and knowledge are the main reasons. Most media outlets cannot afford to buy a computer, get connected, or regularly pay the bills for telephone and Internet access. In addition, most journalists have no experience with the technology. To address this situation, in 1998 the first author of this chapter organized the first Internet workshop for journalists to be held in Togo. For three days, 20 journalists from radio, television, and the print media got the opportunity to learn how to use search engines and gather information. A similar workshop, funded by the U.S. Embassy in Lome, was conducted in 1999 to show how the Internet can be used for research. Togolese journalists also have been able to take advantage of a regional effort at media networking through another project funded by UNESCO.

One problem discouraging the publication of on-line newspapers and magazines is that most of Togo's big companies operate in a total monopoly and do not need to advertise. Also, the country is not yet a consumer society in which fierce competition governs the market. The companies that do advertise avoid doing so in the private newspapers most of the time. They fear retaliations from the regime, which considers the independent print and electronic media as supporters of the opposition. Therefore, little profit is at hand for the independent media.

The youth publication *Cité Magazine* is one of only two on-line at the time of writing. It began its on-line edition in 1997. In hard copy, its circulation is more than 100,000. The on-line version is almost identical to the printed version, featuring stories about youth sexuality, AIDS, entertainment, education, and games. *Cité Magazine* exists because of an arrangement between the management of the publication and Café Informatique, the private ISP, which does not charge the magazine in an effort to promote Togo's Internet culture. The other on-line publication is *Togo-Contact* magazine, hosted by Centre Syfed, which was the country's second private ISP. Mainly academic in content, the publication holds no advertising appeal for the private sector.

The economic situation in combination with the media's shaky structure explain the weak development of the on-line media in Togo. In 1990, at the beginning of the democratic process, there were strong independent newspapers. Three of them—*Furum Hebdo, Courrier du Golfe*, and *Tribune des Democrates*—were critical of the regime. They suffered newsroom attacks by the security forces that resulted in injuries to the staff and devastating equipment damage.[8] Those who had invested in the paper lost hundreds of millions of CFA; after these incidents, those with means were reluctant to invest in the media. Another consequence of the attacks on the media is that private radio stations are very cautious about broadcasting news. Of the 16 private radio stations operating in Togo's cities, none dares to air sensitive political news or debates that could annoy the regime. Things have changed somewhat since 1998, when a new press law praised as less repressive was enacted. However, the implementation of the law was questionable because journalists were always jailed whenever a defamation case was raised against them.

Media professionals are now beginning to show great interest in the Internet. A recent survey indicates[9] that 11 newspapers, two private radio stations, a print journalists' organization, a press house, three media-supporting organizations, and a broadcasting journalists' organization have either an e-mail address, a web site, or both. Interestingly, no government-controlled media organization has an e-mail address or Internet connection. The Maison du Journalisme, a press center run by the independent journalists' organization, acts as a cybercafé where journalists can use the Internet for a minimal fee.

HISTORY OF THE INTERNET IN TOGO

The use of the Internet by the general public in Togo dates to December 1995 through the initiative of Centre d'Assistance de Formation et d'Etudes (Café) Informatique, a private company. However, e-mail and the Internet were first introduced to the country in the early 1990s by a French government scientific research organization to enable researchers to communicate and share information with their counterparts around the world.

According to the director of Internet services at Café Informatique, the server at first provided only a bulletin board system (BBS). At that time, the company's Internet access provider was based in Accra, Ghana. Through that gateway, Café Informatique began to provide e-mail service to its sole client, SOS Togo, an international nongovernmental organization that caters to orphans and abandoned children. The Accra BBS bridge lasted for about one year, after which

Café Informatique implemented its own Unix-based web server. It made full Internet access available to the paying public in 1997. As the first Togolese company to market the Internet, Cafe Informatique manages and owns the domain name ".tg," a suffix that identifies Togo on the Internet. Although use of the suffix is not under direct government direction, the state tried, but failed, to acquire ownership under the cover of sovereignty during bidding for the domain name.

The second Internet access provider to open shop in the country was the Centre Syfed, which began on the Université du Bénin (Lomé) campus. The center is one of 30 located around the world to electronically link French-speaking teachers, researchers, and students. Network designers claim Centre Syfed enables the sharing of knowledge between the subregion and the rest of the French-speaking world at large. To facilitate the spread of the new media in Togo, especially for use in sustainable development work, the RDD/Togo project was begun in 1997 to connect government services, nongovernmental organizations, private-sector professionals, organizations affiliated with chambers of commerce, the university, research centers, and schools.

Togo Telecom was the fourth Internet provider made available to Togolese. The agency is the sole manager of the current national and international telephones wire, telex, dedicated lines, and parcel data transmission (Togopac). In 1998, Parliament passed a law to privatize the telecommunications sector. At the end of 1999, Togo Telecom was opened to shareholders.

QUANTITY AND QUALITY OF TOGO'S CYBERSPACE

Centre Syfed on the University of Bénin (Lome) campus began with only three personal computers reserved exclusively for students, teachers, and researchers. The inadequacy of the equipment is still the main concern, although three more computers were added in late 1999. The company cannot meet the growing demand of its customers and must limit the number of students who want to register. Another cybercafé was opened in 1998 at Centre Africain de Formation à la Maintenance Micro-Informatique, a university-based school that trains computer science technicians. It has eight computers, six of them available for students and two for teachers.

Outside the university, Café Informatique opened its cybercafé with only one personal computer. Subscribers often waited in long lines to surf the web or check their e-mail accounts. Since mid-1998, new Internet Service Providers (ISP) have proliferated in Lomé, and the number of cybercafés has mushroomed. In addition to offering Internet accessibility to the public, the ISPs provide e-mail, fax, and I-phone facilities. In contrast to other countries in Africa, such as Ghana and the Ivory Coast, none of the ISPs operating in Togo comes from outside the country's borders; all are locally based small private businesses that use local expertise. One interesting innovation is the "business center," a cybercafé that allows customers to do word processing, bind various documents, and make telephone calls or send fax messages. The centers also create e-mail accounts for their customers on web-based providers such as Yahoo, Hotmail, Caramail, AOL, Africanet, and Africnet.

It is quite easy for an individual with access to a telephone line to get connected to the Internet in Togo. The ISPs usually supply the modem. However, a shortage of telephone lines is a major hindrance. Although 20,000 new telephone lines were connected in 1998, there are still areas in the capital city that are not reached by the telephone network. According to Ange Dokoué of Togo Telecom, there are dedicated lines for their customers and for individuals connected to their server. Anybody using the Togo Telecom node in Dapaong, the northernmost city, can access the Internet through the line 808-808. Most lines require monthly extension, indicating the rapid growth of Internet usage in the country. Another extension in early 2000 was to add 100 new lines, half of them Integrated Services Digital Network (ISDN).

A lack of qualified personnel was one reason for the delay in Togolese connectivity. A 1996 ISOC conference in Canada trained Togolese attendees and also helped the server on the university campus. Honoré Fiadjoe, director of CAFMICRO, the 1996 ISOC conference in Canada, gave opportunities to some of the Togolese attendees to be trained in the Internet technology. Progress also was made when the state-run telecommunication monopoly was broken up. The third and last reason is relative to the break up of OPTT,[10] the state-run telecommunication monopoly, in 1996. Under the influence of the World Bank, and by presidential decree, the Togolese postal administration and telecommunication office became two separate entities: Togo Telecom for the telecommunication sector and SPT for the postal service. This action marked a breakthrough in the rigid mind-set about the managing and allocation of Togo's telecommunication sources. After a telecommunication law was passed in 1998, it became possible for the private sector to apply for licenses.

As a public backbone, Togo Telecom is more technologically advanced than Café Informatique, although the latter node has been authorized to operate satellite telecommunication connections. Café Informatique charges higher fees than Togo Telecom because its users must dial special telephone numbers to connect. Therefore, someone who has Internet access through Café Informatique and lives in Lomé pays less than those who live in other parts of the country. At the turn of the century, Togo Telecom was one of 17 regional telecommunications companies involved in a project to install a submarine optical fiber cable[11] that was to solve capacity problems, speed up communication, and reduce the cost of data transmission.[12] Even so, the cost of connection is daunting to the average Togolese.[13] A computer bought in country costs a minimum of $2,000, while one ordered from France is about $1,166. However, import duties add 40 percent and then another 18 percent for value-added tax. In addition, there is the cost of the telephone and ISP services, and per-minute charges. Few people in Togo can afford $66 a month to use the Internet.

Despite the barriers, those with the means know about and use e-mail. An e-mail address on a business card is becoming as common as a P.O. box number. The coordinator of a national project estimates that about 30,000 Togolese use e-mail.[14] The number of e-mail users has been increasing so quickly that the newly privatized post office company has bought a server and become an ISP to counter its loss of income from "snail mail."

CULTURE OF THE INTERNET

E-mail is what interests both media professionals and the general public most. The Internet's capacity for research or creative web-site content is still at a premium. One of Café Informatique's directors notes that this is due to a real absence of an Internet culture. "People do not realize yet the cultural benefit the country can acquire from an effective and dynamic presence on the web."[15] This situation is not unique to Togo. A recent regional study[16] finds that lack of knowledge about the Internet's possibilities, poor accessibility, and budget constraints are serious hindrances for increased use of the Internet. The survey found that nearly three-quarters of West African agricultural, research and development centers are connected to the Internet and have e-mail. Very few of them, however, participate in the discussion groups and forums despite the potential for valuable exchanges among researchers. In addition, few of the researchers publish their work on-line.

In Togo, there seems to be an especially weak commitment to developing an Internet culture. One evidence is the poor quality of the web sites and overall content. Two examples are the web sites of Université du Benin (Lome) and RDD/Togo.[17] The university site has empty links, and there is no directory of students or academic work. On the RDD/Togo web site, only two of seven links are available. The director of Café Informatique explains: "The Internet here is evolving in isolation. In other words, if you exclude [those] dealing with the technology and the few people who enjoy it, there is nowhere to discuss and promote the Internet. It is amazing the way I surprise people abroad, whenever I expose what is being done here in Togo. Togo is not even a member of [the international Internet society]."

A search of the keyword "Togo" turns up hundreds of sites. However, only two of them—Café Informatique and Togo Telecom—come from within the country. The others all were created and hosted abroad, especially in the United States and Europe. This has serious implications for the country's role in the growing global economic system, or for tourism or investment. As with Togo's other media, the Internet remains a pure product of the city. There are many cybercafés outside the capital city, but only in the country's other cities. These are used primarily for e-mail access.

CONCLUSION

Internet access and use have greatly spread in Togo in recent years. Infrastructure has been upgraded, and costs lowered. The country is unique in the subregion for allowing competition, and the resulting cybercafés mean access for more people. One reason for the spectacular development of the Internet in Togo can be found in the fact that the country's university graduates are eager to use their increasing competence in the marketplace. Finally, the saturation of the networks in neighboring Benin, Burkina Faso, and Ghana has encouraged many people to get connected in Togo. Togo's next step is to go beyond e-mail use. It must begin to take advantage of the Internet's great potential to do research, to share information both within and outside of its borders, and to join the global marketplace.

NOTES

1. Although Café Informatique, a private company, brought e-mail to the public in 1995, a French government scientific research organization accessed the Internet and used e-mail in the early 1990s.

2. 1997 estimate.

3. Amnesty International 1999.

4. Personal interview with V. Toulassi, April 22, 1999.

5. Togo Law No. 98-004/ PR of Feb. 11, 1998.

6. Committee to Protect Journalists 1999.

7. Ibid.

8. Toulassi 1994.

9. Institut Panos 1999.

10. Togolese Telecommunication and Post Office.

11. Cable SAT3/WASC/SAFE.

12. Togonews.republicoftogo.com.

13. The guaranteed minimum wage in Togo is 13,757 CFA francs, one of the lowest in the CFA zone. $1 equals 600 CFA francs (2000).

14. Interview with William Kossi Savi de Tove, national coordinator of the RDD/Togo project.

15. Interview with Adiel A. Akplogan, Internet productions director at Café Informatique.

16. See http://www.cta.nl.

17. http://www.rdd.tg, http://www.Cafe.tg/genius, http://www.Cafe.tg/gallyjo, http://www.ub.tg.

REFERENCES

Amnesty International (1999). *Annual Report 1999.* http://www.amnestyusa.org/ailib/aireport/ar99/afr57.htm.

Committee to Protect Journalists (1999). *Attacks on the Press 1999.* cpj.org/attacks99/africa99/Togo.html.

Institut Panos (1999). "Média pour une Afrique de l'Ouest Démocratique." MAOD, Lomé.

International Federation of Human Rights (1999).Togo: Des pratiques totalitaires. (January, Number 269.)

Togonews. republicoftogo.com.

Toulassi, Victor (1994). "La Presse Libre au Togo: à quand la mutation?" *Politique Africaine* *54*, 160.

U.S. State Department (1999). Human Rights report on Togo.

12

The Internet in Zambia

Francis P. Kasoma

The use of the Internet and World Wide Web in African telecommunications is having a double effect: It is giving a voice to those who already have it and denying it to the majority who does not. The rich now have more access than ever to information and the opportunity for self-expression, and the poor remain without either. This chapter will discuss this dichotomy with particular reference to Internet communication in Africa, using Zambia as a case study.

Internet technology in Africa is still in its infancy, having started only in the mid-1990s in most countries on the continent. But it is spreading very fast. In early 2000, all but one of 54 African countries had Internet connectivity. This is a tremendous increase, considering the fact that in May 1994 only six countries, including Zambia, were connected. The rapid growth has defied the main problems of poverty and inadequate communication infrastructure that characterize most African countries, Zambia included.

However, the current situation of rapid growth in Africa is deceptive. It has spread only to a few rich people who stay mainly in the urban areas, while the majority of the poor in both rural and semiurban areas remain unconnected. In this sense, the Internet in Africa is an elite rather than a mass medium. This is the paradox Africa is facing as it moves into the new millennium.

THE ZAMBIAN CONTEXT

The development of the Internet in Zambia, which went through a pilot phase between 1991 and 1994, was a result of the far-reaching political, economic, and social changes that swept through the country during this period. It started with the introduction of multiparty democracy in 1991 and the subsequent liberalization of the economy. The dictatorship and the centralized government-controlled economy that had characterized the one-party state ended almost overnight when the United National Independence Party of Kenneth Kaunda was defeated at the polls by the Movement for Multiparty Democracy, led by Frederick Chiluba, who became president in November 1991. Government's previous stranglehold on the economy was relaxed with the liberalization of the economy, especially the sale of state enterprises to the private sector. The liberalization of politics, which also introduced a multiparty system of governance, introduced freedom of expression and speech at a level never experienced during the more than 20 years of one-party rule.

The advent of the Internet helped to promote the free expression of political views as well as commercial advertising and industrial competition. In the telecommunications sector, the changes were paralleled by rapid reforms, including deregulation, which meant the end of the state monopoly in telecommunications, the dismantling of the Postal and Telecommunications Corporation (PTC) into separate entities, and the establishment of a telecommunications regulatory authority. This provided an enabling environment for new entrants to the communication industry unhindered by monopoly regulations that had previously barred private-sector participation.

Since 1993, the government of Zambia has taken a number of measures to create a more vibrant telecommunications sector. These have included the liberalization of telecommunications and equipment, the passing of the Telecommunications and Radio acts in 1994 to establish Zambia's telecommunications regulatory framework, and the licensing of three cellular service providers. In addition, two parastatals and one private company have been licensed to provide Internet services.

THE INTERNET AND ZAMBIA

In 1994, Zambia became the fifth country in Africa (and the very first sub-Saharan country outside of South Africa) to obtain full access to the Internet. This was achieved despite Zambia's status as one of the poorest nations in Africa. It was, clearly, a technological achievement for a country that could ill afford it. It is not surprising that Zambia's Internet connectivity originated in the ivory tower of higher education at the country's University of Zambia, where the use of the Internet for learning and research, rather than for public communication, was the primary aim.

The establishment of Zambia's gateway to the Internet followed three years of experimentation with electronic mail by the university's computer center. In 1991, as a result of the International Development Research Centre–funded ESANET project, Zambia was given a microcomputer and a modem to provide a hub for the first university e-mail system. The rapid growth and development of what was then known as UNZANET was assisted by an arrangement with

Rhodes University at Grahamstown in South Africa, which in November 1991 began to provide a link with the Internet via thrice-daily, computer-to-computer telephone calls. These were paid for by South African Universities Network (UNINET), which was funded by the Foundation for Research and Development (FRD). This arrangement remained until December 1994, when full Internet access was achieved. By this time, some 270 e-mail points were linked to the network.

The technical success of UNZANET demonstrated that e-mail was a viable technology within Zambia. UNZANET also had shown that e-mail had the potential to remove some of the communication barriers that engender a feeling of international isolation in Africa's academic communities. At the same time, it was attractive to a large community of users outside of the academic sector because it offered a fast, easy, and highly cost-effective method of communication when compared to any other available technology.

By early 1993, users were transmitting large volumes of international messages via the Internet, and there was a strong desire among UNZANET users to expand the system. To accommodate this growth and change in direction, the basic infrastructure of the UNZANET system and the way it was funded needed to be reviewed. In particular, it was clear that this growth was based on free service provided by others, which could not be sustained. The Computer Centre, with its responsibilities to the University of Zambia administration, was not in a position to sell and maintain a commercial service to customers from outside of the university. Neither was the university in a position to pay the salaries needed to attract and maintain the high-quality staff that such a service would require.

In early 1994, the university decided to establish an Internet gateway and to sell access to services. ZAMNET Communications Systems was incorporated in May 1994, although it was not able to employ staff or provide service until the following year.

ZAMNET'S COMMERCIAL OPERATIONS

ZAMNET began its commercial operations in March 1995 with three staff members and 30 customers. Access to the Internet was via a terrestrial leased line to UUNET Africa in Capetown, South Africa, providing on average a link of 14.4 kbps. This arrangement continued until January 1997, when ZAMNET commissioned its own direct satellite link to one of the major U.S. backbones. From an initial bandwidth of 64 kbps, this has been upgraded twice. At the time of writing, it maintained a speed of 512 kbps on the downlink, with 120 telephone dial-in lines in Zambia's capital city, Lusaka.

Following a rapid growth of the customer base, ZAMNET in May 1997 began to provide local dial-up in the Copperbelt city of Kitwe. Initially, this was based on a dedicated circuit from Zambia Telecommunications Limited (ZAMTEL), the government-owned telecommunications company that had had a monopoly in the telephone business. Owing to the poor quality and limited bandwidth on the leased line, a VSAT was installed in Kitwe to provide direct connection to an Internet backbone in Britain. Early in 1999, a direct connection to Britain was opened in Livingstone (Victoria Falls) to cater mainly to the academic and tourism sectors.

Owing to the lack of digital high-speed data circuits in Zambia, in 1997 ZAMNET also introduced a high-speed wireless Internet gateway targeted at corporate customers. The wireless system provides around-the-clock access to the Internet and bypasses the inherent bandwidth limitations that characterize the ZAMTEL infrastructure. Organizations using the wireless system include the World Health Organization, UNICEF, Bank of Zambia (the country's central bank), Swedish Embassy, Zambia Electricity Supply Corporation (the government-owned electricity company with a monopoly in supplying electricity), Zambia Revenue Authority, Lusaka International School, Common Market for East and Southern Africa (whose headquarters are in Zambia), Zambia (Coca-Cola) Bottlers, and the University of Zambia Medical School. The demand for the wireless Internet connection was, at the time of writing, steadily increasing.

Other customers included individuals, nongovernmental organizations, schools, small and large businesses, government ministries and agencies, diplomatic missions, and hospitals. The individuals who subscribed mainly were professionals, including academics at Zambia's two universities, lawyers, and doctors. They also included civil servants and businesspeople, as well as industrialists. The country's media outlets, both newspapers and broadcast stations, were also big customers. Almost all had a web site and e-mail capability.

Although most ZAMNET customers lived and worked along the old railway line from Livingstone in the south to Chililabombwe in the north, they could be found as far west as Lukulu, in Mbala and Mansa in the north, and in Chipata in the east. The company also broke into the international market with some customers in Lubumbashi in the Democratic Republic of Congo (formerly Zaire). Until 1998, ZAMNET was located at the university, which is 9 km from the Lusaka business center. Aside from limited office space to accommodate growth, as ZAMNET became more commercial, the university location became a constraint to providing effective service. For example, customers had to travel 9 km either way for support services and to pay bills. ZAMNET then moved to the COMESA Centre complex located near most of the embassies and government ministry offices. ZAMNET became a private company and the largest Internet provider in Zambia. By mid-1999, two other companies had joined the race for the potentially lucrative business of providing Internet services to Zambians. They were Telecell, which also sells cellular telephones, and Zambia Consolidated Copper Mines (ZCCM), the state-owned copper mining conglomerate.

ZAMNET—and, to a limited extent, Telecell and ZCCM—offered a wide range of services. These included dial-up Interactive access, a leased circuit, wireless link access, wireless modems, and local area network (LAN) dial-up. Content services included an on-line job center, the Zambian Yellow and White Pages, web design and individual pages, banner advertising, training programs for individuals and companies, and messaging systems.

TELECOMMUNICATIONS INFRASTRUCTURE

As in many African countries, Zambia has a poorly developed telecommunications infrastructure. In 1997, there was an equipped capacity of 129,232 telephone lines, with only 77,935 working lines for a population of 10 million people with a teledensity below 1 percent. Teledensity in Zambia is higher than average in urban areas. In the Copperbelt, for example, teledensity reaches 2.01 per 100 with Lusaka at 1.63 per 100. On the other hand, Mwense in Luapula barely registers with a teledensity of 0.09 per 100 (i.e., nine telephones for every 10,000 people). On average, household penetration is approximately 5.63 percent, while the average annual growth rate in teledensity of 3.7 percent has barely kept up with the population growth rate of about 3 percent.

There are several constraints to raising teledensity in Zambia. The primary one is affordability. Gross domestic product per capita is approximately $330. Average earnings per month in urban areas range from $40 to $240. In the rural areas, the range is from $16 to $40. These incomes make it extremely difficult for the average Zambian to afford a telephone. Related to this constraint is that once connected, many subscribers cannot afford to continue paying for services. Data from the government's 1993/94 household budget survey shows that few Zambians can afford, or choose to spend, a significant portion of their income on phone service. If one were to add the cost of other services such as electricity and water, the cost becomes untenable.

Low population densities, especially in rural areas, also create barriers to increased telephone service penetration because of high infrastructure development costs. The average population density is 10.3 people per square kilometer, with a high of 46.6 in urban areas and 3.5 in rural areas. Lusaka, with only 13.7 percent of the population, has 33.7 percent of the country's telephone lines.

High Cost of the Internet

Zambians have progressively become poorer over the last few decades, and issues of food and shelter are increasingly more important. Per capita income has fallen almost continually since 1973. By 1999, poverty had increased to the point where some 70 percent of the population lived in households where basic needs were not being met. Life expectancy had decreased from 53 years in 1987 to 45 years in 1997.

With the country in a general condition of poverty, the cost of the Internet access makes it a barrier to widespread use. There are two parts to this cost: payment to the telecommunications company and payment to an Internet service provider such as ZAMNET. To reduce the cost of Internet access for ZAMNET subscribers, the company first provided local-call access by establishing POPS outside Lusaka, in Kitwe and Livingstone. ZAMNET also reduced the cost of the satellite segment by installing a larger antenna. In addition, the combined cost of the satellite segments for Kitwe and Livingstone POPs, using the new VSAT technology, was less than 25 percent of that in Lusaka and yet delivered higher download speeds. ZAMNET planned to change the cost structure for the Lusaka VSAT by the end of 1999 by using new satellite service providers.

Low Computer Penetration

Gaining access to a working computer capable of connecting to the Internet is probably one of the most significant constraints in Zambia. With only 20 percent of Zambian households having electricity, the problems of access to telecommunications pale.

Poverty is not the only problem facing those who want access to the Internet. High tariffs on imported computer hardware and software also make access to the Internet prohibitive. To facilitate Internet access to the public, ZAMNET established a multipurpose public Internet access center where individuals could drop in and use the Internet for a fee. This proved to be particularly popular with young people, tourists, and a small but increasing segment of the media and small business enterprises.

Shortage of Trained Personnel

The revolution in information technology has created a demand for computer-literate and skilled personnel. Finding and retaining such personnel is extremely difficult in Zambia, a country that in 1999 was just introducing an undergraduate degree in information technology at the University of Zambia. Those with computer degrees working in Zambia all were trained out of the country. In 1999, top-quality computer workers were in great demand and commanding high salaries beyond the reach of public-funded organizations such as the University of Zambia. Consequently, the university and other institutions that used computers on a high level had to rely on expatriate staff and the few Zambians with the qualifications.

The shortage of trained personnel in computer science manifested itself in another way: Computer users were unable to get adequate training and assistance, learning instead by trial and error and consequently causing breakdowns of the few computers in use. This reduced the number of computers available since there were few technicians to repair them.

Lack of Awareness of Information Technology

A lack of awareness by policy and decision makers of the power of information networks in economic and industrial development had, by mid-1999, proved to be a difficult problem to overcome. Apart from the University of Zambia, adequate attention has not been given to the provision of information networks including Internet connectivity to the public sector. The computer was only seen as being useful in preparing paychecks at the end of the month. A perusal of the national educational policy showed no mention of computer technology. This revealed a serious lack of awareness by senior policy makers of the role of information technology in education and development. The lack of coordination at the national level for the development of a national information infrastructure was exemplified by official failure to exploit the many international initiatives aimed at facilitating the provision of information network in Africa.

Improving Access in Rural Areas

Zambia is unique in Africa in that more than 50 percent of its citizens live in urban areas. Although the Internet is not readily available to this urban majority, access by those in the rural areas is almost nonexistent owing to a number of factors, foremost among them the lack of accessibility to computers coupled with lack of adequate electrification to power them. The development of rural telecommunications services in Zambia is also very poor. Telephone facilities, which are a necessary prerequisite to Internet connectivity, are almost nonexistent. Where they exist, the facilities are often unreliable and too expensive.

Zambia's rural areas are inhabited by very poor people who survive by doing subsistence agriculture and therefore barely have the basic necessities of life. The computer is the last thing such people would want to own since it would contribute little to their sustenance. The price of a computer runs in millions of *kwacha* (the local currency, which was K2,500 to US$1 in mid-1999). It is doubtful that a rural person would think of spending such a colossal sum of money on an implement whose use in the village is nil.

USES OF THE INTERNET IN ZAMBIA

Media Institutions

One very significant use of the Internet is by the media institutions, both print and broadcast. Most newspapers and stations have an on-line presence that has brought news to places previously not reached. They also have opened up Zambia's media institutions to readers outside the country, giving them the opportunity to keep up with the news and to respond via e-mail to advertisers and editors.

The Committee to Protect Journalists[1] cites Zambia as holding the record for more pending criminal defamation cases and other legal actions against journalists than any other country in Africa. Even so, it notes the country's independent press has remained resilient and undaunted. There can be no doubt that the use of web sites and e-mail by the Zambian media has helped to enhance press freedom. When the government banned one of the *Post's* editions, it was available on the Internet for some time before the government intervened and shut it down. The Zambian press also is able to complain, within seconds of an incident of censorship or arrest, to organizations and governments throughout the world that can exert pressure on the government for denying press freedom. Journalists also are able to network with colleagues in other countries. All three daily newspapers—the *Times of Zambia, Zambia Daily Mail* (both state-owned), and the *Post*—are available on the Internet. So are a number of weeklies and semiweeklies. The Department of Mass Communication at the University of Zambia has also made its teaching newspaper, *Lusaka Star*, available on the Internet, giving access to many people both within the country and abroad.

Political Participation

Use of the Internet by ordinary citizens provides a much-needed outlet for public discourse and political participation. Members of the public who are on-line are able to send their views and comments to political institutions, including government ministries, through the Internet. Some of these messages are addressed to the public at large through the press and broadcasting stations, pressure groups, and nongovernmental organizations. Although no political party has developed a web site, members of many political parties use the Internet to keep informed about developments both within and outside the country. They also send messages to government and other political entities that are interested in their opinions on various issues.

Student and School Use

The use of the Internet by students in tertiary institutions like the University of Zambia has been increasing ever since computer terminals connected to the Internet were made available to students in 1998. Many students are able to do their research by accessing the mountain of information on various subjects. Students and professors both are able to participate in on-line discussions and conferences to enhance their learning. For example, students doing the master's degree in communication for development, offered by the Department of Mass Communication at the University of Zambia, in 1998 "attended" a conference on development communication organized by a university in Australia. It was the first time the students had participated in a teleconference. The resulting scholarly output was impressive. They wrote and presented papers, and benefited from the comments of seminar participants. In another example, one professor developed e-mail correspondence with a worldwide network of scholars after he attended a one-month course on the use of the Internet organized by the World Bank, the University of Illinois, and the Asian Institute of Technology.[2]

In mid-1999, Internet access came to one of Zambia's secondary schools through a special project. ZAMNET provided free Internet access to David Kaunda Technical Secondary School in Lusaka. According to a spokesman, usage patterns and impact on the learning environment were to be studied before the project was extended to other schools.

Healthnet

One of the most outstanding uses of the Internet in Zambia concerns health support services. UNZANET, as the university network was once known, was active in the Healthnet project to introduce e-mail to the health sector. A partnership among the health sector, the University of Zambia Medical School, and the University Computer Centre was instrumental in networking of health institutions across the country. At the time of writing, many remote health centers in Zambia had been connected. Healthnet,[3] a service initiated by SatelLife, an American nongovernmental organization, provides free medical advice and information to medical personnel working in clinics and health centers. Zambia is one of 15 countries in Africa in which Healthnet operates to bring information and networking to otherwise isolated medical personnel.

Healthnet in Zambia was established to address the dearth of medical information. It supplements and in many cases replaces the medical journals and books that are beyond the budgets of most health institutions, including the University of Zambia Medical School. Healthnet provides a cheaper and more reliable data bank through cyberspace telecommunication. Healthnet started with a ground station at the University of Zambia using small antennae, an amateur radio transceiver, and a radio modem to transfer messages between a personal computer at the UNZA Computer Centre and a low-orbit sun-synchronous satellite that passed over Lusaka four times a day. In 1994, Zambia was the first country in Africa to get an official license to operate this system. Since its installation, messages have been shared among a number of African countries, the World Health Organization regional headquarters in Congo (Brazzaville), and the wealthy industrialized countries.

Zambia's medical services for a population of just over 10 million scattered over 752,600 square kilometers is administered mainly through government hospitals, clinics, and health centers. The hospitals belong to the Ministry of Health, although health boards administer them. There also are a substantial number of mission hospitals subsidized through the Church Medical Association of Zambia. Medical supplies are obtained and distributed by a central board of health. In order for this system to work, an efficient network of communication links, such as the one provided by Healthnet, is crucial. Previously, other forms of telecommunication were used. However, telephones, faxes, and the postal service are too expensive, unavailable, or poorly managed. The improved telecommunication infrastructure has helped to improve the provision of health services. It also has helped to improve training in health sciences in the country.

Healthnet has enabled medical personnel and students in Zambia to share clinical experiences and epidemiological data from other African countries in the subregion. Within the country, the network allows authorities to send timely alerts about outbreaks of disease, and to share strategies on how to address them. Health hazards posed by natural disasters can be communicated quickly so that medical assistance is gathered and dispatched in time to save lives. Official reports such as health statistics, budgetary allocations, and similar documents are shared between the Ministry of Health headquarters in the capital city and remote district hospitals and health centers that are connected to the network. Finally, the administration of referral cases to bigger hospitals both within and outside the country (especially with South Africa) has been made easier through Healthnet. Teleconferencing allows medical doctors and other health personnel to exchange ideas on the treatment of patients and other health management issues.

Zambia Legal Information Institute

The School of Law established the Zambia Legal Information Institute in 1996 at the University of Zambia, in partnership with ZAMNET and with financial support from the Legal Information Institute of Cornell University Law School. The Institute's aim is to improve access to judgments, statutes, and other legal materials of the Republic of Zambia both within Zambia and elsewhere. It also connects lawyers, judges, academics, students, and others within Zambia with the growing collection of on-line legal information available around the globe. The institute houses a help line by the Legal Resources Foundation, the brainchild of two enterprising prominent young Lusaka lawyers. The foundation provides on-line advice and legal services for people who cannot afford to pay. Ironically, however, Zambia's poor have little real access to the Internet.

FUTURE DEVELOPMENT OF
THE INTERNET IN ZAMBIA

The young Internet industry in Zambia has faced a number of problems. They include:

- Poor telecommunications infrastructure
- High cost of access

- Low computer penetration
- Shortage of trained personnel
- Lack of awareness of information technology

CONCLUSION

Zambia's entry into the global cyberspace community has not been without contradictions. On one hand, the introduction of the Internet has been necessitated by the unavoidable expansion of the new communication technologies that will be the hallmark of the Third Millennium. However, the new technologies, particularly the Internet, are bound to increase the gap between the haves and the have-nots, between the voiceless and those with the ability and the resources to speak out in the body politic. In an age of free speech, of multipartyism and democratic ideals, this reveals a deep contradiction. How can Zambia subscribe to a political philosophy of liberalization of politics and yet promote a technology that allows only a few people to express their ideas and associate freely with others?

The situation in Zambia would not have been as dire if the Internet had been promoted only by the private sector in the name of economic competition in an open market. The government also joined in the race to provide access to the few who could afford it and ignored the majority of the population with no means of efficient public telecommunication. The fact that ZAMTEL, the state-owned telephone company, has joined the Internet race means that the state has become an active promoter of this lopsided new communication technology. As the Internet becomes more available to the privileged few in Zambia, it is bound to affect the form and direction the democratic process will take. The elite few will continue to protect their interests not only in the social and economic development of the country but also in its democratic process. Still, the state cannot step in to regulate access and technology without violating the principle of free enterprise.

However, the state should not allow this lopsided development to continue unabated. A deliberate strategy must be put in place to prepare the people of Zambia for the new technologies. To start, computer technology education should be introduced in schools, particularly primary schools. (Zambia has almost achieved universal primary school education.) Computers should be provided in all schools, including those without electricity where solar power could be tapped. Schools should be provided with Internet connection so children can be brought up as computer literates able to access the information that the Internet offers. In this way, Zambia will bring up a new generation not only of computer-literate young people, but also of those capable of public discourse in the democratic spirit of free expression. However, this will not guarantee that the teachers themselves are computer literate. In-service training should be given to those currently in the schools, and teacher-training colleges must be equipped to ensure that new teachers are computer literate.

All of Zambia's tertiary institutions must be brought into the global network. The Computer Centre at the University of Zambia has set aside more than 50 computers for use by students, and many departments have their own equipment. The Department of Mass Communication, for example, has 25 computers in a newsroom laboratory.

The provision of computers in Zambia's training institutions needs to be accompanied by a corresponding improvement—and in some cases provision—of telecommunications infrastructure. However, the development of rural services will not happen by chance. The government must take steps to ensure that the rural areas are not left out of the telecommunications revolution. The government could provide incentives to the private sector for investment in telecommunication businesses in rural areas. Unless this is done, private businesspeople will prefer to invest in urban centers at the expense of the rural areas. This could be promoted by waiving taxes and import duties for companies investing in the telecommunication infrastructure of rural areas.

The government itself should turn to Internet communication in its operations, particularly in rural areas. The Internet can be used to reduce the distance and other communication problems government departments and agencies face in communicating with rural areas. The role of the Internet can be of increasing importance particularly in the support of extension workers, decision and policy makers in agriculture, schools, health centers, cooperatives, the police service, and similar sectors. Much government red tape could be eliminated with rapid transmission of information through the Internet.

In this connection, the ZAMNET managing director has recommended that government should promote rural telecenters to provide phone, fax, and Internet services. There is need for our national government to institute a deliberate policy to encourage local entrepreneurs to establish telecenters as part of an integral community program.

VISION FOR A NATIONAL INFRASTRUCTURE

Zambia has made important steps to open up its telecommunications sector. These have included the separation of postal and telecommunication services, the enactment of the Communications Act, the establishment of a regulatory body for the regulation of the telecommunications sector, and the liberalization of the infrastructure and services. However, there is a significant possibility that these bold steps will not achieve the optimum results unless the country can create a shared vision across different sectors.

At the beginning of the new millennium, Zambia stands at the threshold of a major telecommunications revolution through its use of cyberspace, but lacks a clear policy on new communication technologies. Internet communication has grave implications for freedom of expression—the cornerstone of any democracy—and cannot be left to chance or to the forces of free enterprise. Zambia needs to promote the wider use of cyberspace technology in telecommunication even as it confronts its uneven development between rich and poor.

NOTES

1. cpj.org.
2. worldbank.org/wbi/itq-2/.
3. healthnet.org/hnet/hnet.html.

13

The Future of Cyberspace in Africa

Melinda B. Robins and Robert L. Hilliard

"The central challenge we face today is to ensure that globalization becomes a positive force for all the world's people, instead of leaving billions behind in squalor."[1] This comment by United Nations Secretary General Kofi Annan, in preparation for a millennium summit conference in September 2000 by the UN's 188 member states, summarizes the problem, need, and direction for cyberspace in Africa. Annan stated that the technological revolution, especially applied to education, "can bring all kinds of knowledge within reach of poor people and enable poor countries to leapfrog some of the long and painful stages of development." Annan added that a minimal investment in education is all that is necessary, in order to overcome the present lack of infrastructure and illiteracy, especially in the poorest countries.[2]

Annan's words reflect the findings in this book regarding both the role and potential of cyberspace in Africa. As has been shown, cyberspace has, in a number of countries, already begun to leapfrog the development of the older media. The Internet offers the opportunity to heretofore-isolated African countries to become part of the global economy. As noted in this book, many African countries are not able to make the giant move forward on their own. Annan reinforced our conclusion that governments have to work together to make this progress possible, and, as already the key to cyberspace development in much of Africa, that much of the "heavy lifting" will have to be done through private investments and partnerships with foundations.[3]

At the first Africa-European union summit in April 2000, which included 53 members of the Organization of African Unity, the role of nongovernmental organizations (NGOs) was highlighted. As we have seen, NGOs have already played a significant part in the development of cyberspace use. Major goals of the summit were to "raise international awareness of Africa's potential, and plight, to promote its integration into the global economy, and to develop peace and democracy in the region."[4] Cyberspace use in Africa has largely been oriented toward the achievement of these purposes.

The economic problems in Africa, as delineated in this book and emphasized in the per capita yearly income figures cited in Chapter 1, are key stumbling blocks to progress. Half of Africa's population lives in poverty. The gross national product of one small European country, the Netherlands, is greater than the combined GNP of 47 nations in sub-Saharan Africa. It is especially difficult to overcome the depressed economic factors for African countries for several reasons: the European countries that exploited them for so many years finally withdrew without leaving a substantial infrastructure; the dictators and the presidents who have made many African countries fiefdoms have virtually bankrupted them through corruption and "crony capitalism," aided in no small part by industrialized nations such as the United States that poured monetary aid into those countries without accountability requirements and without requiring democratic policies and practices that guaranteed that the aid would be to the benefit of the people and not to the personal benefit of the government leaders.[5]

One of the problems that threatens the development of cyberspace in Africa perhaps even more than countries' economies is the political potential of the Internet. Already many African countries have seen the Internet used as a means to disseminate opposition, minority, and alternative political views that are otherwise suppressed by the party in power's control over traditional media, including the press, radio, television, cable, film, and public meetings. The 2000 national elections in an Asian country, South Korea, may well prove a model for elections in Africa. The Internet was used to "bypass a timid mainstream media and publish what proved to be damning and crucial information about the unsavory records of some parliamentary candidates. The Web also became a virtual Speakers Corner for free political expression," which was barely existent due to the dictatorial control of Korea for the past several decades. The Internet also was instrumental in the organizing of grassroots citizens into a national force that has significant effect on the elections. Lee Kyoung Suk, who ran the citizens' web site, stated that "our site was the only marketplace where people could express their opinion." Professor Park Jai Chang stated that "the civic group owes much to the cyber-networks." Collaboration of civic groups to defeat the old-line government was possible only by meeting on the Internet.[6]

Whether the Internet will play that significant a role in the political crises that afflict Africa as this is written, in mid-2000, is still to be seen. Cross-border and internal wars have resulted in crackdowns on the media by many governments. The Media Institute of Southern Africa issued 82 media alerts in Zambia alone at the end of 1999 because of that country's actions against reporters. In Angola more than 20 journalists were jailed. The Media Institute cited 10 of the

14 members of the Southern African development community as violating press freedoms. The South Africa Human Rights Commission issued a report on government interference and discrimination in the media. In Zimbabwe, President Robert Mugabe has strengthened his control over the media, especially in light of the increasing opposition to his encouragement of violence against the white farmers of the country. The continuing civil war in Sudan between the Islamic government and the Christian and Animist rebels in the south is marked by government strangulation of press freedoms. The government of Angola banned all reporting of the chaotic civil war in that nation and enforced its dictum by raiding media offices and arresting and jailing journalists.[7] And these are only examples of what are more widespread practices.

A summary of the problems and potentials is reflected in the chapters on individual representative countries. Throughout this book, contributors have detailed the myriad obstacles diverse countries share in trying to develop Internet connectivity and usage. At the top of the list, sorely inadequate telecommunications infrastructures make any talk of comprehensive development optimistic at best. Chronic problems of poverty and illiteracy make it moot.

This has been the case in Benin, where overall development has been uneven and limited. In Chapter 4, W. Joseph Campbell describes the indifference and inability of government to wire the country. Instead, he turns to the media for encouragement. The historical role of the independent press in political struggle has shown Benin's journalists to be impressive guardians of democratic values. Benin's return to democratic rule in the late 1980s powered the emergence of a free and vibrant private press. It also bodes well for a future in which the Internet can serve as a conduit for important information for its citizens, once economic and infrastructural problems are remedied.

Although the government thus far has not played an important part in the development of new media technology, nongovernmental organizations have stepped in to fill the gap. Articulate and persistent advocates are working to promote Internet connectivity, in an effort to keep up with the rest of Africa and the world. The new media are seen as crucial to the continuation of Benin's experiment in multiparty democracy, as well as to its economic survival, research potential, professional training, and regional communications.

Benin seems ready to participate in the on-line revolution. It has signed on with international projects to provide mobile cellular service, digital switching equipment, and a satellite-based telecommunications subsystem. It also has been designated one of two dozen landing points for a $1.6 billion undersea fiber-optic cable project to bring a high-speed telecommunications "backbone" to Africa.

In Chapter 5 Asgede Hagos shows how a debilitating war—in this case Eritrea's thirty-year struggle for independence—not only retarded the country's telecommunications systems, but at the same time served as a catalyst for its development. While Eritrea has suffered from the same plagues of poverty, a low literacy rate, and a small market that have marked other African countries' difficulties in becoming part of the global communications infrastructure, the war's decimation of its basic infrastructure in other areas, as well, added to its problems. The need for information about the conflict, both internally and by the Eritrean Diaspora—Eritrea's Virtual Community, as Hagos describes it—resulted in increased use of the Internet both at home and abroad. Aside from web pages "store-and-forward" e-mail became a key link between Eritrea and the rest of the world and e-mail in general among Eritreans abroad—750,000, Hagos estimates—living in various countries.

Since the end of the Eritrea-Ethiopia war in 1991, and despite more recent border conflicts, a number of initiatives promise to spur Internet growth in Eritrea. One is a 1999 memorandum signed by Eritrea and the United States to cooperate in bringing a national Internet gateway to Eritrea as part of the Leland initiative begun in 1996 to strengthen Internet use throughout Africa. Members of the Virtual Eritrea community use the Internet for information exchange and discussions on key issues, and they established an Internet Dehai, or news from home, service. The Eritrean government today recognizes the centrality of information to developmental strategies and, Hagos points out, the free flow of information, as facilitated by cyberspace, strengthens the bonds of diverse communities. The rural-urban resources divide is a problem in Eritrea as in other countries; rural areas lack telephones, electricity, literacy, and other resources necessary for computers and cyberspace use. Appropriate training in all areas is necessary to develop a cadre of competent cyberspace developers, managers, leaders and users. Peace is necessary to avoid resources for telecommunications being drained by armed conflicts. With foreign private investment, regional and international organizations' assistance, and the support of Eritrea's Virtual Community, Hagos sees Eritrea taking its place soon as one of Africa's leaders in the use of cyberspace.

Ethiopia has lagged far behind in its development of information and communication technologies (ICTs) primarily because it has only recently emerged from years of military dictatorship and civil war. Although continuing strife with Eritrea is diverting government attention and resources, Robert White suggests in Chapter 6 that changes are under way that poise the country on the verge of increased Internet development. He notes that nearly 20 years of turmoil and war consumed resources that otherwise might have been directed to development, and inevitably handicapped Ethiopia's emergence into the information age. With lasting peace possibly in the offing, there is good reason for hope.

One obstacle, however, is the inefficiency and corrupt bureaucracy of the Ethiopian Telecommunications Corporation, one of the oldest telecommunications companies in Africa. The Ethiopian government has resisted privatization, slowing the emergence of the private companies that elsewhere have powered connectivity. Whether telecommunications remains a government monopoly or becomes all or partially privatized, extensive infrastructure must be provided in any case.

Observers look to Ethiopia's capital, Addis Ababa, for optimism. Important international organizations are headquartered there, including the UN Economic Commission for Africa and its African Information Society Initiative. Because so many world conferences take place in Addis Ababa, there is an inevitable and substantial spillover of information and awareness of the new technologies. Addis Ababa is also the site of the African School of Information Studies and the headquarters of the Organization of African Unity (OAU). Ethiopia is thus fortunate to be the locus for so much activity focused on information and communications.

A number of initiatives are attempting to increase Ethiopia's presence in cyberspace. The country is included in two U.S. AID projects—the Leland Initiative and the AfricaLink project—that are attempting to extend full Internet connectivity to approximately 20 African countries. Another example is the Ethiopian Art and Architecture database project to digitize Ethiopian art and architecture and make it available on the Internet. The Ethiopian government also is very interested in distance education, a crucial application of the Internet. The African Virtual University, funded by the World Bank, includes Ethiopia among the dozen or so countries participating in this ambitious distance education project. And finally, coffee, Ethiopia's largest and most famous export, has great potential to expand Ethiopia's Internet use as well as boost its economy. A substantial reward awaits those who successfully market it over the Internet.

Perhaps less fertile ground can be found in Kenya, where Internet access and cost are great obstacles, as is a repressive and increasingly threatened government. However, Okoth F. Mudhai in Chapter 7 explores the hopeful place of journalism in the future of Kenya's Internet connectivity. Journalists there have embraced the Internet, and many publications are posted on-line. One important publication, the *Nation*, showed the potential of on-line journalism during the 1998 bombings of the American embassies in Nairobi, Kenya's capital, and Dar es Salaam, Tanzania. The publication achieved record hits during the tragedy, garnering international prominence that could advance the cause of democracy in this East African nation.

However, Kenya's President Daniel arap Moi is far from happy with the media coverage coming from the country's on-line press. He has publicly condemned publications for the news they have disseminated worldwide. Repressive laws on libel, contempt, and sedition, as well as lack of a constitutional guarantee to press freedom, have made it possible for the government to destroy, confiscate, or damage printing facilities. Editors and publishers have been arrested and publications banned, while journalists have been intimidated, threatened, harassed, or imprisoned. This has caused fear and despondency among journalists and resulted in self-censorship by editors.

However, Mudhai finds a hopeful sign as he looks elsewhere on the continent to find that the continuing growth of the Internet is challenging state control. Print newspapers that are banned or suppressed for printing antigovernment information can be published on-line, bypassing internal censorship. Kenyan journalists regularly send via e-mail articles that cannot be published by local newspapers to regional and international publications. In turn, local Kenyan newspapers pick up such articles and attribute them to those foreign publications, a lesser crime in case of any repercussions.

Looking south, a success story can be found in Namibia, where the Internet has developed quickly and explosive growth is projected. In Chapter 8, Protasius Ndauendapo and Chris Paterson detail the rapid changes in the political and telecommunications environments that set the scene for Namibia's enthusiastic acceptance of the Internet. Independence from South Africa in 1990 triggered strong growth in the economy generally and the telecommunications sector in particular, clearing the way for enthusiastic Internet development. At independence, the regulatory framework governing the telecommunications and broadcasting sectors was liberalized to address the challenges and opportunities of the new political, economic, and global environments. Deregulation of the telecommunications sector, coupled with massive investments in telecommunications infrastructure, powered Namibia's Internet growth. Although the early days of the Internet in Namibia were frustrated by insufficient access to bandwidth, this has changed with the introduction of digital circuits and higher bandwidth capacities.

In the media, the country's premier newspaper has had great success as an international information provider for the Internet. A Namibian Internet site also has played a vital role in monitoring press freedom throughout southern Africa and providing extensive and instant international exposure.

The growth of the Internet has been a painstaking process, characterized by minimal financial resources, lack of expertise, lack of buying power among the previously disadvantaged black majority, and a lack of access to the Internet in rural areas and in schools. Even so, Namibia's on-ramp to the information superhighway seems clearer than that in some other African countries.

In Chapter 9, Festus Eribo and Kelly Fudge Albada remind readers that Nigeria is home to the highest concentration of black people on Earth, and at 120 million people has the largest population in Africa. Nigeria's 29-year ordeal under military dictatorship stunted development in virtually all walks of life, gradually decimating the country's political, economic, educational, and technological sectors. As a result, the Internet came late to Nigeria, and accessibility is still embryonic. The mass exodus of Nigerian intellectuals and flight of capital under the dictatorships has exacerbated the situation, as has the fact that international investors shied away from Nigeria because of the instability.

Thus far, the Internet is an urban phenomenon with little impact on the tens of millions who live in rural areas. By world standards, the number of Internet users in Nigeria—perhaps 10,000 in late 1999—is negligible, although the rate of adoption of the Internet and interest in the new technology are on the increase. Although the existing telecommunication technologies are inadequate, the new democratic government is determined to catch up with the rest of the world in cyberspace. The Nigerian Communications Commission has redoubled its efforts to promote the development of telecommunication facilities, markets, industries, services, and skills.

Another point of progress is Nigeria's new constitution, which clearly guarantees freedom of the press. The democratic government recognizes the potential of the mass media, including the Internet, as crucial to the free flow of news and information, distance education, health services, agricultural extension, and electronic commerce. It also is starting to erase the communication gap between Nigerians at home and those in the Diaspora. Nigerian media were quick to seize the opportunity to be present on the Internet. The presence of Nigerian dailies and some weekly newspapers on the World Wide Web has revolutionized the flow of Nigerian news within the country and abroad.

In Chapter 10, Alain Just Coly details how Internet connectivity, access, and use have greatly expanded in Senegal, putting the country on a par with others in West Africa. The use of the new technologies is quickly developing, even if the phenomenon is still largely urban. Users are becoming more sophisticated and organized, as is evidenced by the proliferation of new associations. However, the development of the new technologies is hindered by the cost of equipment and connectivity; a feeble telephonic network, especially in rural areas; a paucity of Internet service providers; and a lack of training.

In many ways, Senegal's situation is similar to that found throughout Africa, although there are also some differences. Senegal's media climate is one of the most tolerant in Africa, and there have been no attempts to curb the growth of the Internet. Editors naturally were interested in the coming of the Internet there in 1996, and many publications have gone on-line. However, uneven site maintenance is a chronic problem. In addition, the promise of the Pan African News Agency (PANA), which is headquartered in Senegal's capital, Dakar, has yet to be realized. PANA, which was set up by the OAU in the late 1970s as the continent's news distribution organization for state-run news agencies, was often seen as a mouthpiece for governments, and has had many financial problems. Its sale to private investors in 1999 may mean its renewal, and may give it an important Internet presence.

Senegal's numerous and lively cybercafés have garnered international attention and been a model for private interests in other developing countries. Most of them are located in Dakar, although they also operate in the tourist area of Saly Portudal, and in the cities of Saint-Louis and Ziguinchor. They have greatly advanced Internet use in Senegal. The Internet also holds great potential for Senegal's educational system. Its participation in both the African Virtual University, sponsored by the World Bank, and the French Virtual University has brought global video conferencing, simultaneous classes held live via satellite, and hyperlinks to further content. Another interesting project is Malick Sy On Line, created by a Senegalese student in France. It is popularizing computer science to students from the Malick Sy Avenue neighborhood, a famous street in the heart of Dakar.

Togo also is overcoming late introduction and obstacles to connectivity. It was one of the last countries in West Africa to open up the Internet to the general public, in 1995. In Chapter 11, Victor Louassi and Melinda B. Robins report the dramatic progress in recent years that makes Togo one of the few countries in the region to have two Internet nodes. However, threatening this progress are ongoing political instability and violence that continue to plague the country. Togo's economic health has suffered greatly, and it has lost many opportunities that could have speeded its connection to the Internet.

One plus, however, is that Togo is legally wide open to Internet development. The absence of laws may be due to a lack of official interest in—or ignorance of—the importance of the new technology. No license is needed for those who intend to become an Internet service provider, and no authorization is required for the marketing of Internet services. However, this may just be a matter of time; Togo's government is very sensitive to criticism, especially that from the independent press. Strong independent newspapers operating in 1990, at the beginning of agitation for democracy, suffered newsroom attacks by security forces that resulted in injuries and devastating equipment damage. It remains to be seen what will happen if an on-line publication contains negative coverage of the government.

Internet use is in its infancy in Togo's media. The few journalists trained to use it have access mainly through the cybercafés, and then primarily for e-mail. The Internet has been slow in coming to the newsroom. Lack of means and knowledge are the main reasons. Most media outlets cannot afford to buy a computer, get connected, or regularly pay the bills for telephone and Internet access. Most journalists have no experience with the technology. In addition, most of Togo's big companies operate in a total monopoly and do not need to advertise.

Even so, Internet access and use have greatly spread in Togo in recent years. Infrastructure has been upgraded, and costs lowered. The country is unique in the subregion for allowing competition, and the resulting cybercafés mean access for more people.

In Chapter 12, Francis P. Kasoma notes that Zambia's entry into the global cyberspace community has been characterized by deep contradictions. While the new technologies have promoted freedom of the press, democratic institutions, and an improved economy, they also have increased the gap between the voiceless and those who have the resources to speak out. Kasoma asks how Zambia can subscribe to a political philosophy of liberalization of politics even as it promotes a technology that allows only a few people to express their ideas.

Zambia's Internet development resulted from the far-reaching political, economic, and social changes that swept the country in the early 1990s, beginning with the introduction of multiparty democracy in 1991 and the subsequent liberalization of the economy. When the government loosened its stranglehold on the economy by selling state enterprises to the private sector, the Internet began to grow. This situation helped to promote the free expression of political views as well as commercial advertising and industrial competition. The changes were paralleled by rapid reforms in telecommunications. Deregulation provided an enabling environment for new entrants to the communication industry, unhindered by monopoly regulations that had previously barred private-sector participation.

In 1994, despite Zambia's status as one of the poorest nations in Africa, the country became the fifth country on the continent (and the first sub-Saharan country outside of South Africa) to obtain full access to the Internet. Many private companies have joined the race for the potentially lucrative business of providing Internet services to Zambian citizens.

Zambia is plagued by poverty and low population densities that create barriers to connectivity. Few Zambians can afford phone service, let alone computers. Even so, there is a new demand for computer-literate and skilled personnel. Finding and retaining such people is extremely difficult in a country that introduced an undergraduate degree in information technology only in 1999.

The Zambian government has been slow to recognize the Internet's potential, using computers mostly to prepare paychecks at the end of the month. The country's national educational policy does not mention computer technology, revealing a serious lack of awareness by senior policy makers of the role of information technology in education and development. A lack of coordination at the national level to develop an information infrastructure has resulted in a failure to exploit the many international initiatives facilitating the provision of an information network across Africa.

Zambia's media, however, have made significant use of the Internet, and most newspapers and stations have an on-line presence that has brought news to places previously not reached. They also have opened up Zambia's media institutions to readers outside the country, giving them the opportunity to keep up with the news and to respond via e-mail to advertisers and editors. Although Zambia's journalists face chronic legal problems, the country's independent press has remained resilient and undaunted. Journalists have taken full advantage of the Internet to complain to the world about censorship or arrest, and to network with colleagues in other countries.

Despite these many problems, the potentials point the way to the future of cyberspace in sub-Saharan African. Even with the debilitations of war, poverty, and corruption, many observers believe that Africa is already in a renaissance. This was, indeed, one of the themes at a year 2000 Africa-European Union conference in Rwanda. Journalist Thomas Moore stated that "for the first time since Portuguese trading ships anchored off the coast of Angola 500 years ago, Africa is determining its own course."[8] Kenyan human rights lawyer Makau Mutua has said that "Africans stand at the threshold of a new epoch . . . [a] democratic renaissance."[9] While there were, in mid-2000, still wars involving the armed forces of 10 countries and 11 guerilla armies, other conflicts were being settled peaceably. For example, Mozambique, which had been the focus of one of the continent's longest civil wars, is moving ahead today in peaceful accommodation. In 2000 an election in Rwanda replaced the long-standing Hutu leaders with a Tutsi president, at this writing hopefully signaling a peaceful renaissance from one of history's most destructive genocidal conflicts. Even in repressed countries, the rebellions are sometimes by forces seeking peace, justice, and tranquility, rather than corruptive power; such an example is Zimbabwe, where the forces opposing the autocratic governments are doing so to achieve a "peaceful end to bad governance."[10] African leaders in a number of countries were involved continuously after war broke out in Congo in 1998 to try to end it peacefully. In 2000, for the first time, both South Africa and Nigeria simultaneously had democratic governments. The opposing sides in strife-torn Burundi sought the help of other African leaders in 1999 to end their civil war. In many countries "bush warfare has given way to parliamentary debate."[11]

A major change has been African self-reliance. No longer do the Western industrialized nations have the prerogative to act like surrogate parents to African nations in crisis. Jan van Eck, of the Center for Conflict Resolution in Cape Town, noted that "foreign powers don't have the leverage they used to have. We're in a completely different era."[12] Journalist Thomas Moore writes: "The continent today rests in the hands of a new generation of political and business leaders. Many were schooled in the West, most were forged not by struggles against colonialism but [against] the corrupt authoritarian regimes that followed. They experiment with democratic models and design grand visions."[13]

South African President Thabo Mbeki has stated that "to achieve an African renewal in politics, in economics, in social life, and in culture we have to act together as Africans."[14] The responsible nations of Africa and their leaders recognize the need for and are seeking effective Pan-Africanism in order to move beyond the traditional barriers separating the countries and achieve cooperative understanding and endeavors to strengthen the economy, culture, and education of each country and of all countries. Hopefully, such cooperation can also provide a buffer against the scourge of AIDS that threatens to destroy much of Africa's recent progress. As this book has shown, the Internet is a most opportune means for achieving these goals. The future of Africa is in cyberspace and the future of cyberspace is in Africa.

NOTES

1. Edith M. Lederer (AP), "Technology Can Liberate Poor, Annan Says," *Boston Globe*, April 4, 2000, A13.

2. Ibid.

3. Ibid.

4. Salah Nasrawi (AP), "Europeans, Africans Gather for Signal Talks," *Boston Globe*, April 2, 2000, A5.

5. Holger Jensen (Scripps Howard), "Africa Needs Debt Relief, Not Lectures," *Daily Local News* (southeastern Pennsylvania), April 8, 2000, A8.

6. Doug Struck (*Washington Post*), "South Korean Election Shows Internet Has a Future in Politics," *Boston Globe*, April 17, 2000, A2.

7. Kurt Shillinger, "In Wartorn Africa, Governments Target Media," *Boston Globe*, Dec. 1, 1999, A2.

8. Thomas J. Moore, "Renaissance in Troubled Africa," *Boston Globe*, April 9, 2000, E-1, 2.

9. Ibid.

10. Ibid.

11. Ibid.

12. Ibid.

13. Ibid.

14. Ibid.

Selected Bibliography

Anderson, Benedict (1983). *Imagined Communities: Reflections on the Origins and Spread of Nationalism*. London: Verso.

Bermeo, Nancy (1992). "Democracy and the Lessons of Dictatorship." *Comparative Politics 24*, 273–291.

Bourgault, Louise (1995). *Mass Media in Sub-Sahara Africa*. Bloomington: Indiana University Press.

Campbell, W. Joseph (1998). *The Emergent Independent Press in Benin and Côte d'Ivoire: From Voice of the State to Advocate of Democracy*. Westport, Conn.: Praeger Publishers.

Charp, Sylvia (1996). "Curriculum Integration." *Technological Horizons in Education 23* (10), 4.

Committee to Protect Journalists (1999). *Attacks on the Press 1998*. New York: Committee to Protect Journalists.

Connell, Dan (1993). *Against All Odds: A Chronicle of the Eritrean Revolution*. Trenton, N.J.: Red Sea Press.

Dizard, Wilson, Jr. (1994). *Old Media/New Media: Mass Communications in the Information Age*. New York: Longman.

Dunn, Hopeton S. (Ed.). (1995). *Globalization, Communications and Caribbean Identity*. New York: St. Martin's Press.

Dutton, H. William (Ed.). (1996). *Information and Communication Technologies: Visions and Realities*. Oxford: Oxford University Press.

Eribo, Festus (1997). "Internal and External Factors Affecting Press Freedom in Nigeria," in Festus Eribo and William Jong-Ebot (Eds.). *Press Freedom and Communication in Africa*. Trenton, N.J.: Africa World Press.

Firebrace, James, and Stuart Holland (1985). *Never Kneel Down*. Trenton, N.J.: Red Sea Press.

Friedman, Edward A., Joshua Baron, and Cynthia Addison (1996). "Universal Access to Science Study via Internet." *Technological Horizons in Education 23* (11), 83–86.

Gaines, Curman L., Willie Johnson, and Thomas King (1996). "Achieving Technological Equity and Equal Access to the Learning Tools of the 21st Century." *Technological Horizons in Education 23* (11), 74–78.

Gatheru, Wamuyu, and Robert Shaw (1998). "Creating an Environment for Economic Growth: Information and Communications—the Potential for Take-off," in *Our Problems, Our Solutions*. Nairobi: Institute of Economic Affairs, 180–191.

Hagos, Asgede (1998). "Mass Communication and Nation Building: Policy Implications for Eritrea." *Eritrean Studies Review 2* (2). Lawrenceville, N.J.: Red Sea Press.

Hedebro, Goran (1982). *Communication and Social Change in Developing Nations: A Critical View*. Ames: Iowa State University Press.

Heilbrunn, John R. (1993). "Social Origins of National Conferences in Benin and Togo." *Journal of Modern African Studies 31* (2), 277–299.

Jackson, William (1997). "U.S. Will Help Africa Establish a Commercial Net Presence." *Government Computer News 16* (33), 42–43.

Jensen, Mike (1998). "Wireless in Africa." *Telecommunications 32,* S6–S8.

Keller, Edmond J. (1988). *Revolutionary Ethiopia: From Empire to People's Republic.* Bloomington: Indiana University Press.

Khvilon, Evgueni A., and Mariana Patru (1997). "UNESCO's Mission in the Promotion of International Cooperation." *Technological Horizons in Education 24* (6), 58–60.

Lee, Kevin C., and Charles A. Fleming (1995). "Problems of Introducing Courses in Computer-Assisted Reporting." *Journalism and Mass Communication Educator 50* (3), 23–34.

Manning, Patrick (1988). *Francophone Sub-Saharan Africa 1880–1985*. Cambridge: Cambridge University Press.

Mansell, Robin, and Uta Wehn (1998). *Knowledge Societies: Information Technology for Sustainable Development.* Oxford: Oxford University Press, 1.

Marcus, Harold G. (1983). *Ethiopia, Great Britain, and the United States 1941–1974: The Politics of Empire.* Berkeley: University of California Press.

Melkote, Srinivas R. (1991). *Communication for Development in the Third World: Theory and Practice.* New Delhi: Sage.

Moseley, Katharine Payne (1975). *Indigenous and External Factors in Colonial Politics: Southern Dahomey to 1939.* Unpublished dissertation. New York: Columbia University.

Mowlana, Hamid (1997). *Global Information and World Communication: New Frontiers in International Relations.* London: Sage.

Naidoo, Kameshnee (1998). *Africa Media Online: An Internet Handbook for African Journalists.* Paris and Dakar, Sénégal: Institut Panos.

Ndauendapo, P. (1999). *The Advent of Internet in Namibia: A Study of Its Sociopolitical, Economic and Legal Impact on the Newspaper Industry.* Unpublished dissertation, Centre for Mass Communication Research, University of Leicester, England.

Pankhurst, Richard (1998). *The Ethiopians.* Oxford: Blackwell.

Panos (1995). *The Internet and the South: Superhighway or Dirt Track?* Media Briefing 16 (Oct.). London: Panos.

Partee, Morriss Henry (1996). "Using E-Mail, Web Sites and Newsgroups to Enhance Traditional Classroom Instruction." *Technological Horizons in Education 23* (11), 79–82.

Pateman, Roy (1990). *Eritrea: Even the Stones Are Burning.* Trenton, N.J.: Red Sea Press.

Reddick, Randy, and Elliot King (1995). *The Online Journalist: Using the Internet and Other Electronic Resources.* Orlando, Fla.: Harcourt Brace.

Rogers, Everett (1976). *Communication and Development: Critical Perspectives.* Beverly Hills, Calif.: Sage.

Ronen, Dov (1974). "The Colonial Elite in Dahomey." *African Studies Review 17* (1), 55–76.

Rota, Joseph, and Tatiana Galvan (1987). "Information Technology and National Development in Latin America," in David L. Puletz (Ed.). *Political Communication Research: Approaches, Studies and Assessments. Vol. 1.* Norwood, N.J.: Ablex.

Sherman, Richard (1980). *Eritrea: The Unfinished Revolution.* New York: Praeger.

Singer, Jane B., David Craig, Chris W. Allen, Virginia Whitehouse, Anelia Dimitrova, and Keith P. Sanders (1996). "Attitudes of Professors and Students about New Media Technology." *Journalism and Mass Communication Educator 51* (2), 36–45.

Stevenson, Robert L. (1993) "Communication and Development: Lessons from and for Africa," in *Window on Africa: Democratization and Media Exposure*, Festus Eribo, Oyeleye Oyediran, Mulatu Wubneh, and Leo Zonn (Eds.). Greenville, N.C.: Center for International Programs.

United Nations Development Program (1999). *Human Development Report: Globalization with a Human Face.* New York: UNDP.

Webster, Frank (1999). "What Information Society?" in Hugh Mackay and Tim O'Sullivan (Eds.). *The Media Reader: Continuity and Transformation.* London: Sage.

Yohannes, Okbazghi (1988). "Behind the Ethio-Eritrean Federation: The ConspiracyThesis." *Journal of Eritrean Studies 3* (2), 67–75.

Index

Abacha, Sani, 122
Acacia Initiative, 41
ACC Statement on Universal Access to Basic Communication and Information Services, 27–32
Accra BBS (bulletin board system) bridge, 142–43
Adam, Lisa, 20
Adane, Fanta, 82
Addis Ababa, 62, 63, 80, 82, 85, 166; hotels, 82
Aduda, David, 94, 96–97
Advisory Network for African Information Strategies (ANAIS), 23
Afeworki, Estifanos, 64
Africa, 15–16; economics, and telecommunications, 12; and exploitation by European colonial powers, 2, 5, 14; illiteracy, 4–5; Italian colonies, 61; perception of by Western media, 14; poverty, 99, 164. *See also* Africa, and cyberspace; African women; HIV/ AIDS
Africa, and cyberspace, 1–4, 15, 16, 19–20; future of, 163–72; Internet service providers (ISPs), 21, 23, 25–26; and lack of communications infrastructure, 2–3, 5–6, 13–14; and political

expression, 164–65; structure, 19–23, 25–26. *See also* Internet, the, and use in Africa; *names of specific African countries*
Africa II Gateway Project, 21
Africa Internet Group, 23
Africa Internet Developers Association, 22–23
Africa Network for the Prevention and Protection Against Child Abuse and Neglect, 97
Africa One, 23, 54
Africa Online (AfOL), 25, 93
Africa Optical Network, 21
Africa Policy Information Center, 36
AfricaLink Directory, 21, 80–81, 167
African Gender Institute, and WomensNet initiative, 38–39, 41
African Information Society Initiative (AISI), 21–22
African National Congress (ANC), 94
African Regional Network Information Center, 23
African School of Information Studies, 166
African Virtual University, 84, 167, 169
African women, 33–34, 41–42; barriers to communication technologies, 38–40;

About the Editors and Contributors

KELLY FUDGE ALBADA is Assistant Professor in the Department of Communication at East Carolina University in Greenville, N.C.

W. JOSEPH CAMPBELL is Assistant Professor of Communication at American University in Washington, D.C.

ALAIN JUST COLY is a journalist for *Le Soleil*, in Dakar, Senegal. He writes frequently about new technology.

FESTUS ERIBO is Associate Professor of International Communication and Co-ordinator of African Studies at East Carolina University in Greenville, N.C.

ASGEDE HAGOS is Professor of Mass Communication at Delaware State University in Dover, Del.

ROBERT L. HILLIARD is Professor of Media Arts at Emerson College in Boston, Mass.

FRANCIS P. KASOMA is Professor and Head of the Department of Mass Communication at the University of Zambia.

VICTOR LOUASSI is a journalist in Togo.

OKOTH F. MUDHAI is a journalist in Kenya.

PROTASIUS NDAUENDAPO is Head of the Information and Library Division of the Namibian government.

CHRIS PATERSON is Assistant Professor of Media Studies and Broadcast Journalism at the University of San Francisco.

MELINDA B. ROBINS is Assistant Professor of Journalism at Emerson College in Boston, Mass.

ROBERT G. WHITE is Professor of Government and Political Science at Humboldt State University in Arcata, Calif.